LONG SLOW TRAIN

LONG SLOW TRAIN

THE SOUL MUSIC OF

SHARON JONES
and the DAP-KINGS

DONALD BRACKETT

Backbeat
Books

An Imprint of Hal Leonard LLC

Published in 2018 by Backbeat Books
An Imprint of Hal Leonard LLC
7777 West Bluemound Road
Milwaukee, WI 53213

Trade Book Division Editorial Offices
33 Plymouth St., Montclair, NJ 07042

Printed in the United States of America

Book design by M Kellner

Library of Congress Cataloging-in-Publication Data is available upon request.

ISBN 978-1-61713-691-7

www.backbeatbooks.com

Dedicated to James Brown and Sharon Jones,
the hardest-working performers in show business,
and to the Dap-Kings, the substance of soul

"The heart of youth is reached through the senses; the senses of age are reached through the heart."

—NICOLAS-EDME RÉTIF, *The Human Heart Laid Bare*, 1797

CONTENTS

FOREWORD
What Is Soul Power?

I t's impossible to forget your first encounter with this woman and her band. In my experience, it was a mild November night in Toronto in 2007, and Sharon Jones and the Dap-Kings kept us waiting. We had to be patient, because to witness a performance by Sharon Jones was to experience a musical force so strong as to render one bone-weary from exhilaration. It is to walk home damp with sweat after a night you'll never forget from a band with an engaging lead singer who knows not only how to entertain but how to power your nervous system with lasting energy. This performer embodies what amounts to a perfect definition for an utterly unique source of natural energy: soul power. Listening to her is basically like plugging into a living, breathing, and dancing electric current.

This particular Toronto concert was originally booked in a club along the city's main thoroughfare, Bloor Street. But the venue, Lee's Palace, was too small. Tickets sold very quickly, so Jones and the band needed a hall that was larger and grander in scale, a place big enough to accommodate their own grandeur. They settled for a club east of Lee's Palace called the Phoenix. After the doors opened, around eight o'clock, the crowd meandered its way into the club in an orderly, Canadian manner. By nine, the room was chock full of people anticipating a great night. I've been to enough concerts to know when the buzz in the room is a good omen of what's to come, beer consumption notwithstanding, and this was one of those special nights—the kind you tell your kids about when bedazzling them with how live club music used to be.

Everybody in the house knew Sharon Jones's music by word of mouth. She didn't get much airplay on radio, despite her intimate accessibility: a powerhouse of sound with a band that could only get that good after playing hundreds of one-nighters around the world. The Dap-Kings were so musically tight that even a passive listener had to sit up and take notice. They were the real thing: no synth-drums or flaccid guitars, nothing but a dynamic rhythm section supporting three horns and a keyboard player. At first, their claim to fame was backing Amy Winehouse on her superlative record *Back to Black*, released in the fall of 2006. This is when most people discovered them, only to find out a little later on that they had their own lead singer, a woman named Sharon Jones. This was also a soul performer whose power could make most other entertainers feel as if they were literally standing still.

Jones and the Dap-Kings had originally hit the scene in 2002 with the release of their first record, *Dap-Dippin' with Sharon Jones and the Dap-Kings*. It was a critical success, but most people generally agreed that the band's best work was always achieved live onstage. In some ways, Jones and the Dap-Kings preferred the concert stage to the recording studio, for they were on an inspired and inspiring mission: a soulful mission that could only succeed by reaching out to touch their audiences in person. And so the band continued to tour, to hone their presentation, and always seemed to leave audiences wanting more. By the time the Dap-Kings reached Toronto, they were no longer just bubbling under and over: they were the hot ticket that November night because the show at the Phoenix was their best chance to connect with all of us. It was also our best chance to experience something unique. The title of Hendrix's first record, *Are You Experienced*, could just as well have been a question aimed at listeners before and after encountering the Jones treatment.

By 2005 and the release of *Naturally*, Sharon Jones and the Dap-Kings were beginning to preach a deeper African American experience, especially with their contemporary funk version of "This Land Is Your Land," originally written and performed by Woody Guthrie. He wrote the song in 1940, deliberately to take the piss out of "God Bless America," penned by Irving Berlin and made famous by the singer Kate Smith. The version by Jones and the Dap-Kings took ownership of the song and transformed it from an anthem for the downtrodden into an R&B standard that encompassed the African American experience in less than five minutes. It was a bold move that made me uncomfortable on first listen. I was accustomed to hearing a song about poor white people from a legendary white folksinger, and it didn't even occur to me that any black artist could bring it home as well as Sharon Jones could. And she did it with abundant commitment and a deep historical context. After years of hard work, often on the fringes of the music industry, this woman had earned the right to sing it her way. In fact, she did everything her way.

I'm a music lover, and I'm always interested in what people are listening to. If I see a friend walking to work with earbuds in, I'll always ask, "What's on your iPod this morning?" I'm always curious to get a tip on an artist I've never heard before, while also gaining some insight into other people's tastes. This is how Sharon Jones and the Dap-Kings first came into my personal world, when a friend at the office of the radio station where I work handed me his earbuds and said, "Check this out." It was Sharon Jones singing her *Dap-Dippin'* version of "What Have You Done for Me Lately?," originally recorded by Janet Jackson, but with Jones committing three times the energy. Jones totally transformed that song and made it her all her own, which is an important aspect of her craft: to go deep within herself and connect with a song's story by giving it some real soul. In other words, she plugs the song into herself and lets the soul current flow.

The word "soul" first became associated with black musical artists such as Otis Redding and Ray Charles in the mid-'60s. It was a word used by music critics to try to describe a unique sound that wasn't exactly pop or blues—or rock 'n' roll, either. The word was a hybrid solution to the dilemma of characterizing something really new; a word to describe a muscular musical force that quickly became a distinct genre. In a sense, it was similar to the word "cool," which described a quieter type of jazz music coming out of the West Coast of the United States. If anything, it was also a good way to try to categorize something so hot that white thermometers couldn't measure it.

Soul music, by definition, incorporates all forms of modern American music, but especially R&B and gospel. It also works on a different level than any other brand of music: it operates with an unfiltered groove that you can feel in your nervous system while it transforms your mood and even your basic state of mind. It's not three chords and the truth, or a pop song written by a committee and overproduced to within an inch of its life. It isn't processed or melted down or combined with any other ingredients that might spoil the purity of the source. The recipe for soul music is so basic that it taps into our wider humanity, regardless of the color of our skin. As Irwin Stambler describes it in *The Encyclopedia of Rock, Pop, and Soul* (St. Martin's Press), "R&B and soul remain the bellwethers of mass audience music, embraced in turn by each succeeding generation of teens and young adults." In other words, it lasts—and for good reason. It thrills.

And so it was for all of us by 11:30 that night at the Phoenix. From the first downbeat, Sharon Jones and the Dap-Kings immediately grabbed us with their authenticity: no fancy Auto-Tune or click tracks here. They were the real deal. This woman who never took any singing lessons was genuine, original, and full of grit. Sharon Jones sang "from herself" and taught us all that bearing one's soul will cure you of whatever ails you, be it a broken heart, an unrequited love, or a loss of self-worth. To paraphrase John Lennon, in his apt description of the founder of rock 'n' roll, the late Chuck Berry: if they gave soul music another name, it would be called Sharon Jones.

This marvelous profile by Donald Brackett tells the wonderful story of an ideal synonym for soul: Sharon.

— *John Corcelli*

• • •

John Corcelli is a Toronto-based music journalist and critic who works with the Canadian Broadcasting Corporation. A regular contributor to CBC programs such as *Inside the Music* and *Sunday Edition*, he is the author of the book *Frank Zappa FAQ: All That's Left to Know About the Father of Invention*, published in 2016 by Backbeat Books.

ACKNOWLEDGMENTS

My deep gratitude to Alex Kadvan, manager of Sharon Jones and the Dap-Kings; to Saundra Williams and Starr Duncan Lowe, Jones's beloved Dapettes; to Pastor Margo Fields; to Sharon's sister Willa Stringer-Jones; and to all the folks at Daptone Records.

And thanks to the editors at Backbeat, Bernadette Malavarca and Tom Seabrook. My additional personal appreciation of John Corcelli, Barbara Kopple, and Maureen Dougherty for their cooperation.

INTRODUCTION
A Diamond in the Rough: Roots in the Real World

"Too short, too fat, too black and too old . . . "
> —Perennial refrain from record producers responding to Sharon
> Jones in the early days of her music career, as related by Jones
> in an interview with *Mother Jones Magazine*, 2011

There's a great song by David Crosby called "Long Time Gone" that retroactively evokes the spirit of Sharon Jones for me: "It's been a long time coming, going to be a long time gone." We won't see the likes of her soon, if ever.

Sharon Jones was almost lost to history, then she was found again, and then, sadly, she was lost again. A second anniversary already; my, my, how time flies when you're dead. It's been two years since one of the greatest funky dames in soul music took her final bow and sang her final, fiery encore at sixty. It's been a year since her final album with her fabulous band, the Dap-Kings, suitably titled *Soul of a Woman*, was delivered to hungry audiences almost on the first anniversary of her sadly anticipated but still shocking departure. It was lovingly released to global acclaim and to the near worshipful responses that often accompanied assessments of her legendary rise and fall and rise again.

At first glance, this might appear to be a hard luck story, and you could even be forgiven for thinking it's one of the greatest hard luck stories in music history. It must have seemed like Sharon Jones was living in a Hollywood movie that couldn't quite decide if it was a tragedy or a comedy. After all, it's the story of a woman who struggles valiantly along on the fringes of the music business for decades, trying to break in and find a place for herself; then she finally gets her break at forty years of age and has a good decade of increasing notoriety, only to have her band borrowed by the producer of a young white British jazz-blues singer half her age for a record that wins five Grammys and catapults said shaky girl to stardom almost overnight; then her stellar band is taken on the road by that new pop superstar for a raucous world concert tour that eventually ends in doom and gloom; then Jones recovers her band and returns to her interrupted creative journey, finally beginning to garner the respect she so deserved after another good decade of recording and performing, before suddenly, and finally, being interrupted once again, this time by a debilitating illness, pancreatic cancer.

But that hard luck aspect is only on the surface. Underneath the surface of struggle, it's the story of what we can probably all agree is the hardest-working woman in show business, only bending that famous James Brown emblem slightly to accommodate the shift in gender. The tale is epic in its heroism and stubborn stick-to-it-ness, and it puts me in mind of a line from a great song by a fellow late-blooming career struggler on the musical path, Sixto Rodriguez, who worked in obscurity for years in the big shadows of Dylan and Ochs and others, often taking day jobs in construction, without ever realizing that in some parts of the world those albums he made in the early '70s—which had lapsed into a silent void in America and Europe—had transformed him into something of a myth, a legend, and even a cult figure of considerable prominence. In his sad and idiosyncratic folk song "Because," he intones the ultimate rendition of this dilemma: "'Cause they told me everybody's got to pay their dues and I explained that I had overpaid them."

Sharon Jones had definitely overpaid her dues. But what keeps her story from lurching into either tragedy or comedy, or even into a commonplace hard luck litany, is the simple fact that unlike many others who were overdrawn at the bank of karma (and she certainly was), by all accounts Jones never once surrendered to the temptation of feeling sorry for herself. A weird irony in her career parallel to the jazzy white girl who made it big with Jones's band in tow was the odd fact that despite achieving the highest pinnacle of success, that troubled younger artist lacked the basic self-esteem to ever really succeed in life—or, indeed, even to survive living though it.

In stark contrast, Jones's spirit was apparently too strong to give in to that most human of all foibles—self-pity—and instead she didn't just represent soul music onstage or on records, she represented a tangible soul embodiment where it really mattered: she somehow managed to *perform* her life itself with the same grace, charm, humor, candor, and unpretentious raunch that she did onstage.

Following their traditional performance pattern, when her band the Dap-Kings started a Sharon Jones concert by playing a few instrumentals to get the crowd warmed up to a fever pitch and ready for their main attraction, they would introduce her by having the M.C. and guitar player Binky Griptite boom out, "Ladies and gentlemen, 110 pounds of soul excitement, Miss Sharon Jones!" She was all of that and more, with not an ounce of falsehood in her sturdy frame.

So no, this is not a hard luck story. This is a tale of triumph over adversity and the lifelong commitment to a pure and positive spirit. It's more of an epic underdog narrative. This is the saga of Sharon Lafaye Jones, May 4, 1956–November 18, 2016, and her six decades of raw, untutored, ramshackle, rambunctious, and infectious life energy.

Performing at a concert in 2014—the year she was valiantly fighting off the illness that would eventually claim her only two busy years later—and going onstage to perform one of her typically boisterous and sensual sets, she was asked by Max Blau of *Spin* magazine how it felt to be suddenly performing with a totally bald head. It just wasn't part of Jones's character to try to escape from reality or to pretend it wasn't happening by wearing a wig onstage. As reported somewhat jubilantly by

Blau, she declared, "It's going to be different. I'm just going to go with it. That's what soul music is all about!"

Sharon Jones was definitely different, and she was definitely what soul music is all about. She went with it, all right—all the way to the end. Jones brought a bombastic and gritty new take on a well-established musical genre into the stratified spotlight of contemporary pop by being totally true to herself, and by meeting the right band for her music and the perfect producer for her sound at the right time.

This is the chronicle of her early struggles, her rise to fame, her discovery by Gabe Roth of Daptone Records, and her musical and artistic triumph and its attendant challenges. It's a tale focused solely on the music of her soulful revivalist style, and her artistry in interpreting a glorious tradition in a vitally new, purist manner. In particular, it emphasizes her place in the context of contemporary soul music, while also offering a short history and definition of soul as a style and its major female exponents for deeper context. Her whole personal and creative life was an ironic, paradoxical, sad, magical, sensual celebration of what it means to be alive on earth and to be blessed with a soulful voice that can share the human condition with the world.

Jones would struggle to break into the business the old-fashioned way, singing in wedding bands (a thought that fills me with both delight and dread in equal measure) and talent shows, where she was always viewed with some degree of skepticism, often as a result of what I would call her rugged and unconventional beauty. She fought her way into the hotly competitive field of studio session work, often appearing as Lafaye Jones, keeping busy, but her dreamed-of solo recording contract was slow in materializing. Two of her backup singers in an early wedding band called the Good and Plenty Girls would eventually become her sizzling backup singers, decades later, with the Dap-Kings: they became the Dapettes. Loyalty loomed large in Jones's world.

When I spoke to Saundra Williams (who along with Starr Duncan Lowe worked in wedding bands with Sharon while Jones was also working as both an armored truck and prison guard, and later backed her up on the big stages) for this book, she confirmed with some merriment that, yes, when they first encountered the tiny Jones in about 1990, she was indeed wearing her guard uniform with a holster and her "little gun." Indeed, her singing partner and fellow Dapette, Starr Duncan Lowe, also told me that she had a "big knife." That about sums up the Sharon ethos right there: speak softly but carry a big knife. She was also, Duncan Lowe confirmed, always ready for whatever action might arise. Jones didn't want to shoot or hurt anybody, but if she had to, she certainly wouldn't hesitate. Duncan Lowe emphasizes that it was clear as soon as they met that "this was a strong woman you didn't mess around with."

Jones was exactly the kind of tough dame with a heart big enough to withstand the struggles of rejection in the music industry and then, later on, her confrontation with mortality, both of which she approached with the same defiant aplomb. She never did stop dreaming, however, remaining undaunted even when she was working as a prison guard at Rikers Island, where the heavily armed angel would sing Whitney Houston ballads to lonely inmates. All I know is that if I were ever incarcerated with a bunch of violent lowlifes, I would certainly appreciate being serenaded outside my cell by Sharon Jones. After all, I suspect she may have been one of the greatest soul singers in the late twentieth and early twenty-first centuries, including all of the ones whose names are household brands—and especially since she didn't just *sing* soul music. She *lived* a sacred life, in addition to a highly sensual one.

In an interview for vulture.com in February 2014, Jones explained to Lauren Schwartzberg just how she managed to cope with "one damn thing after another." She remarked that she "knew I was going to be famous later in life" ever since her mother sent her as an eighteen-year-old to visit a neighborhood tea reader, Madame Cohen, who told her, "You'll travel, play music, be happy, and be well off." At the time of the interview, Jones wistfully declared, "I'm almost fifty-seven years old and things are finally happening for me," with her usual sunny demeanor, even though, less than a year beforehand—just when she had reached her full artistic and financial powers—she had been given an ominous survival chance of less than 10 percent. Destiny is such a double-edged sword: it first sets you free and then it cuts you loose.

As Schwartzberg listened to Jones tell her life history, she felt almost like she was listening to the plot of a Russian novel: the stint as a prison guard and as an armored truck guard; the brother who lost his way as a result of some ill-advised psychedelics and then later died; the mother who shot a gun at her own husband because he was cheating on her during her pregnancy; Jones's own relationship hell; and her arrival as a late-rising singing star who had been living with her mother in the Queens projects barely a couple of years before reaching #15 on the *Billboard* chart.

Jones's final struggle seems to have been watching the televised election of a president who appeared to represent everything that was anathema to her, and who she only half-jokingly blamed for the stroke that quickly laid her to rest. It might have been the final indignity in what many of us would have described as an unfair life in which she was cheated out of her musical success until the last few years, and then cheated out of it again once she finally had it. But not Jones—that wasn't her way, and no matter how hard her climb to the top had been, or how briefly it would last, she always saw a bright side to what befell her that most people couldn't even imagine. Her inner light shined on brightly.

She had an immediately recognizable sense of style and grace, even right out of the starting gate, and a personal delivery (directly from my heart to you, as the old Richard Penniman song has it) that was characterized perfectly by Jon Pareles, in his *New York Times* obituary of Jones, when he called her "a powerhouse soul singer with a gritty voice, fast feet and indomitable energy." It was this combination of singing and shouting that could instantly connect us with her brand of gospel-charged soul and funk, and that was transmitted to us via a uniquely raw voice—a sound that "had bite, bluesiness, rhythmic savvy and a lifetime of conviction."

Jones was also the peaceful cease-fire in the battle between Motown Records, trying to reach out to wider multi-racial audiences across America with Smoky Robinson, and Stax Records, trying to stay true to an ultra-raunchy brand of in-your-face blackness best exemplified by the percussive mania of Sam and Dave. She traveled from the root to the fruit of soul in the blink of an eye, and she wanted us to be completely messed up by her sound—in a good way. From the beginning, she also referenced, though totally unconsciously, what we could call the mythic and mystic origins of soul music: in the sanctified beats of faith out of control, of church clapping gone mad, of testifying private feelings publicly, of the steam locomotive train track's repeated rumble of click clack, of the secret power of dimly lit juke joints off the main streets of popular culture, of the urge for dancing in the streets while still indoors, of tracing the tracks of her tears for all of us to see and hear.

This book's title conveys much of the spirit and content of its hopeful and optimistic narrative, and lord knows our culture could use more hope and optimism these days. This is especially evident in the fact that Jones began as a Southern church singer who, like James Brown, was taken over (possessed, one might say) by the raucous energy of a different sort of soulful singing, but one no less sacred in the final analysis.

Our narrative places Sharon Jones in the context of historical soul music and provides an overview of her importance in that genre by demonstrating how she stretched the classic soul vibe and merged the raunch of Otis Redding and Wilson Pickett with the female power of Etta James, Lucille Bogan, and Marva Whitney. I will quickly establish my personal position on her historical importance—one that ranks Jones as not just the equal of Aretha Franklin, Gladys Knight, and Tina Turner, but in many respects their superior. They got the glory, though, and Jones seemed to accumulate more heartache by the ton. But she took whatever cards the Creator, or else the casino of fate, dealt out to her, and she carried on like a trouper—and, toward the end, maybe even a saint.

But damn, this woman had struggled. She had early struggles, she had late struggles; her whole damn life had been one long struggle. But here's the thing: after Lafaye, *struggle* was probably her other middle name. In 2013, while preparing to complete and release her album *Give the People What They Want*, which would go on to be nominated for a Grammy Award for "Best R&B Album," Jones was dealt her health blow, and the project had to be delayed. This period of her life and career is well documented in a heart-stirring film by Academy Award–winning filmmaker Barbara Kopple (director of *Harlan County, USA*, and *American Dream*) called *Miss Sharon Jones!*

In a final demonstration of her indomitable spirit and grit, toward the very end of her challenging life Sharon Jones insisted on creating a new song—yet another sparkling Daptone single, ironically written for the soundtrack of the film meant to chronicle her own mortality—and she titled it "I'm Still Here" with typical tongue-in-cheekiness. Even though she was barely five feet tall she loomed large in our lives, and she always seemed to grow taller the longer she sang, until in the end she seemed even taller than Aretha with Tina sitting on her shoulders.

It remains to be seen how and even if the Dap-Kings will manage to continue on without their heart-blistering and spirit-baring frontline singer. They obviously can't simply replace someone like her. Do they become the kind of fine, purely instrumental soul-funk unit they've already proven themselves to be over the years (à la their heroes, Booker T. and the M.G.'s)? Do they become creative consultants and work with other producers to provide the firm foundation for another gifted singer to bounce around on? Do they call it a day? Stay tuned.

Sharon Jones was not limited to happy or sad songs, since true soul music alerts us to the fact that sorrow and happiness are not mutually exclusive—that life is not an either/or scenario but a complete package of both sensation and spirit. Jones was making medicinal music as a manual to the human heart, an operator's guide to the machinery of survival under any and all conditions: she was all about the mechanics of bliss, not the mechanized menu of momentary pop pleasure. In an age where some so-called soul music is merely syncopated schlock, Sharon Jones was a mother lode of the real deal—the kind that lasts.

Jill Scott put it very well when she remarked to *Billboard* in 2014,

"Soul music is about longevity and reaching and touching people on a human level, and that's never going to get lost." For a while during her long and obscure struggles in the music business, it appeared that Jones might be lost or even permanently forgotten—passed over, perhaps, by performers who were either luckier or prettier. But no one was pluckier, and once you identify what made her so special, it's easy to realize that she wasn't merely pretty: she was beautiful the way goddesses are. There was something ineffable about her. Still is. She beat all the odds stacked against her in a world fixated on glamour and glitz, but of course she couldn't beat the odds of a rigged mortality.

Perhaps the perfect testament to her hybrid talents for conveying both the scared and profane in life was the fact that she was given two memorials. The first one, on December 14, 2016, was at the Brown Memorial Baptist Church in her adopted hometown of Brooklyn; the second was on December 17, at the Imperial Theater of her homeland in Augusta, Georgia. Thus, when she was laid to rest—when her struggles had ended and her life, spirit, and creative work were being celebrated—it was totally suitable for one event to be in an old traditional church and the other to be in a classic neighborhood theater. The altar of worship and the performance stage were both equally holy places for her. In fact, throughout her brief but intense time in the spotlight, she often seemed to transform the stage into her own kind of altar.

So, Jones has finally been found again and forever, and now can never be forgotten or replaced. But the year 2016 was a terribly sad one for losing some of our greatest musical talents: Bowie, Prince, Cohen, and Jones, among others. Time flies in the hyperactive world of pop music, but since Jones departed our earthly environs to sing in a more ethereal choir—one which I'm sure would have welcomed her like a homecoming queen—the Sharon soul legend has only grown deeper. This tiny titan called Sharon Lafaye Jones cast a very long shadow on our contemporary cultural stage, and in a compelling way, her final song says it all: she may be gone, but luckily for us, her music is still here.

JUST IN TIME

Sharon Jones at Last

1956

On May 4, Sharon Lafaye Jones is born in Augusta, Georgia.

1965

Sharon puts on her first public performance, as the angel in the Christmas pageant at the North Augusta Baptist Church.

1969–1970

As a teenager, Sharon moves to New York City with her mother, but she continues to return to her hometown regularly during the summers. In 1969, she becomes a member of the Universal Church of God in Queens, New York, where bishop Elijah Fields encourages her to take up piano and become the resident church musician. She would go on to lead the choir, known as E. L. Fields Gospel Wonders, and would remain a lifelong member of the congregation.

1977–1995

Sharon Jones's professional music career is limited to wedding bands and sporadic session work on various dance records during this period. In the '80s and '90s, she starts singing in a wedding band from Staten Island led by John Costellano called the Good and Plenty

Girls. They quickly become a regional favorite in the tri-state area.

1996

Sharon gets a call to sing backup at a Desco Records studio session for '70s soul legend Lee Fields. Co-owners and producers Philip Lehman and Gabriel Roth (a.k.a. Bosco Mann) bring her in on a tip from a sax player, Jones's boyfriend at the time. The other two session singers never show up (or so the legend goes—actually she planned it that way) and Jones cuts all the background parts herself, then proceeds to record an impromptu prison rap over "Switchblade."

1997–1999

Jones sings frequently alongside Lee Fields, Joseph Henry, and Naomi Davis as part of the Desco Super Soul Revue, backed by Desco's house band, the Soul Providers. Desco releases a handful of singles in her name. In the UK, the blossoming "deep funk" scene shows support for these Desco releases, paving the way for Jones and the Soul Providers' first international tour in 1999, where her command of the stage earns her the overnight title "Queen of Funk."

2000

Desco Records folds; the Soul Providers will not perform again, so Jones and Roth regroup in another formation. The group is now Sharon Jones and the Dap-Kings.

2001

In anticipation of a summer residency, the group lands at a club in Barcelona, where a rough 8-track recording studio is rigged up in the basement beneath the Afro-Spot. After a few weeks of tracking and mixing, the band's full-length debut album, *Dap-Dippin' with Sharon Jones & the Dap-Kings*, is completed. Though a few hundred copies are pressed to sell on the road, it will take several months and the birth of a new record label before *Dap-Dippin'* is given a wider release.

2002

Saxophonist Neal Sugarman (whose organ-driven Sugarman Three combo will give Desco two of its most prominent releases) and Gabriel Roth join together to form Daptone Records, with the intention of continuing where Desco had left off. They release the *Dap-Dippin'* album in May.

2003

Daptone Records relocates to a dilapidated two-family house in Bushwick, Brooklyn. The entire Daptone extended family—Sharon included—converts the upstairs bedrooms into offices and the first floor into what would become their highly regarded analog recording studio.

2004

After spending the past three years touring extensively and building steadily upon a growing reputation as the unrivaled frontrunners of old-school soul and funk music, Sharon and the Dap-Kings return to the studio, which is now outfitted with a 16-track tape machine, to record their second album, *Naturally*. The Dap-Kings' lineup now consists of Binky Griptite and Tommy "TNT" Brenneck on guitar, percussionist Fernando Velez, drummer Homer Steinweiss, saxophonists Neal Sugarman (tenor) and Leon Michels (baritone), Dave Guy on trumpet, and Bosco Mann (Gabriel Roth) on bass. (Michels left the band soon after the release of *Naturally* to form Truth and Soul Records.)

2005

Naturally hits the streets in January and sets Jones and the Dap-Kings loose on a relentless touring schedule, encompassing more than 250 shows during twenty-one tours in fourteen countries on three continents by year's end. They make their late-night TV debut on *Late Night with Conan O'Brien*. Sharon also appears as "Ella Elephant" on Verve Records' *Baby Loves Jazz: Go Baby Go!*

2006

In honor of Jones's fiftieth birthday, Daptone Records presents a Soul Revue at New York's Irving Plaza to a sold-out crowd. The lineup includes Naomi Shelton and the Gospel Queens, the Budos Band, the Mighty Imperials, and Antibalas. This year also marks the first time Jones and the Dap-Kings tour Australia; eventually, they slow their touring schedule to make time for a return to the studio to record what will become *100 Days, 100 Nights*. Sharon performs with Lou Reed at a special show at Brooklyn's St. Ann's Warehouse, while her band goes into the studio with Mark Ronson and Amy Winehouse to record her multi-platinum, Grammy Award–winning album, *Back to Black*.

2007

Sharon tours with Lou Reed in Australia as part of the stage adaptation of his 1973 album *Berlin* and steals the show with her rendition of "Sweet Jane" during an encore at the Sydney Festival. The Dap-Kings act as the backing band for Amy Winehouse on her first US tour, which includes performances on *Late Show with David Letterman* and *The Tonight Show with Jay Leno*. Jones and the Dap-Kings perform at SXSW, prompting a feature in the *Village Voice*. On October 2, *100 Days, 100 Nights* is released to widespread critical acclaim. YouTube premieres the black-and-white video for "100 Days, 100 Nights," and Sharon Jones and the Dap-Kings tour the USA and Canada.

2008

Sharon Jones and the Dap-Kings perform "100 Days, 100 Nights" on *Late Show with David Letterman* in February and sell out New York's Beacon Theater for a special Valentine's day show before appearing at the Womad Festival in Australia and New Zealand in March. Despite having been on the road for practically the past six months, they complete a full festival tour. They return to New York to appear on *Late Night with Conan O'Brien* (performing "Let Them Knock") before winding down their summer touring.

2009

Jones and the Dap-Kings start the year with a West Coast tour and a performance on *The Late Late Show with Craig Ferguson*. They cover Shuggie Otis's "Inspiration Information" for the lauded *Dark Was the Night* charity compilation, and also appear at an associated benefit show on May 3 at New York's Radio City Music Hall, alongside David Byrne, the National, Feist, and the Dirty Projectors. The *Brooklyn Vegan* blog notes of that performance, "Sharon Jones and the Dap-Kings' onstage power, especially in that massive room, was something no one all night had come close to." Sharon then goes into the studio with David Byrne to record a song for his Imelda Marcos tribute album, *Here Lies Love*, before she and the Dap-Kings record "Baby (You've Got What It Takes)" with Michael Bublé. Then, after concluding a full summer of touring, they finally return to Daptone Studios to begin recording their follow-up to *100 Days, 100 Nights*.

2010

In January, Sharon joins Michael Bublé for a duet of "Baby (You've Got What It Takes)" on *Saturday Night Live*. In March, in preparation for the release of their fourth full-length album, *I Learned the Hard Way*, the band set off to Austin, Texas, for a busy run at SXSW that includes showcases curated by AOL and NPR. They then travel back home to New York City to play WNYC's Soundcheck and to celebrate the release of the LP on April 6. The album continues to climb the *Billboard* charts, reaching #2 on the Independent Albums listing and #6 on the R&B/Hip-Hop chart, and will go on to move over 100,000 copies in its first four months of release. Jones and the band spend much of 2010 touring in support of their new album, covering the USA, Canada, Europe, Australia, and New Zealand.

2011

On January 18, Jones and the Dap-Kings open for Prince on his "Welcome 2 America" tour at Madison Square Garden. Prince then invites

Jones and members of the band to perform with him during his song "A Love Bizarre." After the show, they are invited to play Prince's after-party downtown at the Darby. They then continue to tour the USA and internationally, opening for Prince in Paris and Ghent.

On July 24, 2011, Sharon Jones shares the stage with Stevie Wonder, as well as fellow Daptone family member Charles Bradley, for an evening of soul music collaborations at the Hollywood Bowl. In September 2011, she and the band go into Daptone Studios for a month to write and record their fifth full-length album.

2012

Jones and her band dedicate a lot of time to the continent of Europe in 2012, undergoing five separate tours altogether. In between these tours, they put the finishing touches to their next album, *Give the People What They Want*, while Jones also joins Daryl Hall on his inaugural "Live from Daryl's House" tour.

In May of 2012, Jones and the Dap-Kings collaborate with the National Symphony Orchestra and John Legend, performing Marvin Gaye's classic "What's Going On" at the Kennedy Center in front of two sold-out audiences. Sharon has the honor of meeting First Lady Michelle Obama after she attends the second performance.

On August 18, Sharon Jones and the Dap-Kings play a homecoming show in Williamsburg, Brooklyn, following a few more European trips. They then return to the studio in September to record six classic cover songs for Martin Scorsese's *The Wolf of Wall Street*, before selling out Davies Symphony Hall over Thanksgiving weekend.

2013

At the start of the year, Jones and the band return to one of their favorite places—Australia—for the sixth time since 2005. The highlight of the trip is headlining a Daptone Super Soul Revue on the opening night of Sydney Festival in front of 50,000 screaming fans. Joining the band once again is Charles Bradley, alongside the Budos Band, the Menahan Street

Band, and the Sugarman Three. Then, in March, a trip to Quito, Ecuador, marks a brilliant debut at the Ecuador Jazz Festival at the beautiful old Teatro Nacional Sucre.

In early May, Daptone Records announces the release of *Give the People What They Want*. NPR's "Wait, Wait Don't Tell Me" invites Jones and the Dap-Kings to be the house band for its live broadcast on May 2, which is relayed from NYU's Skirball Center for the Performing Arts to 600 movie theaters around the country. They are joined onstage by Steve Martin, Paula Poundstone, Mo Rocca, Tom Bodett, and the show's hosts, Peter Sagal and Carl Kasell.

One week after performing on the NPR show, Sharon Jones is hospitalized for dehydration and exhaustion. Ten days later, on one of the most difficult days of her life, she is diagnosed with a Stage 1 cancerous tumor of the bile duct. She releases a statement explaining her situation, and Daptone indefinitely postpones the release of *Give the People What They Want*. On June 11, Sharon undergoes a seven-hour Whipple operation at New York's Columbia-Presbyterian Hospital. The surgery is successful, and a few weeks later, Sharon temporarily moves to Sharon Springs, New York, to rest and recover from the surgery.

Despite the surgery's success, the doctors at Columbia-Presbyterian recommend a six-month course of chemotherapy. Jones remains in Sharon Springs, undergoing chemotherapy at the Bassett Center in Cooperstown, New York. In late August, Cabin Creek Films starts work on a documentary about Sharon's life. The film is to be directed and produced by Academy Award–winning director Barbara Kopple and co-produced by David Cassidy.

On October 9, Daptone Records announces a new release date for *Give the People What They Want*, while also releasing an animated video for the single "Retreat."

2014

On January 14, *Give the People What They Want* is finally released. That week, Jones and the Dap-Kings appear on *Ellen*, *The Tonight Show with*

Jay Leno, Late Night with Jimmy Fallon, and *Conan.* On February 6, they play their first full show since Sharon's diagnosis at New York City's Beacon Theater. The show and the preparation leading up to it are filmed for use in the movie *Miss Sharon Jones!* Throughout 2014, they tour across the USA, Canada, Europe, Australia, and New Zealand. They perform on *Later . . . with Jools Holland* in the UK, *Inas Nacht* in Germany, and on Canal+ in France, and at the Glastonbury Music Festival, Montreux Jazz Festival, Rock Werchter, Rock en Seine, and more.

In August, Sharon Jones and the Dap-Kings reprise their rendition of "What's Going On" with John Legend at the Hollywood Bowl in front of a sold-out crowd. In September, they tour Europe as part of the Daptone Super Soul Revue with Charles Bradley, Antibalas, and the Sugarman Three. Sharon participates in a tribute to Stevie Wonder in Memphis, put on by the Memphis Music Consortium, an organization that encourages local kids in to get involved in music. In December 2014, Jones and the Dap-Kings host three historic nights at the Apollo Theater as part of the Daptone Super Soul Revue, while *Give the People What They Want* is nominated for a Grammy Award for "Best R&B Album."

2015

In January, the doctors find a small tumor on Sharon's liver, and she undergoes an ablation surgery to remove it. She and the Dap-Kings tour across Brazil, playing to many sold-out crowds. In March, Sharon participates in a David Byrne tribute at Carnegie Hall, where she brings the crowd to its feet with a great rendition of "Psycho Killer." The film *Miss Sharon Jones!* premieres at Toronto International Film Festival to a standing ovation and much critical praise. Sharon watches the film for the first time.

Sharon and the Dap-Kings embark on a co-headlining tour with Tedeschi Trucks Band across the USA. Every night, Sharon and the T.T.B. duet on Etta James's "Tell Mama" during the encore. In September, Sharon begins another course of chemotherapy. Meanwhile, Sharon Jones and the Dap-Kings release their first album of holiday classics and originals, *It's a Holiday Soul Party.* They appear on *Conan, The Late Show with Stephen Colbert*, and *Michael Bublé's Christmas in Hollywood.*

2016

On February 22, Sharon Jones is a special guest at Philip Glass's Tibet House benefit at Carnegie Hall, where she sings David Bowie's "Tonight" with Iggy Pop. She and the Dap-Kings then record a cover of the Allman Brothers' "Midnight Rider" for a Lincoln Motor Company TV commercial featuring them and the actor Matthew McConaughey. In March, Sharon undergoes the Y-90 treatment—a targeted radiation therapy to treat her cancer.

On April 16, Sharon and her band play the outdoor stage at the grand opening of KEXP Seattle's new studio. From late spring into summer, they open for Hall and Oates on the East Coast, the West Coast, and in the South. In July, *Miss Sharon Jones!* opens at the IFC Center in New York City and the Nuart Theater in L.A., and then across North America. It runs at the IFC Center for a full month, with many sold-out screenings. In August, the *Miss Sharon Jones! Original Motion Picture Soundtrack* is released on Daptone Records, featuring a new song from the band called "I'm Still Here." In November, the film is released on DVD and certified fresh on Rotten Tomatoes with an audience score of 95 percent.

In July and August, Sharon undergoes a week of radiation therapy treatments aimed at her spine (where the cancer has spread) and begins a new course of chemotherapy. "I'm Still Here" wins "Best Song in a Documentary" at the Critics' Choice Documentary Awards, while Sharon is among the winners in the "Most Compelling Living Subject" category at the same awards ceremony.

Sharon Jones passes away at Bassett Medical Center in Cooperstown, New York, on November 18, 2016.

SAILING AWAY
Coal Becomes Crystal Under Pressure

"There is a sound that comes from gospel music that doesn't come from anything else. It is a sound of peace. It is a sound of, 'I'm going to make it through all of this.'"
—YOLANDA ADAMS in *Points of Power*, 2010

The secular entertainment known variably as blues, rock, soul, and funk is considered by some people to be the devil's music. Maybe it is, but if so, it's a devil with a human heart that helps us to live and to cope with our choices, no matter how ill advised they may have been.

In Randy Newman's 1972 satirical ode to the African diaspora, "Sail Away," his unreliable narrator intones the virtues of their ensuing voyage in sarcastically hopeful terms. The nasal voice opines that, in America they'll all have food to eat so they won't have to run through the jungle and scuff up their feet. They'll just sit around drinking wine all day and sing about Jesus. Thus the devilishly seductive shipmaster invites them on his dark journey: "We will cross the mighty ocean to the Charleston Bay. Sail away, sail away with me, it's great to be an American." History as irony writ large.

On her final album—one she didn't live to listen to with the rest of us—Sharon Jones sang a song about another contrasting kind of end-lessly sought liberation, but one involving forgiveness and the hoped-for redemption that often accompanies it. On her poignant song of letting bygones be bygones, "Sail On," Jones purrs about a former friend or lover who gets thrown out of their home and reminds them that when she herself came knocking on their door under the same circumstances, they told her to *sail on*. "Two people stranded without a helping hand, two people stranded without a friend."

If the song sounds a little like a hymn, that's because that's exactly what it is: a hymn to doing unto others. In a similarly spiritual vein—one even more explicit—the video released to support the classic gospel tune "Call on God," which closes Jones's posthumously released 2017 album *Soul of a Woman*, contains some touching archival footage from ten years earlier that reveals a degree of religious fervor that might surprise some of Jones's fans more familiar with her ripping secular raunchy funk stylings.

They might also be taken aback, given that many of them only discovered and fell in love with her realness in the twenty-first century, that she had penned that song in the late '70s for the E. L. Fields Gospel Wonders group, the choir she sang for at New York's Universal Church of God. The song was so powerful that she and the band wanted to hold it in reserve for an all-gospel tune album they were planning, but her early departure prevented that spiritually flavored record from being completed.

At Jones's New York memorial service in 2016, her old friend and pastor, Margo Fields, the widow of E. L., delivered a moving rendition of the song with reunited members of the Gospel Wonders. Following the service, the Dap-Kings brought the Gospel Wonders to their studio to add their soaring choral voices to back up Jones for the final track on her final album.

As Fields expressed it to *Rolling Stone*, "Sharon always wanted to add background vocals to the song and she would have been happy to know that her old friends had come through to sing with her one final time." Indeed, it's also a great reminder to those who may not be familiar with Jones's roots in sacred music just how integral her sanctified faith was to her secular art.

When I interviewed her for this book, Margo Fields told me that Jones possessed that intensity from the very beginning.

> Sharon came to New York from Augusta at an early age. She joined the Universal Church of God family at the tender age of thirteen under the leadership of the late bishop Elijah Fields, located at Rockaway Avenue in Brooklyn, New York. Pastor Fields encouraged her to go to the piano. With no piano lessons or any vocal training, Sharon learned to play starting with two fingers and following the bassist Ronald Lee and guitarist Willie Jordan. With God as her teacher, she grew to become the church musician and its choir director.
>
> She also spontaneously arranged and wrote original gospel songs, and even wrote a play entitled "Pray for Me" to raise funds for our Women's Day. Sharon's character was that of a young lady who began singing in the church but from there her voice took her around the world. The play she wrote would eventually become her lived reality.

To many of the faithful, of course, that sounds like a deity's plan playing out across a lifetime; to many others of us, it sounds like creative visualization and pure personal willpower on a grand scale. Either way, it's pretty impressive. And for Fields, the young Jones demonstrated a sense of faith and self-determination that would hold her in good stead throughout both her career and her life.

Pastor Fields, originally from Virginia but now a spritely seventy-six-year-old New Yorker, confided to me that she and her husband recognized that there was something special about the young Sharon from the first moment they set eyes, and ears, upon her. The late bishop Elijah, in particular, noticed that when their little orchestra started to pick up the pace and rock the congregation, a certain little girl in the back began bobbing up and down, twitching to and fro, and pounding the pew in front of her like a frenzied drummer. It was hard to miss the kid in the back since she was almost spinning like a barely contained top, even while sitting down.

"Girl, get yourself up here," he gently requested, with the girl in question maybe suspecting she was about to be reprimanded for over-exuberance. Instead, pastor Margo vividly recalls, the bishop was clearly discerning the spirit overtaking the girl: "He told her to go play the piano, knowing that God, and her own spirit, would guide her hands." In this case, it was only two of her tiny fingers that God guided, and apparently that guidance continued right up until 2016, when the little woman, by now a famous soul and funk star recording "Call on God," went on to join an invisible orchestra.

Pastor Margo told me that Sharon, with whom she developed a deep relationship, was always what she liked to a call a "churchy girl." By that, she meant a person whose initial inspiration in life was the church, and one who never really left the church behind. This despite the fact that Margo could never bring herself to see any of her protégé's live concerts, since she couldn't cope with "watching her shake her butt off up there onstage."

Yet still the admiration the pastor felt for this spunky girl came through loud and clear in our discussion. Eventually, Margo relented and accepted a ticket to see Sharon perform at the fabled Apollo The-ater, a site of such cultural importance within the African American community that even a religious leader would be familiar with it. She was placed in the balcony with a fine view of her little angel's transfor-mation into a vibrant and sensual life force set loose upon the audience, and admits that she was a little nervous that Jones might wave up at her and single her out. She didn't, of course, but she did direct a few reverent winks in her direction, which made Fields beam, in spite of the raunchy circumstances.

Margo explained to me in no uncertain terms that there was no way to separate soul music from gospel music, and that her concept of "soul power" was something we all had originally but that most of us had lost, and that it was most evident when we fire ourselves up, lose ourselves, and let the Creator take over. Indeed, anyone who has seen either James Brown or Sharon Jones at the Apollo knows for a fact that *something* has taken over.

One of the most charming distinctions that Pastor Margo made for me between the music and dancing of the church's gospel music and that of the secular theaters and clubs of soul music was a somewhat counterintuitive one. It had to do with "crossing your legs," but not in the way we might first imagine. She stipulated that, in gospel dancing, your legs are always side by side and never cross over, while in soul and funk music, the singers' and dancers' legs are perpetually crisscrossing over themselves and do not remain sedately parallel. If you crisscrossed your legs while dancing in church, people would shout, "Go sit down, you're not out in the world now."

I found this delightful, like most of what Margo Fields shared with me—especially the fact that Sharon was possibly the most determined, ambitious, stubborn, and independent person she ever met. "She wouldn't ever take no for an answer," was how the pastor put it, and "she did what she wanted, the way she wanted"—much to her credit, in the end, since so many people provided so much professional discouragement over the years, and yet she not only persevered and persisted, she triumphed despite all odds.

But for me, the most important insight that Margo offered me in our illuminating chat was that, "You can take the girl out of the church but you can't ever take the church out of the girl." This observation was borne out by the fact that when she did see Sharon perform live, or on video, she felt, "To me, she was still in church, no matter what she sang—just look at the way she sings and moves."

Was she still testifying, I wondered? "Exactly so, exactly so, uh huh!"

Mrs. Fields offered another keen insight into Jones's character via the fact that throughout her life, Sharon continued to contribute financial tithes to her church; and whenever her busy international concert tour schedule permitted her to return home to New York, Jones always found time to not only appear at the church personally but also to join in the congregation's rousing singing. Naturally, hers was always the loudest and most boisterous voice.

This is why, in order to fully understand the soul power of Sharon Jones properly, one really needs to fully explore her musical ancestral roots. And that ancestry is easy to trace in its tracks, from the sacred to the secular and all the way back again. That's because her trail is practically a map in itself—it's the geography of her imagination and her artistry, one moving historically backward from New York to Georgia, and from Georgia back to Africa. It's a map that helps us to pinpoint the musical evolution of this consummate churchy girl, crisscrossing legs and all.

• • •

For about thirty seconds I toyed with the idea of calling this book *The Gospel According to Sharon* but veered away to avoid any unintended irreverence, even though that's a clear picture of the style she began with and never really left behind: *gospel fury.* Her sound was a riveting battle between the sacred and profane fighting inside of her. It strikes me as even more pertinent in the context of a comment by Paul Oliver in his fine study *Songsters and Saints*: "Soul Gospel was a variation on black gospel pioneered in the 1950s by a number of church quartets, including the Soul Stirrers and the Pilgrim Travelers, as well as solo artists such as Aretha Franklin. While religious in subject matter, soul gospel was marked by its raw, often sexually charged display of emotion." Sounds like the perfect description of Jones to me.

Sharon Jones made perfectly clear the formative roles of both religion in general and gospel music in particular in her life when she spoke to National Public Radio in 2016, only a couple of months before she left us. "I never took any kind of vocal lessons or teachings of how to—I never even took piano lessons," she said. "A voice just came to me and said: go play the piano in church!" And she couldn't have been any clearer when she explained how she choose her career and her beliefs over a more conventional family life: "I just want to give my love to

God." Somewhere along the way, of course, she decided that she may as well give it to all the rest of us as well.

Unless we understand how central the role of gospel music was in both the personal and professional life of Sharon Jones, we won't be able to appreciate the fact that she never stopping singing it or testifying to its message, no matter how much she sashayed, shimmied, shook, rattled, or rolled. That fact also helps to clarify the radical stylistic transformations from the spirit-possession music of West Africa to the churches of the American South to the streets of its northern cities. It's also perhaps a surprising fact that the new secular soul sound she explored was still deeply spiritual music, even if she might be the only one who interpreted it quite that way.

One of Jones's fellow soul vocalists, Saundra Williams, who knew her well and backed her up for years, offered an ideal summation to the AOL Build Series: "Man, Sharon's voice is like a freight train, you just better get outta the way!" The implication for me being that those boxcars were chock full of the holy ghost, or at least some comparable and highly combustible fuel, but were also mingled with the contraband cargo of raw sex appeal. That train, in the words of the great song by the Reverend Blind Gary Davis, is bound for glory, and all travelers are welcome to come aboard.

Such are the odd and disturbing paradoxes of involuntary African emigration to America. The ironic gospel tune pushes and pulls at the heart of the historical black diaspora into their American nightmare, via the grand musical creations that emerged before, during, and after the departure of the slave ships. Those forced travelers were the vibrant bearers of a glorious new musical tradition that traversed the ocean with them from Yoruba to Charleston, and then migrated from Memphis to Detroit—and eventually everywhere. Jones would eventually ride her soul train all over the planet.

Along the way, first by sea and later by highway, these forced migrants would internalize the combustible faith-fuel forced on them by presumably well-intentioned if misguided Christian missionaries and invent gospel, blues, jazz, rhythm and blues, rock 'n' roll, soul, funk, and, later on, hip-hop, in one of the most creative explosions of self-expression in history. Several generations after that original voyage, an African American artist with the spirit-fire of James Brown would sing his own loud national anthem of black pride in quite a different and defiant tenor. And it's with creative figures like him and those who followed in his stylistic tradition that we can see and hear the truly incredible evolution from gospel to soul and eventually even to funked-up rap. The circuitous voyages of sacred music leading to the secular soul sound can all be equally exotic, and they all reveal that at the heart of each tradition is one shared inherent core meaning: liberation.

Sharon Jones had personally absorbed this musical message of liberation early in life. When she was nine years old and she bravely stood up in a traditional Baptist church to sing the hymn "Silent Night" as a solo, the little angel portrayed by Jones suddenly realized a new sensation, the feeling of being transported out of her body and carried on the wings of her voice into another realm, a special realm, a sacred realm. And I certainly suspect that anyone, regardless of race or faith, could benefit from hearing what Jones does to embody that Holy Spirit, so gentle and mild, in her bluesy, *adult* rendition of "Silent Night" forty-six years later on her *Soul Time* album with the Dap-Kings.

In an interview with Elio Iannacci, features editor for *Fashion* magazine, published posthumously in 2016, Jones remarked on how her early childhood musical awakening felt, and the first time she could remember ever singing. "They cast me as an angel. I was just a little girl, just a child. It felt so good! I felt like I was only half a person before I sang anything. When I started singing that carol, I remember feeling like I was completely me, for once." This now strikes me as perfect typecasting. To those who knew her personally, I've discovered, she actually seemed angelic, although she was certainly a hot and sweaty version of one.

The word "gospel" literally means "good news," but the really good news is the fact that gospel music morphed into blues, blues morphed into soul, soul morphed into funk, and funk was practically Sharon

Jones's middle name. It took her unique penchant for eliminating barriers to help us see, and hear, that true soul music transcends the artificial boundaries and genres we tend to place on art in general and on music in particular.

When blues music went on a blind date with gospel music and had too much rhythm and blues to think, that unlikely marriage of heaven and hell gave birth to something called soul. In some ways, the parents of these sacred and profane styles didn't want their kids going out together, let alone settling down and starting a dance-mad family that would shake up the musical world forever.

Thus we enter the saga of Sharon Jones at the beginning of her long hard climb to the stellar soul heights, in the hot, holy, Southern church pews where fervent worship was the only spiritual dish on the community menu. When we listen with the right ears—perhaps even ears sanctified to some extent by the broadest and most inclusive context possible—we can easily discern something utterly obvious: Sharon Jones began her life as a gospel singer and remained a gospel singer throughout its six decades. She even ended her time on earth where she began it, singing "Go Tell It on the Mountain" and "His Eye Is on the Sparrow," among other iconic gospel tunes, on her peaceful deathbed in New York in 2016, more than half a lifetime away from her first public solo as a child choir singer.

We can accurately trace the tracks of her tears and follow her soul journey back to its origins, when she first encountered the devil in the jumping church choirs of black Augusta, where she joyously watched her sisters Willa and Dora letting loose and she learned from the masters the power of the spirit. Jones's second primary and life-altering demonic encounter would be with another Georgian native: the devil's chief disciple, James Brown, a friend of her mother's. Like Jones, Brown had absorbed the reverential frenzy of faith and then shifted his allegiance to the raucous energy of the life force itself.

In our interview, Dapette Starr Duncan Lowe gave me her personal testimony as to the coherence of this continuity between different musical styles that all stem from the same source, in the same way rivers all flow (eventually) back to some ocean or other. "The notion of the *good news* of the gospel actually ends up turning into the 'feels good!' of all soul music. It's like, this 'feels good!' and I'm gonna tell you why!"

In the big, sprawling Jones family, with Sharon and five boisterous siblings—Dora, Charles, Ike, Willa, and Henry—the church was the center of not just a community of faith but also one of living, breathing, and sweating music. But the church, as we'll clearly see and hear, was never fully left behind—in fact, Jones carried it inside of her right to the end, just as her idol Brown did. The daughter of Augusta native Ella Mae Price and Charles Jones, a resident of the adjacent county of North Georgia, she was the youngest of six children in a large family unit augmented by the fact that Ella Mae also raised her late sister's four children as well as her own. As Jones told it, she was born in a hospital storage room because the brutal Jim Crow laws of the '50s South prohibited her mother from having a room. It would be her very first rejection—an existential denial of equality—in a lifetime of rejections by a superficial and gloss-obsessed music industry prior to her mid-life triumph.

In 1960, when Jones was four years old, her family moved to the Bedford Stuyvesant area of Brooklyn, New York, her mother needing to escape an abusive husband. In this she was ironically again shadowing James Brown, whose father took him away from South Carolina to Georgia, similarly to escape a broken marriage; from there, he too would migrate to New York. Even more ironically, the Jones clan had moved to the same locale where nearly four decades later she would accidentally meet Daptone Records founder and writer, performer, and producer Gabriel Roth, the abundantly gifted man who would give her a long-awaited chance to make her mark in authentic soul music.

Jones would be fully forty-six years old before releasing her first album under her own name, and with her own band, under Roth's visionary tutelage. Meanwhile, she was about six years old when James Brown was exploding onto the scene at another kind of church, the fabled Apollo Theater in New York, and seven when he released his seminal *Live at the Apollo Theater* in 1963. As children, she and her huge sibling tribe would take turns imitating the dancing and singing style of the mercurial Mr. Brown. By the time Jones was nine and old enough to realize the power of what she was hearing, Brown had invented a completely new kind of American music, especially with his release of *Papa's Got a Brand New Bag* in 1965. At the risk of being irreverent yet again, I'll describe her prepubescent exposure to the sensual abandon of Brown as a kind of John the Baptist moment, anointing her with the holy power of his new, bump-and-grind scripture.

Jones's sister, Willa Jones-Stringer, recalled for me a startling childhood moment when Sharon was a young kid who suddenly jumped up to offer her own "testimony": "When I grow up I'm gonna write and sing songs, and I'm gonna buy my mother a house!" It may have taken her a while, but that's exactly what she did. In fact, Willa told me that even as a girl, Sharon felt responsible for the entire family. After graduating from Thomas Jefferson High School and attending Brooklyn College, the future funk queen instantly began to enter talent shows backed by local soul bands, while still a regular church choir singer, thus establishing early on the twin creative polarities of her seemingly conflicting commitments. To Jones, however, there was no contradiction between these two poles, since somehow she intuitively perceived them as an alternating current, conveying a life force that belonged to her alone, no matter how she chose to express it to others.

She was both a generator of and an amplifier for an energy that couldn't be denied. But the real origin of her skill at transmitting divinity through the body was an innate supernatural ability predating even soul music that harks back to the beginnings of gospel music, to what used to quaintly be called the *negro spirituals*. The volatile and exuberant new forms of expression they engendered might be better described as *afro-physicals*. Yet even more important than the blissed-out state their music provoked in us is the historical link each elder statesman (or woman) provided for future fellow practitioners of their craft.

There's a creative conduit flowing between an innovative performer such as James Brown and a vital incarnation such as Sharon Jones—one that operates in the shared communal language of music. They both liked to sing with the angels but also to dance with the devil, and I'm reminded of Tennessee Williams's remark that he never wanted to get rid of his demons because then he might also lose his angels. Brown in fact often stated his intentions very clearly in action, apart from his main objective of being the most famous and celebrated performer on earth: he wanted to be beyond good and evil. He had not an ounce of false modesty (or any modesty) in his quivering frame when he declared that he and his fellow howlers "sang like angels." "I'd like to go back to gospel," he once explained to *Rolling Stone*. "Really, I never left it. Or it never left me. The public may not know it, but the Sex Machine first did it to death for the Lord. I want to, I can testify. Gospel singing saved my life, except that I didn't get to sing it in church that much, I sang it in prison."

Brown did so literally: he was harmonizing in jail cells in Georgia in 1949, having been sentenced to a term of eight to sixteen years for breaking into cars. Ironically, the woman he most inspired to sing soul, Sharon Jones, would also have a history of serenading prisoners, though from the other side of the bars as an armed guard. "People cried when we sang," Brown recalled in his breathy raspy voice. Sharon Jones did, too. She also decided that she too wanted to make people cry with her voice, and she did that as well, eventually.

Such an emotional link is even more obvious when we consider the direct and immediate creative conversation between Brown and Jones— one that ensures that the historical inheritance has the quality of being a lived experience. A classic is something that never finishes saying what it has to say, and that's vitally true of gospel and soul music, especially the kinds practiced by figures such as Brown and Jones. The soul music journey is never really over. In fact, one generation of singer/songwriter/performer might continue to say precisely what their forebears were saying, in a kind of accumulating wave that never reaches any shore.

As we'll soon see and hear, continuity is everything here: not just the connections between varying styles but a far deeper spiritual continuum between totally different musical genres. But genres meant nothing to a dame as forceful as Sharon Jones, and in 2010, when she was becoming famous as a soul music revivalist extraordinaire, she declared to *FaceCulture*, "Church and church singing, that's my calling, that's my blessing, and it's still what I do. It's all church singing."

In our conversation, Starr Duncan Lowe confirmed to me the same sentiment expressed by Margo Fields—the notion that you can take the girl out of the church but not the other way around. "The gospel 'feeling' never leaves you. That's because it's part of the DNA embedded in your body and soul. It's only the 'setting' in which your music is performed that gives it a different brand or label, such as gospel or soul or funk, or anything. The setting you're in makes you adapt yourself to that environment. It's all about the context. But that gospel music feel"—what Pastor Margo called the churchy feel—"that's part of the fiber of who you are, it's *what* you are. It's in your spiritual DNA."

• • •

The apparent nostalgia I detect in spiritual music such as gospel is of a very specific and deep sort. It's a unique longing built on the bones of African American oppression, a longing that saturates the exuberantly faithful who publicly testify their belief in churches utterly unburdened even by social decorum. From my perspective, one of the secret ways to both appreciate and enjoy the pleasures of gospel music is not a religious one at all, though it's spiritual in nature. It rests on a principle that can easily be traced as gospel morphs into blues and blues merges with rhythm and then morphs into both soul and funk music. Each one of these stylistic evolutionary leaps is an embodied meaning that reflects, distills, and crystallizes the core values and time of the culture that birthed it.

I propose that gospel music is a nostalgia for a *future* state and place, not a past one: a nostalgia for a future of salvation and the place where it might theoretically occur; a place called heaven. Few genres of music have influenced mainstream American popular sounds and entertainment quite as profoundly as gospel, with artists such as James Brown and Sharon Jones just the jutting tip of a vast and sonorous iceberg. Long before it would morph so ironically into blues or soul or funk, gospel had itself already emerged from a much earlier fusion of West African song traditions: the scarring experience of slavery, of "sailing away," of superimposed Christian devotional practices, and the social nightmare of being black in the American southern states.

Eventually, as the African American spirit possession and worship traditions grew more active, and post–civil war reconstruction catapulted waves of migrating, newly freed individuals away from the rural South and northward into the industrialized urban zones, the influences of this musical genre became all the more prevalent. Its ultimate transformation into a non-religious realm, and even the non-black domain of popular secular entertainment, would be one of the most amazing artistic evolutions in cultural history—one that can still be felt in the shimmy of Sharon Jones or the wiggling genius of the late Prince. One of the most obvious places to look at this transplanting of generic roots into shocking new soil is in the morphing of thematic lyrics and song content: a shift in emphasis away from a worshipped patriarchal creator deity, *He*, into a down-to-earth romantic figure worshipped for distinctly different reasons, *She*.

Perhaps the most influential of the many examples of this technique is the legendary performer Sam Cooke, who with his group the Soul Stirrers would morph an ancient tune such as "Wonderful," with its message of faith—the firm belief that the Lord will provide whatever is needed—into a peppy pop tune about his lover initially delivered when he was still Dale Cook—"There's not quite another, quite as sweet as you, I love my girl, she's so lovable"—plumbing a message of undiluted desire, especially in the way he alone could transmit it.

For me, though, it was Sister Rosetta Tharpe (1915–1973) who truly was one of the towering bridges between gospel and rock, fusing them into an unheard-of rebellious romp, pumped along by her masterful electric guitar riffs, delivered in her totally unique rendering of a classic gospel shaker such as "Down by the Riverside." Jones perfectly straddles this ongoing genetic and stylistic link between a prayer (*give me guidance*) and a promise (*I'll be true to you*) in its tumultuous transition from the pulpit to the bedroom. Yet paradoxically, this unique female performer, the glorious Sister Rosetta, was already twanging out adrenaline-charged steel guitar gospel riffs as early as 1944. And in the hands of a primitive genius like Tharpe—with "Strange Things Happening Every Day" in 1945 or "Up Above My Head" in 1946, or even boldly revamping a classic like "Riverside" in 1948—a fresh, new, and as yet unexplored and unnamed musical style and tradition was being born right before our eyes and ears. I'm also delighted to report that in recognition of her visionary musical status, last year Rosetta Tharpe was finally nominated for induction into the Rock and Roll Hall of Fame, and that she's up where she belongs, wildly praying right next to Bo Diddley.

The merger of African harmonies and rhythms with Christian narratives of hope and salvation produced an incredibly potent shield for both survival and sustenance. The eventual arrival of the electric guitar and amplification would transform these rural delta folk-blues roots and field-chant lamentations into a dynamic and utterly new kind of urban sound, one that continues to evolve dramatically every hour of every day. The gospel music that Sharon Jones, her sisters, and their community grew up singing was the direct result of the forced Christian conversion of West African slaves in the American South, culminating in a roof-rattling kind of liberation sound that allowed its practitioners to rise up, above, and beyond not only the early physical bonds of oppression but also the social and cultural boundaries of their poor neighborhoods in big American cities in the north. Its secular manifestations would take the embodied meaning of faith and pump it full to bursting with the life forces of desire, lust, sensual abandon, and a new kind of ecstatic dancing that would prove every bit as transformative as its original African roots.

Even though the gospel songs that grew from the soil of fieldwork laments shared the same roots as blues and jazz, the religious-versus-secular component kept them quite separate until all three literally burst into popular music almost at the same time. Over time, the borders between these styles became less mutually exclusive, especially once composers such as the pianist Thomas Dorsey (1899–1993), often called the father of the bluesy gospel song as we know it today, started to filter it into the mainstream society around him. His lively blues renditions were actually known as "dorseys" and had an evangelical passion capable of fueling engines as powerful as the one that drove overwhelmingly captivating titans like Ray Charles and James Brown. That fuel would in turn combust the engines of singers traveling in a straight line all the way to Sharon Jones in the twenty-first century.

In the Baptist churches the family of Sharon Jones was attending, both while still in Georgia and soon in her early childhood in New York, the songs that started her blood circulating at a faster-than-normal rate were those taught by parents to their offspring long before the kids could possibly comprehend their theological origins or meanings. "Deep River," "Wade in the Water," and "Amazing Grace" have all, of course, become stalwarts not just of black religious culture but of American culture in general, becoming, in other words, icons, emblems, or logos of spirituality that cross over the sacred, secular, and racial divides. Even more remarkable is the fact that barely a single note of these tunes has been altered since they were first being intoned to relieve deprivation in the Southern fields over a hundred years earlier.

Gospel music is often called the quintessential American musical language for the way it reflects the interaction of independent but integrated portions of a piece delivered by a wild and free group format, and how it quotes historical musical gestures in a myriad of new ways—some so new that they were no longer officially termed gospel but rather soul. The Nigerian origins of what we might call "spirit-roots" music (whether sacred or secular) can best be summed up as passionately human but no less divine, and encompassing the twin roles of religion and music in black culture. But it was the *sanctified* variety of sacred music, contained in houses of worship where the parishioners were encouraged to *testify* their belief, that Sharon Jones grew up with as a kind of *furious faith* and absorbed deeply as environmental nourishment, hoping it would heal the difficult and often violent parental relationship she saw in her childhood.

Like gospel and the blues that ravished it, soul music could also be identified as a personal storytelling medium, and it still remains a vehicle for channeling deep feelings, whether the story is one of religious conversion or of how someone's lover betrayed them. From my perspective, many of the most important and influential gospel artists who would bend the genre toward soul were women, some of whom were overlooked either because of their gender or due to difficult life circumstances. Sharon Jones would become all too familiar with what it felt like to be overlooked.

Clearly, without gospel there would never have been a starting point for soul and R&B music. Whether the song has an upbeat tempo or a slow one doesn't matter, because these musicians are still going to produce music that is either *about the blues* or is telling a story of the blues, which is exactly what gospel has done from the beginning: it's just blues music about the word of God. Its derivatives—soul and funk—would merely bring those blues back down to earth. Indeed, such songs transcend all arbitrary emotional or stylistic boundaries, as evidenced by a classic such as Dorsey's "Take My Hand Precious Lord" (1932), which has been covered by artists as diverse as Nina Simone and Chaka Khan. And the forward motion or momentum of such songs is so intense that four years after Mahalia Jackson sang it at the funeral of Martin Luther King Jr., Aretha Franklin sang it at the funeral of Mahalia Jackson. The Dapettes, Jones's vocal partners Saundra Williams and Starr Duncan Lowe, would naturally also need to sing it for their soul sister at Jones's own memorial, joined by the choir of her youth, the Gospel Wonders. The heartbeat of both prayer and lust goes on and on: this train never stops. Sharon Jones, for one, took the rocking advice and words of her famous gospel mentor, Madame Mahalia, literally to heart, and she applied them passionately. In fact, it sometimes strikes me that Sharon Jones is Mahalia Jackson on amphetamines.

• • •

In the late '70s, Jones composed and sang lead vocals on a single 45-rpm record released on the little Hall Records label from Virginia, appearing with E. L. Fields and the Gospel Wonders on two tracks, "Heaven Bound" and "Key to the Kingdom," arranged and produced by the Universal Church of God Inc. No one paid too much attention to it back then in '78, so the self-produced record sank like a stone tossed into the ocean, still twenty long hard years before Jones's discovery by Daptone Records near the end of the twentieth century.

"Heaven Bound," in particular, is rousing to the spirit and arousing to the body, with its insistent shouts of "Wanna testify, gotta testify" over a resounding boom-boom rhythm that bears a striking sonic resemblance to a song by the pop group Chic, "Le Freak," a simple tune that by 1979 had kick-started the disco phase of rhythm and blues that would dominate the next decade. It definitely seems to my ears as though Sharon Jones got there first, but the music industry, not always the most prescient of businesses, didn't know what to make of her futuristic invention of something that today we can easily call by the obvious name "gospel funk."

Jones firmly believed that if she ever started to appear to be higher than everybody else, God was always available to bring her down a notch—to let her know she's not. She described her feeling of gratitude to *Fashion* magazine as that of being appreciative of her audiences and so fortunate to be out doing her concert performances. As she put it, "I'm so thankful for them, for God, for having me be able to shout and keep my voice open. It's just about me being humble for my blessings."

Even when she's in the throes of a tremendously sensual and foxy soul sashay, she's still never far from the pews where she first started singing. In church, she explained, she would not hold back—not that she ever did onstage, either, for that matter. She described this to NPR as letting it all out, when what she called an "anointing" came over her, just as it seemed to on the secular theater stage, when she appeared to invite the devil inside her out for a party. "I just opened my mouth and the words came out, the air just flowed. And it was from that that I knew God had watched over me and had me ready."

Back in the '70s, Jones was only *singing* about being heaven bound, though she was doing it in a manner that merged old-fashioned sacred gospel testifying with contemporary soul-dance grooves that certainly appeared to prophesize a new and paradoxical language of holy funk. By now, of course, she really was heaven bound. If gospel music offers the hope of a future redemption, its salty cousin, soul music, offers the strength to carry on despite the fact that redemption may not be forthcoming. There's a pain at its core, maybe even an emotional bruise that enjoys being rubbed to remind us of an injury.

Most people at one time or another have had a sprained ankle or wrist they had to favor gently until it healed. But soul music involves something deeper and more troublesome: it's about favoring a sprained heart. Sharon Jones lived with a sprained heart for years: first in the South for not being white, then later in the north for not being conventionally pretty, then in the music industry for not being young enough. But she also showed us all how not just to survive but to play *through* the pain of a sprained heart, and that was her secret gift.

PANTHEON OF SOUL
Tower of Power

"When I'm onstage, I'm trying to do one thing: bring people joy. Just like church does. People don't go to church to find trouble, they go there to lose it."
—JAMES BROWN, in Martha Bayles, *Hole in Our Soul*, 1994

As Jones's pastor, Margo Fields, explained to me, "When you see Sharon doin' what people call that soul music, she still bein' churchy. No difference really, same emotion . . . just more motion." Not to mention those devilishly crisscrossed legs of hers. In that same vein, and with perhaps a hint of nostalgia, Jones remarked to the *Soul-Zangers* show in 2010, "Listen to it. The best soul music is still from the '50s and '60s, from when I was growing up. Nothing has changed for me. And soul pretty much ended in the 1970s, when it turned into that disco thing." If you detect some disdain there for *that* disco thing, that's probably because disdain is exactly what all true soul and funk players felt for its mongrel nature.

If all this sounds like we're conducting an archaeological dig at a historic site called Jones, that's because that's exactly what this is. And the search for her roots is made all the more satisfying when we realize that even a sparkling diamond was once an encrusted lump of coal. When we excavate the small but sturdy building called Sharon, it becomes instantly clear that her musical house has several floors, all connected by a single spiral staircase. Beneath the basement is the lower foundation, which is where the gospel music masonry lives; the basement itself is where the soul music lives; the ground floor is occupied by funk; and the attic, well the attic is once again suffused with gospel music, much to most visitors' surprise.

In the same progressive manner, I've been fortunate enough to receive input for this book from a number of the people who knew her best, including her manager and the Daptone-based band that formed around her almost three decades ago. But my even greater good fortune was to have contact with her vocal partners, Saundra Williams and Starr Duncan Lowe, who knew and worked with Jones when she toiled in the entertainment wilderness at several jobs to support herself and her family while trying to get her big break, back in the late '80s and through the '90s.

I've never been fond of the term "backup singers." It just doesn't do justice to the basic guts behind the glory, especially when applied to the stylistic finesse possessed by Williams and Duncan Lowe. As we also know, Jones herself started as a so-called backup singer—or, preferably, a vocal partner—and one who loyally brought her harmonizing Dapettes along with her once the big show finally beckoned. Their input has proven priceless as a means of stalking Sharon through the jungle of both her anonymity and her celebrity.

When it comes to the meaning of soul power, and the core of all soul music, the dear Dapette Starr Duncan Lowe was quite explicit when she explained where the music she sang with Sharon Jones came from:

> Music is just a central kind of language which is redefined and named according to its different styles. But at the basis of it all is the same thing: bringing energy into people's lives, recharging their battery. It's also about imprinting a feeling on their memory, so that way into their future life, when they think about a certain experience, they also think about the music they associate with that experience, whether it was good or bad. When

we three ladies sing together, there's a vibration to it, a certain structure of some sort that resonates with people forever. That's a joy to know.

Let's call that, in passing, a person-to-person transmission of the architecture of joy. That perfectly sums up an ideal definition for both gospel music and soul music, and even funk music and blues music. In fact, Duncan Lowe strongly clarified for me that soul and funk were really just blues, but speeded up, and that gospel and soul . . . well, of course, that was also blues, but a lamentation of a more joyful sort. She also explained that this is the meaning of an exclamation that gospel singers, and by extension their listeners, often make spontaneously: "I feel fire shuttin' in my bones." Meaning, she told me, that one feels a *power* that shuts you down from the inside: another ideal definition for the dictionary of soul and funk.

That might have been why, Duncan Lowe explained, every show they did together contained a section where Jones stopped singing for a while and started (almost) rapping about "the ancestors." By this she meant the ancestors of their music, but also their ancestors from Africa, who brought their culture with them during their forced voyages and managed to brilliantly disguise their rootsy spirit music in the new African American styles they invented: gospel, blues, soul, and funk. (And yes, whether we like it or not, even into the exotic urban styles known as rap and hip-hop.)

An equal honor was the chance to interview the influential Mrs. Fields, whose recollections went back even further, to Jones's teenage years, when she so clearly demonstrated that she was destined for great things, even if those things did make her pastor a little nervous when it came to the secular bounce of Sharon's bumping and grinding delivery. Fields was still canny enough to recognize what she called "the spirit in action," no matter how carefully it was disguised.

I also spoke to the person who knew Jones the longest: her elder sister by three years, Willa Jones-Stringer, who took me for a stroll down memory lane that was both inspiring and wistful—well, that was perhaps the icing on the cake. Willa is a modest and self-effacing lady who knew Sharon from year zero, when she came home from the hospital, and her insights into what made her "babygirl sister" so special provided a bonanza for the archaeologist of her now famous site.

Though, as Jones-Stringer explained, the family migrated northward as early as when Sharon was four, and therefore couldn't be said to have absorbed many conscious experiences of literally "growing up in the South," they did return every summer to visit their father, until he passed away in 1969 and the family took up permanent residence in Brooklyn. So Sharon did remain, as Willa put it, a "Southern girl at heart," and she certainly had occasion to experience some of the more unpleasant sides of life in the South for African Americans passing through the crucible of the civil-rights era.

This was something that Jones herself referred to in the celebrated Kopple documentary film on her later years, notably when returning to be filmed singing in a Baptist church as if just an average member of the congregation. While driving past a small store, she wistfully recalled how she and her sisters would enter to buy some candy and be referred to loudly by the shopkeeper in a common but nonetheless repellant epithet. That kind of ostracization tends to stay with a girl, even after she's grown to womanhood and thence on to New York–based and finally international stardom.

Once again, and in a steady refrain, Willa also referred to the preternaturally spunky, self-assured, and occasionally even stubborn hardheadedness of the baby of the family who grew up insisting that she was going to take care of everybody else. And so she did, finally buying her mother a house in South Carolina to liberate her from the stigma of poverty in the urban housing projects of Brooklyn. The other thing Willa professed to me, just as strongly as their pastor had done, was the basic fact that all of the family—and most definitely Sharon herself— felt their religious faith was the foundation of their lives. As Willa put it to me, "That faith was something deep, something that never left her no matter how famous or celebrated she became. It was also true that Sharon believed with total conviction that God had given her a gift, a gift that was meant to be shared with the world." Something else that she also eventually did on a grand scale.

Willa's response to my frequently asked question for interview subjects, "What is soul power?" also brought a familiar refrain: "It's a life force, a source of energy that comes from within, everybody has it but not everybody discovers or uses it. The thing that allows some people to do so is a connection to the Creator that they never lose, no matter what." She added that what made a special person so special, in her estimation, was they never let their own power—even their soul power—go to their head.

Special people remain humble and unassuming, regardless of how outsized their talents, abilities, or worldly recognition might be. Like Margo Fields, Sharon's elder sister emphasized to me that it was the "holy ghost" that kept great people on track and made them even greater. Indeed, it would be the same thing that kept Sharon stable while she was struggling in her early days, and again as she maintained her stability when she was challenged with an insurmountable health threat. As time went on, and the weaker her sturdy little body became, her faith just got stronger.

Willa's most prized memory—apart from Sharon's kindness as an adult, and her concern, having experienced poverty and its injustices, for helping other people less well off than herself—was of her little sister's principal character trait. "She was one tough little cookie, all right. She never ran away from a fight. She didn't know how to take no for an answer, she did what she wanted to do, regardless of the obstacles placed in her way." She was no stranger to anger, by the way, and her big sister confirmed that Sharon would explode frequently and then declare, "That was good. I feel much better now." When Sharon felt better, everybody felt better—that was her true gift.

Jones was also a tough cookie with a heart of gold, and one for whom all music, regardless of the style or format, was spiritual in nature. That, of course, included the secular kind so frowned upon by her early churchy girl roots. It was as if the little girl had a direct pipeline not just to gospel sounds but also to the throbbing propulsive forward and circular motion of both West African folk-music traditions and African American urban soul-funk traditions.

The latter art forms were mostly just coming to be born as Sharon was herself reaching puberty, and one can only imagine what it must have felt like for a teenaged Sharon to be swept away, not just by the raging inferno of James Brown but also by the feminine mystiques of Aretha Franklin and Tina Turner. She could easily see, as Willa put it, that "music of whatever kind is spiritual, since it helps you release yourself, liberate yourself, and especially, to lose yourself."

From Willa's close perspective, the thing that meant the most to Sharon was her good fortune in encountering the people who ran what would become the Daptone Records label, first in 1996 and then more formally in 2002. They were, she said,

> a close knit family, almost as close as our own family. They felt what we felt and we felt what they felt. It was special. They always stick together no matter what goes down. As a matter of fact, sometimes I think the folks at Daptone, and her band, the Dap-Kings, might even really miss her more than we ourselves do. Sounds strange to say. But they had a deep connection with her, played with her every night, traveled together. In a way, they knew her even more intimately than a family could have done. In fact they were her second family, for sure.

Summing up that professional relationship, personally and artistically, Willa Jones-Stringer put it in a manner that more and more people would also use when trying to find the words to describe what they loved about Sharon Jones: "Uh huh, she did for them what she did for everybody else. Whatever was happening on the outside, Sharon kept it real!"

Everyone I spoke to about Jones would claim that this was practically her job description. One thing we know for sure: in that same vital vein of keeping it real, it just bugged the hell out of Sharon Jones that so many people misunderstood or misconstrued the true meaning of blues, rhythm and blues, soul, or funk music, not to mention the gritty guts of gospel music. It greatly riled her that by the end of the twentieth century, audiences could actually believe that Mariah Carey, say, could be considered R&B or soul music. Or that even someone as otherworldly gifted with jazzy-bluesy channeling skills as an Amy Winehouse might be considered as such, and win armloads of Grammys for so hauntingly imitating Billie Holiday and Dinah Washington. That just drove her nuts.

For Jones, Carey and Winehouse and the rest lacked true soul power. Theirs was a pop masquerade—pop camouflaged as R&B—and it lacked the *blood* that makes for real soul power. Apart from being the name of a stellar song released by James Brown in 1971, with the original J.B.'s, "Soul Power" has as many different definitions as there are listeners to and practitioners of the craft itself.

• • •

For deep-funk legend Lee Fields (no relation to Elijah or Margo Fields), the notion of Soul Power first and foremost involves an essential and copious amount of sheer heart—something Sharon Jones possessed in boatloads. Leslie Derrough of *Glide* magazine declared that Fields was living proof that doing what you love does not have an age limit, with the same of course being so true of his protégé, Sharon Jones. As he told *Glide* himself at the age of sixty-five, only a few weeks after Jones's passing, "I feel that every human being's purpose is to do what their inner voice says to do." And this early member of Kool and the Gang, who released his first single in the superheated soul year 1969 and continues to take our breath away as the real thing, must also have instantly recognized the realness hiding inside tiny Sharon Jones, waiting to burst out.

Burst out she did, stealing the show as Fields' backup singer and revealing bigger and better solo things yet to come, as well as sharing their mutual fondness for memories of singing in church and whooping it up for the Lord. The role of the church in soul stars such as Fields and Jones is always just a heartbeat away form the sensual swagger they exude as popular entertainers. "Sharon is definitely amazing," Fields told *Glide*. "A human being like her is a spirit. We go back from the beginning, from the very beginning of her career. I was there first and I saw her, I saw this amazing budding flower."

A human being is a spirit. That's a religious notion that even sexy and sonorous beings such as Jones or Fields will never let you forget, mostly because their early spiritual upbringing in the gospel sonic realm won't let them forget it either. The salvation pulse is always there, beating just beneath—or is it above?—the domain of physical desires. But it's that emotion and motion that constitute a true soul star.

Jones always passionately considered herself first and foremost a certain kind of emotive singer, and apart from her primary and lifelong allegiance to gospel, she made it clear that no one should even dream of contacting her to sing anything that remotely smacks of pop. She told the *Sun Sentinel* as much with her customary bluntness in 2011: "I feel like this: when you call me in to do something, you must want me to do some soul-singing. Because you *know* I'm a soul singer! Don't ask me to come in and rap. And don't ask me to come in and sing pop. I'm not trying to be a pop singer. I'm not saying they're bad musicians. But how can Taylor Swift or Justin Timberlake win Grammys for R&B and funk? They're pop singers! I'm a *soul* singer!"

Anyone who's ever heard the ferocious Jones deliver the sanctified secular goods we call soul music knows, or at least feels, that they're also vividly witnessing a kind of atavistic spirit possession and hearing a special kind of funked-up gospel testimony. When she swirls her small stocky body across the stage like a ceremonial voodoo doll, there's no question that a living tradition has been transmitted from Yoruba culture in West Africa to pop culture in America. The propulsive devotional aspects of her soulful presentation can hardly be denied: it's a stirring frenzy of faith and funk, transcending and unifying both of them into a musical message embodying a new sonic language of lust and longing.

While Jones's gospel roots help explain how she remained possessed by the spirit, unless we trace some of the core footprints on the historical path of soul music from the classic masters of the '60s and '70s, we won't be able to appreciate exactly what mission Daptone Records and its star attraction, Sharon Jones and the Dap-Kings, had in mind when they reached back to the sound of Memphis for their inspiration in an act of homage that has few equals in popular music. They weren't imitating anything, they were simply rejecting the synthetic surface of twenty-first-century pop-oriented soul, itself a pale shadow (pun intended) of the real thing they had all grooved to while growing up. To do that effectively and convincingly, they also had to abandon the digital world entirely in favor of the analog domain of four decades ago. The special soul sound they longed for, and which they clearly seemed to have found and creatively cemented through their lengthy collaboration, was that gritty groove of funk that probably started with James Brown and ended (or at least went on permanent vacation) with a perfectly formed performer like Prince.

On NPR's *Fresh Air*, the interviewer, Terry Gross, greatly amused both Roth and Jones by drawing an obvious parallel to the bombastic, over-the-top way that James Brown was usually brought onstage—which was hyperbolic, to say the least—and the charming way that the Dap-Kings always introduced Jones to the stage, especially for performances of their debut album, *Dap-Dippin'*. "As far as the live show goes," Roth explained, "it is really influenced not just by James Brown but by all the other soul revues that were going on in the late '60s. There's a sense of showmanship in that and an excitement that you don't see in a lot of shows nowadays."

Soul music did not arrive in our world like some interstellar gift dropped from a spaceship. After running away from church, leaving liturgy behind and starting to sing of personal woes usually associated with love and loss, the blues still met stylistically with gospel illicitly in clandestine juke joints in the red-light district of culture, where a new and drastically different kind of rejoicing commenced. This was the original fusion music, resulting in the soul sound—the next in a ribald parade of permutations where music appears to go wherever it wants to in order to tell a human story seemingly divorced from scripture. But only seemingly.

Historically, we can easily designate the great Ray Charles, a.k.a. "The Genius," as one of if not *the* first to forge a path out of the church and into the nightclub, away from the sacred (on the surface at least) and toward the musically profane with an alternative kind of worship shifting gears. Charles (1930–2004) was a gifted visionary raised in Albany, Georgia, who can clearly be seen as a signpost pointing to a brand new musical map, the cartography of future soul as caused by the continental drift of gospel banging headlong into blues and beyond. Ever since he started his signature rocking back-and-forth with an iconic composition like "I Got a Woman" in 1954, it's impossible not to see him as a lighthouse illuminating the path that would sprout artists such as James Brown in '64, Stevie Wonder in '74, Prince in '84, and Sharon Jones in '94, as if the tumbling decades were themselves rhythmically birthing new branches of an ancient musical tree.

Determined by unique vocal techniques, performance practices, pentatonic scales, and musical gestures, the gospel traditions turned on their soul head by Ray Charles can be easily identified merely by comparing a classic such as the sacred "None but the Righteous" with Ray's own secular "Hit the Road Jack." There's an antiphony between the lead singer and the rest of the choir that is literally shadowed by Charles in his song as he leads the vocalists, who remain in tune regardless of his vocal acrobatics, and they engage in a call-and-response motif that echoes the main theme. It's a kingdom come of soul-stirring majesty.

For a performer such as Sharon Jones, looking for alternative deities to the one she had already embraced in churches as a youth, Brown may have loomed like a kind of musical/biblical prophet. One can't overestimate his impact and influence on both Jones and her future band, the

Dap-Kings, who were modeled somewhat on both his fabulous early Flames and later on with his incendiary J.B.'s. Musical history often seems like a conveyor belt of shared styles, each fusion nourishing the one to follow. Technically speaking, all music is fusion music.

As we've seen and heard, the first fusion was West African music with Christian scripture to make gospel; the second fusion was gospel with blues to make soul; the third fusion was soul with rock to make funk; the fourth fusion would eventually join funk with spoken word to make hip-hop. But for Jones, it all began with the astonishing virtuosity and pure power of James Brown. Sharon clearly idolized him as a precocious nine-year-old, when she and her yelping sisters would channel Brown in front of the mirror at their family home. Singing on both sides of the sacred and secular highway would come naturally to Jones, whose booming voice came to embody the paradox of the holy musical roots at the heart of the soul style. What Jones borrowed from Brown was not so much a style as a sense of limitless energy and the compulsive commitment to entertain us beyond our own perceived pleasure limits.

Stylistic borrowing is often sanctioned in one cultural tradition, in this case the black sacred/secular paradigms of a shared folk patrimony, while it's robustly shunned in another one, the commercial white industry so often guilty itself of misappropriation. Reverence is often a risky business, but as we'll clearly see and hear, the conscious and careful borrowing and blending of sounds is as integral to musical evolution as is the cross-pollination and mutation of forms in the flower kingdom. From the love affair of gospel and blues, to the courtship of soul and rock, to the marriage of funk and hip-hop, the whole jungle of music history is but one long saga of radically sired offspring with an obvious family resemblance.

We can all benefit, however, from an accessible study of this remarkable tradition as it mutated across genre borderlines in books such as the splendidly titled *The Holy Profane: Religion in Black Popular Music* by Teresa L. Reed. The reason I find the title so aptly alluring is that it so simply exemplifies one of my main themes: the continuity of fervent religious faith throughout the transformation from seemingly sacred to apparently profane music, as exemplified in the rise of both James Brown and the reincarnation of Sharon Jones and the Dap-Kings. It's one of the key reasons why the paradox of faith fills to the brim great love songs by pop superstars such as Marvin Gaye in his torchy "Can I Get a Witness?," or Wilson Pickett in his pleading "99 1/2 Won't Do," or even the glorious Supremes in their shimmering "Come See About Me." This central irony—one that encompasses as diverse a later range as Stevie Wonder; Earth, Wind, and Fire; Tupac Shakur, and even (surprisingly enough) the flagrantly violent and sexually charged idiom known as gangster rap—is something that Reed explored very effectively. Her appreciation for the folkway streams is an ideal vehicle for grasping one of my main preoccupations here: that the *holy profane* was a new brand of social and community faith being experimented with by edgy figures such as Ray Charles, James Brown, and Sharon Jones. But its roots are nevertheless clearly visible outgrowths from a shared spiritual soil just below the surface.

Jones would have often heard whispers about this or that person who had once sung in a church but was now "out there in the world," describing these artists as backsliders, defectors from the faith community, fallen from grace. The central puzzle here is how the black church, as the most vocal opponent of secular sins, could have spawned so many gifted interpreters of "the devil's music." It's a central irony at work in the soul and funk music industry, namely the curious amalgam of the sacred and secular which turns our attention back to the origins of gospel, all the way back to West African cultural practices prior to Christian conversion. Back to a harmonized time period where no such division between holy and sinful even existed, and when the supernatural was accepted as a key part of everyday life.

I believe the answers to these questions about cross-cultural currents and belief system modifications are also at the very heart of what made Sharon Jones capable of not just accepting or embracing but also celebrating and memorializing a deep proportional harmony, an elegant golden ratio between sin and pleasure that perfectly prepared her to become an Empress of the Holy Profane. From West African villages to Augusta, Georgia, and then northward to New York City: the continental drift and trajectory of soul music would be riddled with a multitude of puzzling shapes and sounds, a storm of shifting emotional shadows on a contour map that's still being drawn to this day.

By now it's abundantly clear that an arbitrary social, cultural, and religious construct was superimposed over the West African indigenous traditions that were transplanted from their homeland first to the American South and then, after the "emancipation," following the reconstruction north to Chicago, Detroit, and New York. In a sense, when gospel singers ventured outward, away from the altar, they were actually only following an almost atavistic past history and returning to a more harmonious mode of behavior—one that ideally suited their core ethnic character. This new form of emotive testifying was a hyper-theatrical format especially suited to hugely emotional endowed performers such as the irrepressible Sharon Jones.

• • •

That there still exists a hearty strain of Pentecostal fervor in black secular street music is even clearer when we examine and listen to the stirring sounds of a triumphant figure like James Brown. He was not only the preeminent inventor of contemporary soul and funk as we know it today but also clearly the most influential performer to impact and inspire a young impressionable Sharon Jones. Some wags have even dubbed her James Brown in drag.

Showmanship and sanctification in black American culture have always converged. Classic R&B gestures designed to exhort the listening dancers to ever more frenzied levels of transport are glaringly overlaid with the possession by the Holy Spirit, which was the traditional aim of the sanctified church. This parallel is not only not new but indeed rather ancient: it also totally prefigures our current subject.

An early concert performance by James Brown and the Famous

Flames, or later with his fabulous J.B.'s, as well as one thirty years later by Sharon Jones and the Dap-Kings, would have the key ingredient to an invitation for the spirit to enter the singer and audience and would also *give them utterance*: emotional and psychological freedom, physical intensity and spontaneity, and poetic abandon coupled with an extreme degree of artistic expressivity. Obviously, white audiences who were more sedate and less familiar with West African concepts of near Dionysian dancing or palpable spirit possession would have found Brown's acrobatics and his embodiment of the traditional ring-shout quite frightening and overwhelming.

Watching Sharon Jones live, or even in footage, listeners can obviously relate to the deep connection between the crafted soul showmanship of artists like her and the unfettered frenzy of parishioners at a sanctified service. Listeners to performances by artists of Baptist origin such as Aretha Franklin, Gladys Knight, Patti Labelle, or Jones in their prime will easily come to believe that the link between West African spirit possession and African American soul music is not only a roots connection but also a living force, alive and well in the urban streets, clubs, and theaters of the new world. Yes, it *was* a new world, but one totally transformed by the sheer poetry and beauty of people who were forced to come here against their will and yet ironically ended up musically freeing the very culture that had oppressed them.

There's an ever-expanding genre swing in action here, with soul music often placed under the catchall category of rhythm and blues. However, although all soul music can be classified as R&B because of stylistic similarities and the latter's obvious influence upon it, not all R&B can be classified as soul, within which there's a more passionate emotionality, especially noticeable in the percussive horn sections and shimmering vocals. R&B is frequently more pop and more commercial, and clearly, after the death of Marvin Gaye in 1984 and his last hit, "Sexual Healing," what was known as traditional soul music appears to have come to an end. Frankly, any listener who thinks that Sam Smith or Ed Sheeran should be classed as soul needs a new prescription.

As inherently fusion music, soul and funk have a hyper-original and paradoxical blend of raw simplicity and emotional grandeur. The fusion could be called a *merger* of gospel revival and quivering doo-wop in the early growth seasons of soul. Like James Brown before her, Sharon Jones *appeared* to shift her allegiance from the altar to the nightclub, but she maintained a persistent strain of spirit-possession in her delivery. The Dap-Kings would later write volume two of this dynamite soul saga featuring Sharon Jones in Brown's role of lust-spirit avatar. Daptone Records would stubbornly sustain that classic '70s style, almost as if hip-hop had never even happened. (Hip-who?) It was definitely a future past that Daptone wanted to go back to with Sharon Jones for frequent visits, but not as tourists or even as historians—they were more like guru worshippers.

Readers seeking an accurate roadmap to the transformative mutation of sacred spirit music into secular soul music, and beyond, would be best served by the following creative and historical listening arc of albums offered up effectively in this short timeline:

Gospel: Mahalia Jackson, *Live at Newport*

Gospel to soul: Sam Cooke, *Portrait of a Legend*; Aretha Franklin, *Amazing Grace*

R&B to soul: Ray Charles, *Birth of Soul*; James Brown, *Live at the Apollo*

Early Motown: the Supremes, *Gold*; Percy Sledge, *When a Man Loves a Woman*

Later Motown: Marvin Gaye, *What's Going On*; Stevie Wonder, *Original Musiquarium I*

Deep soul: Otis Redding, *The King of Soul*

Memphis soul: Al Green, *Let's Stay Together*; Ann Peebles, *Straight from the Heart*

Neo-soul: Macy Gray, *On How Life Is*; D'Angelo, Voodoo; Erykah Badu, Baduizm; India Arie, Acoustic Soul

British soul: Amy Winehouse, *Back to Black*; Adele, *21*

To this list I would also of course add all eight records released by Daptone of Sharon Jones and the Dap-Kings, as well as almost every other release by their fellow Daptone artists.

For a great taste test and flavor comparison, try playing anything at all by Mr. Brown and then drop on a two-part Dap-Kings single from 2004 that was later included on their *Soul Time* compilation in 2011. "Genuine Pts. 1 and 2" is exactly that, with its screaming, J.B.'s-like horn section and tight bottom, and it's totally true to the kind of music that Jones and her band grew up listening to and loving, while at the same time paradoxically feeling completely and authentically all their own. Its message is as simple as it is punchy—"Got to be gen-u-ine . . . if you wanna be mine!"—and it's possibly the heaviest bump-and-grind groove that Jones and the Kings ever put down.

Most of us writing about its genealogy agree that soul was a merger between gospel and secular forms of pop music, and we also agree that soul's social and political significance transcended more disposable pop fashion. Where some pop-culture historians differ is in our perspectives on this important period of social and cultural American life, and therefore what soul did and still does to reflect currents active in everyday living patterns.

A similar expression of the style paradoxes involved here was made by Mark Humphrey in his *Holy Blues: The Gospel Tradition*: "Holy blues is an oxymoron if we believe blues to be the devil's music, a tenet held by many reformed blues singers and the saints of many African American churches. Blues is unholy, sacred music is unbluesy. Blues celebrates pleasures of the flesh, gospel celebrates release from worldly bondage. One is oil, the other is holy water, they are unmixable." I diverge drastically from such either/or interpretations, if only because life is too short for such quibbles (especially a life as short as Sharon Jones's), and also in light of the accomplishments of Ray Charles, James Brown, and many others in ideally mixing the oil and water right before our eyes and ears, and in our accelerated hearts.

The history of American popular music is replete with—and in many ways is the actual history of—breaking taboos continuously and artfully. From magnificent African American inventions such as blues, jazz, R&B, and rock 'n' roll to soul is a vast litany of style liberations and a fresh new liturgy of the holy profane. The faith chain that connects with the lust life was very clear to a consummate fusion artist such as Jones. When asked by Adrian Lee of *Maclean's* magazine in 2014 about when she first fell in love with music and singing, Jones said, "It was always there right from the beginning, but no one ever remotely thought she'd be a 'big singer' one day, instead of only singing in churches and choirs, and wedding bands. But I felt that it was God who gave me the gift to sing." Someone sure did.

Even blatant rejection over the years didn't stop her, though it did slow her down a bit. "Life has its time and everything in life is meant for you," she admitted. "I never doubted myself, I doubted the music industry out here, that they would ever accept me. Thank God I didn't give up, I hung in there and met those guys at Daptone Records." We're pretty sure "those guys" felt the same way about her—and they've said so many times over the years. Equally clear is how strong the perpetual force of what I've called her positive *gospel fury* was throughout her life. This notion of the holy profane is precisely the roadmap for appreciating a figure like Sharon Jones, since toward the end of her life, after shaking and baking the devil's music, it wasn't widely known by either the public, her fans, or the music industry that she was secretly planning to release a new and totally *traditional* gospel record. I would kill to hear a Sharon Jones album of songs by Sister Rosetta Tharpe, and I'm sure I'm not alone. It's a bold move that harkens back to Daptone's independent origins and demonstrates a deep commitment to Jones's religious roots, which the label plans to continue exploring for a long time to come.

The parallel devotional roads of prayer and sensuality have never been more evident. By dedicating itself to situating gospel so firmly within its soul and funk catalogue, Daptone was also making another kind of testament abundantly clear: gospel music has guts galore. Audiences may have grown harder and harder to reach by the end of the

1990s, or maybe the message was getting harder to hear above the computerized noise of the times. Soul music had definitely evolved to a point where two drastic mutations were taking place, the first being the baroque anger of rap and hip-hop, the second being the polished but pale dilution of Michael Jackson's pop version, both of which would be counterbalanced to some degree by the brilliant androgynous swoon of Prince in his soulful prime.

Just as the analog twentieth century was drawing to a close, in the early dawn of the digitally slick era a tiny Brooklyn production company and distribution label run by fetishistic and compulsively funk-driven young music lovers would start to feel a deep yearning for what made soul music great in the first place. Rap and hip-hop were two radical fusion styles that also developed out of a drastically different urban setting in the last couple of decades of the twentieth century, and they too changed the musical landscape of the mainstream (meaning white audiences) in similar but divergent ways.

Soul had changed white pop music in the early '60s in a way just as dramatic as the way we saw hip-hop change white pop music in the '90s. Soul music elevates feeling above all else; secularized gospel embracing blues profanity, it deals almost exclusively with that most important subject: the vagaries of love. Its sound remains based largely in a church context as a completely vocal art, wherein the singer works out the feelings of the audience in real physical time. In this sense it still remains somewhat sacramental. Naturally, rhythm and blues as a stylistic emotional expression was always looked down on. It was low-class music, it was wild music, it was sexual music, it was even "dirty" music. But as far as fans were concerned, it was the most glamorous sound in the world. This was heavenly to them back then. And it was heaven all right—a dirty heaven but still heaven nonetheless.

The original sound of that otherworldly soul music domain was, of course, distinctly different from the slick and polished pop music that had evolved by the end of the twentieth century—as different, so the saying goes, as chalk from cheese. Gabe Roth and Neal Sugarman were desperately looking for a way out of the pixilated digital domain of synthetic music and a way back to the haptic realm of the human touch. Maybe it was pure luck, or maybe it was something we can attribute to fate, karma, or just the law of consequences, but the way they found to move *forward* by looking *back* suddenly appeared to them right on their own doorstep, in the most inconspicuous and modest form imaginable.

The imaginative folks at Daptone were looking for a way to revitalize contemporary soul and funk music in an honest and authentic way that didn't smack of either retro or nostalgia. Imagine their surprise when they just happened to discover a bouncy, gospel-soul apparition called Sharon Jones—a mature and fiery dame who was more than ready to shake, rattle, and roll both the spirit and the body. What she also offered, almost as a bonus, was a crash course in the secret ingredient that links gospel to soul and funk. All these musical styles actually want the same thing: they want you to be nearly ill with longing. Whether it's a longing for salvation or for satisfaction really makes no difference, and often it can be a longing for both at the same time.

DAPTONE DISCOVERY
Made for Each Other

"People don't like getting force-fed music. We try to make records we love and that have a high standard. People reward our being discerning with loyalty to our label, and they expect a certain sound and a certain quality."
—GABRIEL ROTH, cofounder of Daptone Records, to *PopMatters*, 2010

Even if destiny rules when it comes to providing us with our opportunities, good old-fashioned concentrated effort and hard work always pays off in the end. This is true of Daptone Records and its fabled discovery of Sharon Jones in 1996. It only took her thirty years to become an overnight sensation. In the emotionally charged romance of retrospect, it could be easy to mythologize the chance encounter between Daptone's Gabriel Roth and Sharon Jones as destiny or karma, but the magic they would eventually generate together still took a while to build up steam. It was still clearly love at first sight, or first hearing.

Although Roth's earlier recording ventures with the Desco label had rapidly evaporated, his Daptone dream quickly arose from those corporate ashes, with Jones and the Dap-Kings forming the centerpiece of his new label's new artistic image. The sudden frontline singing star— sudden after long years of struggling, of course—was naturally enough being compared with funksters such as Lyn Collins and Marva Whitney, merged with the more bluesy inflections of LaVern Baker or Ruby Johnson. But the real truth is, she was always only Sharon being Sharon, right from the beginning.

She demonstrated quickly that as a band's frontline, featured performer, she was an unstoppable force, a personal and stormy weather pattern that the rest of the band simply had to desperately try to keep up with. She also quickly established her basic repertoire of song material—love troubles with men, feminine power unleashed, hard times in life, but all without a trace of the moribund self-absorption of younger and hugely famous stars who shall remain nameless. It was truly a brand of tough blues, but one proffered in a sassy shimmy and usually adorned with sparkling sequins—maybe even a kinky kind of spiritual glitter.

For Neal Sugarman, Roth's cofounding partner in Daptone, the encounter was blessed by the performance gods, as he expressed in his posthumous appreciation for her on the Daptone site in 2017:

> There was no question from the very beginning how amazing Sharon was as a front person. It was remarkable how she could make every single person in the audience feel like she was singing directly to them. That's a gift that I've really only experienced with her. She was always super gracious, she never had an ego or felt like she was better than anyone else. She was small, but when she went on stage, she doubled in size, every time she put a microphone up to her mouth she doubled. Then she could go offstage and suddenly be barely five feet again.

Considering Jones played no musical instrument herself, apart from the microphone and those vocal chords, Sugarman was stunned by her innate musicality. "She was never thinking about *anything* when she picked up an instrument, she was just naturally musical," he said.

Looking back from this afterward vantage point, it's equally impressive how much Jones, her remarkable band, and their creative little label influenced the entire pop music environment at the time they emerged.

"Established acts like Solange Knowles and Raphael Saadiq began dabbling in various retro-soul offerings, but more substantially, an entire cadre of independent label soul artists arose alongside the Dap-Kings," Oliver Wang declared for National Public Radio's *The Record*. Wang also noted that this sudden flowering included renewed interest in older soul survivors such as Lee Fields, Charles Bradley, and Nicole Willis but still offered blossoming attention for younger artists including Lady, Mayer Hawthorne, Myron and E., and Nick Waterhouse. "Jones and the Dap-Kings weren't the sole reason behind this explosion," he aptly concluded, "but they were undeniably one of the most productive engines powering it."

Sharon Jones was definitely leading out in front of all the young new retro-wavers, and this is mostly because she so easily stacks up against the '60s originals. She might be one of the real missing links back to soul giants such as Otis Redding. For Quint Davis, the organizer of the New Orleans Jazz and Heritage Festival and someone who witnessed her early ascent, she was "a classic powerhouse singer with her own unique thing, incredibly infectious, for real. Her personality and her enthusiasm for what she was doing was so strong it shone through everything, she was relentless and she hung on until she got the people frenzied every time. She was a power source." Indeed, she was the brand new battery behind the engine of the Dap-Kings, and the studio sparks flew almost immediately.

Speaking to the folks at Reverb.com's *Soundcheck* show, Sugarman was unrestrained in his combination of pride for the label he'd started with Roth and the obviously gifted singing star they both uncovered after years of neglect. "We started this label with the full-on intention to make the best soul music records of our era," he said. That's not just ambition talking there—that's pure passion simmering out. "I started out originally as an artist on Desco Records . . . and what made it special even then was being a label that also had its own recording studio. That's also a huge part of what we wanted to do with Daptone, too. It was unique as an artist to have everything in-house: business, promotion, marketing upstairs in the same building where the music was created, produced, and mixed."

Alison Fensterstock of *Pitchfork* described the dilemma that Jones had faced for decades well in her posthumous profile piece: "Gabriel Roth was finally the enthusiastic buyer for what Jones was selling." That sums it up perfectly. Until Roth, label executives were puzzled, to say the least, by Jones's slightly eccentric and unconventional attributes. Fenterstock also observed that Jones and Daptone, as if by synchronicity, were at the forefront of a new-millennium vogue for vintage-style hot soul and throbbing funk. Some of the artists whose star rose with the revival, including veterans such as Jones, remembered the historical sounds from the first time around. Others, like Black Joe Lewis and the Honeybears, St. Paul and the Broken Bones, Eli "Paperboy" Reed, Alabama Shakes, Mayer Hawthorne, and Leon Bridges, were students turning the pages of their history books and updating grooves with slick Hammond organ, sharp horn sections, hip-tickling grooves, gospel-toned shouts, and sweetly yearning ballads to make you swoon and sway. "It was music made for dancing," Fensterstock remarked, "and it filled up the floors again in the halls of rock 'n' roll."

From the perspective of Brooklyn, the home base for Sharon and her boys (and the ladies), the reasons for the rewarding acclaim for their old-school soul sound had come together as a result of the small, hand-built, analog recording studio in a little brick row house. They saw two elements as the key to their success. Firstly, their out-of-fashion tape recording equipment, which gave the Dap-Kings a resonance that recalls the heavy tracks cut some four decades ago at Stax/Royal Recording in Memphis; the Muscle Shoals Sound Studios in Sheffield, Alabama; or Malaco's studio in Jackson, Mississippi. Secondly, the almost spiritual-revivalist, family attitude that permeates everything the label and the musicians do together. This isn't nostalgia, folks. It's realism.

That Daptone authenticity is also of course what first attracted producer Mark Ronson when he was seeking a "real-thing" kind of sound for his monster hit *Back to Black* with Amy Winehouse. History lives right here in Brooklyn, so why try to synthetically simulate or digitally imitate it elsewhere? That was the lesson the hip young Brit pop wizard learned from the Daptone family. Ironically, though, in learning that lesson he also inadvertently derailed the forward motion of the Sharon Jones train by borrowing the Dap-Kings from her to record and tour with doomed Amy. One other accidental side effect of that borrowing was the painful fact that the general public would later mistakenly think that Jones was then subsequently jumping on Winehouse's wobbly wagon, when in reality it was obviously the other way around. Luckily, history occasionally gets corrected and written anew.

As Fensterstock also noted, "This is the kind of American music whose commercial fortunes may ebb and flow but as an art form it is everlasting." But what's most important for Roth, his band, their label, and its growing audience—and what really counts most in the end—is Sharon Jones's unmatched ability to connect with her listening public. This attitude is best exemplified by Roth's oft-quoted notion that what comes from the heart reaches the heart. It was an insight that applied from the moment he met Jones in 1996 and recognized what she carried around inside her, just waiting to burst out, or maybe waiting for someone to give permission for it to burst. Burst it did. The phenomenon known as "Dap-Dippin'" was born in 2002, with Roth serving as midwife, and the soul storm known as Sharon Jones was reborn in turn, with Daptone Records getting all due credit for her late-term delivery.

In his NPR profile of Jones, Wang emphasized how her soul was surpassed only by her spirit—an intriguing distinction. Wang knew whereof he spoke, and he also knew just how lucky he was to have seen her in her exuberant prime. He was among the first fortunate few to see her in her early Dap-Dippin' days following her first solo featured record with her boys, in a tiny club called the Elbo Room in San Francisco's Mission District. He'd already become familiar with her from her earlier guest spots on several Desco/Daptone tracks, in addition to her first star turn, but he hadn't really quite appreciated how much power Jones could pack into her stout frame while she "sang, sweated, stamped, strutted, and slayed." He also described her, accurately, as one of the greatest second acts in American music history—a rise to acclaim that never seemed to diminish in wonder the more he contemplated both her bad luck and her good fortune.

It's this very odd mixture of hard luck and good karma that makes Jones so fascinating in the end. After her brief flirtation with touring in the mid-'70s, as a backup singer for a Long Island R&B girl group called the Magic Touch, she had pretty much sunk beneath the oblivious waves of pop history for a long twenty years in the musical wilderness. One of her Dapettes in later years, Saundra Williams, told me that she had fond memories of working with Sharon and Starr Duncan Lowe when they were known as the Good and Plenty Girls (the perfect name for these three); they were also known as the Triple "S" Threat when performing at private receptions with the John Castellano Band in the early '90s. "My favorite part of watching Sharon onstage was watching her inter- act, with the audience, with the band," Williams said. "Every show was wonderful with her, just watching her be herself, and she gave a thousand percent of herself on every stage."

When I interviewed Duncan Lowe—and, by the way, for a music critic, few things could be more gratifying than having a soul queen exuberantly sing songs to you over the telephone—she personally con- firmed even more of that instantaneous intimacy that was such a big part of the legendary Jones ethos. To call the Dapettes "close" would be a drastic understatement. Talking to me about Starr, Williams told me, "She's my rib." Talking to me about Williams, Starr told me, "I'd sing 'Tic-Tac-Toe' or 'the cow jumped over the moon' with her—anything. In 1991, when both Saun and I were auditioning for the same gig as a singer to accompany Sharon in the Castellano wedding band, it was just such a feel-good moment. It felt like the energy suddenly clicked on like a light switch, it was just meant to be, it was fate."

Duncan Lowe too has no regrets over their early dues-paying strug- gles together. "Working in the wedding bands early on was very helpful and instructive. It made us develop character and stamina. We would sometimes be performing for four hours straight at a reception, then take a break and do another four at a different one. You hone your craft that way, and get to use those skills later on in the profession. In Sharon, especially, it helped her develop a kind of charismatic stamina."

Upon listening to this, I was immediately struck by the contrast to certain young and famous, diva-like singers who shall remain nameless, who deliver maybe sixty or ninety minutes and are then whisked away exhausted in their limousines before the applause even stops. This is especially so in the case of the extremely young performers who make it big even before their characters are fully formed and become transformed into spoiled divas before they can possibly cope with the pressures. The long, slow route is sometimes better, if not for your bank account then certainly for your real identity as a person.

The same way that people describe their past life flashing before their eyes, it must have felt to the soon-to-be (ten years later) Dapettes that their *future* life was flashing in front of them upon meeting Jones. The odd irony here is that the three ladies were involved in an early singing audition together that would foreshadow Jones's first gig at Desco Records, where she brazenly offered to do all three slated vocal spots by herself. Perhaps that was even the moment when it first occurred to her to bring her former wedding bandmates into the soon-to-be-born Daptone fold. I like to think so. Watching grainy footage of the Good and Plenty Girls performing at weddings is startling, mostly because they are already in a certain tight and seductive groove together that can't be denied. The only ingredient missing is the collective rhythmic genius of the Dap-Kings behind them.

Speaking to *Beyond Race Magazine*, Jones herself would concur. "Having three singers is a powerful thing," she said. "I didn't study any musical theory you know, but I do know harmony when I hear it, and when you get everybody hitting it together you get that ring. Retro? What the hell is retro about me? I am soul. When I open my mouth, soul comes out." You'll notice, I expect, that she didn't refer to her vocalist cohort as backup singers. That's because they weren't: they were fellow musicians, whether they were entertaining a wedding party or entertaining thousands of fans at Madison Square Garden. They were the embodiment of what entertainment is all about, and they killed it every time.

This was also during her surreal stint as a corrections officer and armored guard, before she inexplicably roared back as an *overnight* sensation with Daptone Records. As if making up for lost time, she rapidly began specializing in what Oliver Wang rhapsodically referred to as "vintage-sounding gutbucket funk singles." During his apprenticeships with both Pure and Desco, Gabriel Roth had clearly achieved a technical mastery of the real analog magic touch he was looking for. He was then in the market for a certain soul-drenched someone who could capture that authentic vocal vibe but without seeming to appear to be merely copying, mimicking, or channeling its storied past glory. Suddenly, Sharon Jones was embodying it in a visceral way, right before his eyes and ears.

Sharon and her band quickly began to reincarnate a long line of diverse but equally soulful entertainers such as Willie Bobo, the Funk Brothers, the Four Tops, Etta James, Otis Redding, the Blue Notes, and even Nile Rogers and Chic, by way of Sly Stone and Stevie Wonder. It would be a long, strange, and winding road from her hallowed gospel roots to the steaming funk train of later on.

All along the way, her Dap-Kings were right there behind her, rushing to catch up, to keep up, to lift up this amazing dame in front of them, while the astonishing Gabe Roth, the man who was smart enough, or visionary enough, to finally buy what she was selling, was busy doing double duty as label executive and producer/engineer. And, at his antique-looking 8-track tape machine and analog mixing board, he had only one simple but challenging job: find the magic, support the magic, and preserve the magic.

• • •

Gabriel Roth and his creative alter ego, Bosco Mann, are really three or four geniuses for the price of one: a superb bass player, a label executive, and an engineer/producer, all contained in the same hyper-talented individual. The rest is herstory. Back in 2010, when Daptone Records was then celebrating its first decade as a new and thriving label specializing in authentic soul and funk music, it aptly described its own business ethos better than any journalist ever could have: "Delivering the New Sound of Old Soul since the turn of this century and establishing itself as a place where quality, heart, and feeling are the staple of every one of its releases."

This philosophy was never more true than with Daptone's initial excursion with Sharon Jones into what would soon become the cult of Dap-Dippin', and the label quickly provided ample evidence of that dedication with a busy series of shows and special re-releases designed to map out this unique territory. It seemed that this band, producer, and lead singer were simply made for each other. As Roth rhapsodizes on the Daptone website, "She has established herself as one of the greatest soul singers in history, and because of that, she has always been the backbone of our whole label. When you listen to a Sharon Jones and the Dap-Kings record, you're listening to a *real performance*, people feel that and they react to that, and Sharon just seems to soar over the top of the whole thing."

After ten years of hard work in the studio and on the road, Daptone, Jones, and the-Dap-Kings were suddenly riding high. Like its new star, the label too was a slow-moving train a decade in the making. Some things are just worth waiting for. Daptone had plenty to celebrate about and to share with the growing community of devotees for its brand of true grit and soul grind. The Brooklyn label had, as its founders liked to put it, "launched itself into the forefront of the soul explosion" with Jones's 2002 debut, and "had remained at the head of the class ever since." Once again, the label's founders would do the best job of describing the secret to their success, even though hordes of critics and journalists can often find more complicated ways to encapsulate it. "We were able to stay rooted in this idea that people want to hear good music," Roth summed it up on Daptone's tenth-anniversary sampler, "That's our business plan. We're gonna try and make really good records. Period."

Given how far they've come and the challenges they've faced along the way, Roth and co. are certainly entitled to feel proud of the achievements of what they often refer to as their tightly knit Daptone Family, and their label's website gleams with the joys of hard work and survival in the telling of its story. They're especially pleased with the fact that they don't make their music or run the business side out of a generic steel-and-glass tower in a corporate amusement park somewhere, but rather do it all in a rickety old row house: an actual residential home in Brooklyn's Bushwick area, which they're rightly entitled to call the House of Soul.

The label's now-legendary old-school analog studio occupies the first floor of the building, while the second features mountains of shelves filled with actual vinyl pressings, along with more contemporary (though less alluring) CD and DVD formats, as well as a few scattered office desks occupied by dedicated members of the sales and promotional staff. Emotion trumps marketing in the label's overall strategy, not for world domination but simply for soulful inspiration, dished out the old-fashioned way. One of its most accurate self-assessments is the following: "Some labels develop a brand—Daptone has built an identity."

Not surprisingly—at least not to me—Starr Duncan Lowe had some salient thoughts on what made Daptone Records the right place— maybe even the only place—for Jones to have ended up:

> Daptone is just as unique as she is. They wanted to pay homage to what's pure, and so did she. In a way they paid homage to that *Stax* soul sound of the south, but they also paid homage to her own personal purity too. The music they make is beyond labels or styles, sometimes you don't know what to call it, but, you know, "This sounds good!" That's their secret. Now, that funk they produce and record . . . what does it mean? Not so much a style of music in itself. Funk means a kind of *grammar*, it's an

emotional blueprint for all these different styles of music. At the bottom of it all, it's a marriage between the drums and the bass, it's a love affair between the drums and the bass.

The two patriarchs of this family-toned operation who presided over the love affair and marriage, Gabriel Roth (the bassist) and Neal Sugarman (the sax player), really did build it from the ground up, literally with their own hands, and they readily admit that their first decade was one of struggle, perseverance, and, in the end, a gestation period of family growth. If Daptone was a kind of musical blind date when it was first founded in 2001, one year before its debut Sharon Jones release, the pair's gestation period included a short stint as Desco Records, which was practically a living audio museum. On that short-lived label, Sugarman released his own first two records as the Sugarman Three, and it was from this launching pad that he and Roth established a gritty appetite for what we can honorably call idiosyncratic soul- and funk-flavored sounds.

On their website, Sugarman easily characterizes what makes them special. It's also easy for their avid listeners to identify what makes them unique: they're absolutely analog, and using tape machines offers them a special character that creates a definite sonic feel—something more organic. Daptone followers also love the same vinyl records as the producers and band themselves. For Sugarman and Roth, vinyl isn't romantic, or nostalgic or quirky, it's just the best format, as is tape, analog and mono. Vinyl isn't just a format to them, it's also an aesthetic.

That original foundational format also brought together the skeleton of what would eventually evolve not only into the body of Daptone but also the heart and guts of the Dap-Kings band and their core personnel. Before that, the label released tunes by the Daktaris and also inaugurated a band called Antibalas, a dynamic, mixed-genre group that helped catalyze something of an Afrobeat renaissance. The Mighty Imperials were also part of this stable, a precocious band of inspired sixteen-year-olds, among them the gifted percussionist Homer Steinweiss, who remains the drummer for the Dap-Kings to this day.

Among the other volatile ingredients just waiting for that second correct combustible combination were other Desco recording artists, including Sharon Jones, Lee Fields, and Naomi Shelton, all backed by a group known as the Soul Providers, featuring future Dap-Kings guitarist Binky Griptite, bassist Bosco Mann (Roth), and an additional percussionist, the flamboyant Fernando "Boogaloo" Velez. Eventually, they would be joined by the dynamic Dapettes, who still sound as delightful as the Good and Plenty Girls did in the day.

Thus the basic recipe for the magical analog sound that would fuel both the Dap-Kings with Sharon Jones and Daptone itself as a label were all in place and just waiting for ignition and liftoff. Some of that popular fuel, it's fair to say, would also be accidentally provided by the aforementioned young British producer Mark Ronson, when he borrowed the Dap-Kings for freelance service as a studio band in the making of his 2006 mega-monster hit for the talented but ultimately unfit-for-duty Amy Winehouse.

In his 2010 profile of Gabe Roth for *Waxpoetics*, written around the time of Jones and the Dap-Kings' fourth album, Brad Faberman summed up the scene quite nicely. "Behind two of the most important R&B singers to emerge in the last ten years there's a pair of shades and a Fu Manchu mustache. These belong to Gabe Roth. The singers of course are Sharon Jones and Amy Winehouse." I might even go further and say that the three most important R&B singers of the last twenty years are Sharon Jones, Amy Winehouse, and Sharon Jones.

Speaking to Roth for his profile, Faberman expressed some natural curiosity about what makes the driven musician tick. What was it that made him want to do everything himself? "I was never really that ambitious with music," Roth replied, "we were just trying to make good records for fun. Me and my friends Philip Lehman and Mike Wagner were just messing around in the basement, we weren't really taking anything seriously. It all came out of that."

Since the Paris-based Lehman had his Pure Records label doing reissues and compilations, however, it offered a vehicle for the trio's friendly play to turn into some serious creative business. Roth acknowledges that Lehman's own musical knowledge, as well as his radically rebellious do-it-yourself attitude, rubbed off on him at this formative stage. Lehman's somewhat eccentric energy, Roth has attested, really kick-started the whole recording enterprise for him. After hooking up in 1995 and starting out by doing a few 45-rpm releases—a radical and eccentric format at that time—they were off and running.

Originally, Lehman was playing drums, Roth was on bass, Wagner was on guitar and trombone, and then they were joined by Fernando Velez on congas, in a loosely knit combo mostly slapped together just for studio projects. Roth is the first to admit that, at the very beginning, it wasn't even really an actual *band*. But they dreamed up the name the Soul Providers almost as a pure lark while recording a goofy ersatz "soundtrack" for a nonexistent movie called *The Revenge of Mister Mopoji*, essentially presenting themselves as a fictional band, which in a sense is exactly what they were.

Back then, the band's sax player was Ed Hrbek, whose main historical importance to us now is that he introduced Roth to his future singing star, Sharon Jones. Thanks, Ed. In a couple of years they would meet the exuberant Binky Griptite, who joined on guitar; Roth's roommate at the time, Martin Perna from Antibalas (which means "bulletproof"), was on baritone and tambourine, with Leon Michels on tenor. Paul Brandenburg played trumpet on the first record; Anda Szigali, who toured with them, was followed by Todd Simon, Victor Axelrod, and Earl Maxton. So, the entire extended musical commune consisted of bits and pieces from Antibalas, the Soul Providers, the Mighty Imperials, and the Sugarman Three, all stewed together into what Roth characterized as one big happy family, working together in different hybrid ways. Although the players didn't know it at the time, the raw uncooked ingredients for the Dap-Kings were all there in the mix.

Making their recordings all the more alluring for some of us fetishists was the fact that they mostly concentrated on vinyl formats alone in those days, and were mostly inspired by the hard '60s Stax sound and by James Brown's multi-label ethos, as a result of Lehman's massive collection of obscure funk 45s that so impressed both Roth and Wagner. They also absorbed and channeled discs such as Matala's *Independence* and tunes by Fela Kuti, Hank Carbo, Eddie Bo, and other gutsy, rootsy players. Bassist Roth was himself also greatly influenced by superb players such as Fred Thomas and heavy-duty musicians like Bootsy Collins, as well as both the gospel vibes of *Sam Cooke and the Soul Stirrers* and the R&B vibes of Ray Charles, Little Willie John, and old Bobby Bland.

Personal and professional differences with Lehman made their creative collaboration short lived, but Roth quickly bounced back thanks to a deal with a boutique label for a production-only imprint that seemingly evaporated into thin air but left one very substantial trace in its wake. He had personally invested in studio recording equipment and already begun assembling the rough material for Sharon Jones's debut album (*Dap-Dippin' with Sharon Jones and the Dap-Kings*) in the basement of a friend's residence in nearby Williamsburg. This was followed by a month-long musical residency in Barcelona, which gave Roth, Jones, and the band a chance to meld together into the formidable and tight creative unit they still are today (sadly minus Sharon, of course).

The first Desco releases were limited-edition works that nevertheless captured some of the fire that would become Roth and his collaborators' signature style from then on. Roth would dream up the name, logo, and design style for Daptone merely to have some sort of image to stick on these initial cottage-industry pressings. They really did give the phrases "back to basics" and "back to the roots" a whole new meaning; the word "homemade" acquires a fresh take when looked at in light of such humble beginnings. Today, even though they're quite successful by any standards, Daptone's releases still *feel* homemade, and that's the way they like it.

There's also another phrase that could very well be their artistic slogan: "Chance is the fool's name for fate." Chance materialized once again when Sugarman approached Roth to produce his third album, *Pure Cane Sugar*, for which he'd been struggling with a raft of independent labels to ink a distribution deal. Roth recalls that at some point in that seemingly endless battle to break in and through the industry gatekeepers, he sat down with Sugarman and said, "Let's just do it ourselves." With that pronouncement, Daptone was born for real, with an agreement that Roth would be involved only in the creative side of performing and producing, and that Sugarman would undertake the tasks of business strategy and selling product. Their first and lasting caveat for the whole affair was that they would "follow their own compass" by making only the music they both loved to hear themselves, and to make it in the old-school technical-production manner they each wanted to showcase.

Incredibly enough, this counterintuitive, artist-driven ethos actually began to click with audiences and record buyers who had clearly become just as bored and unimpressed with the corporate-industry mentality and digitally besotted production style of the day as the two founding Daptone partners were. Maybe it was some kind of end-of-the-century zeitgeist. Roth and Sugarman then creatively refined the sounds of both *Pure Cane Sugar* and *Dap-Dippin'*, releasing them as more formally produced albums, as well as launching a wave of gritty 45s born from the same sessions. In keeping with the back-to-basics model, these releases were all distributed and sold from the kitchen table of Sugarman's own Brooklyn apartment.

It was at this early developmental stage that Roth and Sugarman also searched for a proper studio, eventually settling on the two-story family house in the Bushwick district of Brooklyn. This is where the family aspect of their operation came into play, as on a shoestring budget (meaning literally no budget at all) they turned to friends and cohorts, flinging themselves into a communal renovation project and knocking down walls, ripping out electrical and gas systems, making use of whatever imaginary resources they could muster. This even included Sharon Jones herself helping with the wiring, Charles Bradley installing radiators, Fran and Kenny Gonzales buying construction supplies (in exchange for credit on future recording sessions), while members of the Budos Band jacked up the sagging ceiling, using old tires salvaged from the street and fabric cuttings pilfered from local textile dumpsters to create isolated sound booths, while repurposing gas pipes as curtain rods. In all, it gave the do-it-yourself movement a whole new, soul-infused texture. "One of the reasons this studio means so much to me is because we all worked so hard to build it." Roth explained to Faberman. "It wasn't some kind of manifest destiny in my head."

Yet manifest it truly did, with the studio not only starting to yield releases by Jones and the Dap-Kings but also bringing to life albums by others from their growing roster of labelmates. The Budos Band joined in 2005 and launched three self-titled records of what has been described as Staten Island–based Afro-Soul; Naomi Shelton and the Gospel Queens released *What Have You Done My Brother?*, establishing themselves at the forefront of a new wave of gospel-soul; and Dap-Kings guitarist Thomas Brenneck produced a disc for his bouncing Menahan Street Band.

Savvy Daptone then re-released some of the earlier Desco material, including the Mighty Imperials' *Thunder Chicken*, the Sugarman Three's *Sugar's Boogaloo* and *Soul Donkey*, and the Daktari's *Soul Explosion*, as well as lesser-known gems by the Poets of Rhythm, Bob and Gene, and Pax Nicholls. These would quickly lead to a separate sub-label called Ever Soul, focusing especially on 45s by Eddie and Ernie, Hank Mullens and Darrell Banks, Dirt Rifle and the Bullets, Lee Fields, and Binky Griptite and the Mellomatics. In addition to generating vinyl, the bands involved were also touring feverishly and promoting the label's philosophy with blistering live shows, while the label's analog studio started to be used more and more for independent recording projects by artists looking for an authenticity that couldn't quite be found anywhere else or replicated by computers.

Meanwhile, the band at the center of this cyclone, Sharon Jones and the Dap-Kings, continued to enhance their profile by releasing one album after another of sizzling soul and funk, all while still maintaining the down-to-earth philosophy of camaraderie and collaboration that put them on the musical map in the first place. "We want to preserve this unified sound," is how Sugarman put it on their site. "We wanna do stuff our way. Having that family element is important to us." It's that basic focal point that makes them exactly what they are: practitioners of perfectly produced soul and funk music. Suddenly, Daptone seemed like an instant empire recipe. All it needed now was to add a sprinkle of Sharon and shake.

A number of other behind-the-scenes ingredients were equally essential to the overall mix and vibe: Nydia Ines Dávila, a Daptone VP who helps runs things as the label's marketing manager; manager Alex Kadvan, an old university chum of Roth's who has been a crucial part of the blend for almost two decades now; and Wayne Gordon, the label's chief master tape operator (that's right: actual tape!). For Roth, as principal visionary, engineer, producer, bassist, and founding father, the key element moving everything forever forward remains his core idea of hands-on craftsmanship, something that is impossible to replace with either fancy expensive technical gear or convoluted digital computer gimmicks.

The Daptone site characterizes this ethos most accurately: "Music made for love, not for market pressure or trend hopping." Ironically, by making sounds that disregarded all trends, Roth and co. may just have kick-started a whole new industry trend for reassessing the power and punch of that true analog tape magic. In other words, what used to be the classic old Stax sound has evolved into the new postmodern Daptone sound. (We'll be discussing the critical overlap between Stax and Daptone more anon.)

When Faberman asked Roth why he thought Daptone was going so strong while so many other areas of the music industry were falling apart, the multi-faceted artist expressed his personal doubts that the industry sky was falling as a result of the digital formats, streaming, and Internet in general. "I mean, it's kind of the best time ever for independent artists and independent labels," he said. "I don't think there's any trouble in the music industry. It's great for artists and great for people listening to music, I think it's been great for everybody." He went on to stipulate that the only people who really suffer now are the major commercial and corporate labels and that—not surprisingly, given his creative approach to the business—he thought it was just fine that they were finally suffering a little after enforcing a monopoly for so many generations of musicians and listeners alike. "I have no problem with that," he said.

• • •

There's an old folk adage that all good things come to those who wait long enough. Sometimes, on rare occasions, it actually seems to be true. When she spoke to Noel Murray at the *A.V. Club* in 2010 about how difficult it was for so many young artists such as Amy Winehouse to cope with their early celebrity, Sharon Jones gave a telling response about how she may have handled stardom at twenty instead of fifty. "I probably could have handled it okay," she said, "but I would have also probably have been on some stupid major label, and you do one song, and if I don't do it right I wouldn't have stuck around. So to me, everything worked as planned. Who knows how things would have happened back then. I was wild when I was young, getting involved in stuff. And thank God I'm where I'm at now."

Another way that faith formed itself as a sort of armor in these ladies, and especially in Sharon Jones? Perhaps the very fact that faith is inherently about what Duncan Lowe called "things hoped for but not seen." This, she told me, had a huge impact on her career:

> Not just as part of the basis for her music, but also the fact of faith as the raw material for having a *vision* of the future, and then seeing it happen as it unfolds, *recognizing* it as your vision. That's how she managed to present her soul to the world, she had a big character, a strong character, but almost no ego at all. She was given, or she created a "total persona." But after the show was over, there was just her and the universe, and she

always gave thanks for having the opportunity to do what she did. Which, of course, was also her own vision for herself and her future.

The implication here is that lots of people have a vision for their future, but not everyone recognizes it when it suddenly appears before them, and too many people assume that they themselves are solely responsible for it if they do, rather than giving thanks for it. "After a show, she still had to go home alone, to do the dishes or whatever, but she always gave thanks, the same way she gave her show, from the heart."

Yes, where Jones was at was just fine with her, and commenting on the concept of retirement from something that didn't really even seem like work in the first place but more like a celebration of her joy and sorrows in this life, she quipped, "Retirement? What's that? I know our label's gonna grow, and you know what? Instead of me retiring, I want to be able to find other talent, and find some young soul singers, and keep the Daptone label going, y'know?" We do indeed. Jones also stipulated that the only thing she ever wanted was to finally be recognized by the music industry. Now she is, at long last, being not just recognized but also acclaimed. She never got tired of being grateful for the love that her fans showered on her, and she never took it for granted. She was a lively dame first, a beloved star second, and a demanding diva never.

Gabe Roth's first encounter with Sharon would be charmingly accidental, and it feels similarly Jonesian in spirit. He was looking for backup singers for a 1996 pre-Daptone album, and one of his band members, the aforementioned saxophone player, said his girlfriend was a terrific singer and also knew two others who could fit the bill. Legend has it that three singers were supposed to arrive for the session, but only one showed up—Jones.

The actual story is even more precious, in retrospect. There were actually no other singers invited, only Jones, who showed up for what would have been a short and modest $50 gig and then bravely volunteered to do all the vocals herself for $150. It was pure theater of the spunkiest sort. Most of her spunk just seemed to come out of her own character and life experience, while some of it—the super-theatrical side—may also have been learned, absorbed, or practiced in her youth by following the example of her main idol James Brown.

Sharon Jones found her own feminine version of his unique ferocity, and she controlled the stage and the audience in a very similar fashion. Anyone who ever met James Brown knew they were in the presence of someone who was always right. Such a stance caused considerable trouble for Brown, a man of prodigious and often counterproductive appetites. Jones had a more benign and still faith-grounded version of the same stance: for her, it was God who was always right. Either way, the link with and love for Mr. Dynamite was always strongly self-evident, in Jones's work just as it was in so many other African American artists of his era. After all, one can only imagine the impact on young black artists of hearing Brown defiantly declaim one of his seminal songs, "Say It Loud, I'm Black and I'm Proud." Maybe especially so for an unconventional-looking young woman such as Jones, for whom it must have felt like an invitation to look in the mirror and start to love herself. As she put it so reverently to *Fashion* magazine, "What Mr. Brown said, it made me walk away, go out with the band and take a chance."

The chance she took was a big one, perhaps especially because she had heard that same old restrictive refrain from so many record producers over the years, and eventually it would become a kind of personal anthem for her: proving them wrong. Sometimes, destiny seems to step in, or at least in retrospect it seems that way. The 1996 recording session that made all the difference in her career arc—the source point for her whole career, in fact—was originally organized by that exotic little soul label called Pure Records, then run jointly by Lehman and Roth. Now a long-forgotten part of mature soul-music history, it was also the stepping-stone that would lead Jones to Roth's new label, which would be expressly formed around little old *her.* It was also a long blind date they would go on together for the next twenty years.

Jones's positive spirit and stick-to-it-ness—which by now has become part of her received legend—always held her in good stead, even in the face of the man troubles that accidentally brought her together with her future producer, chief songwriter, bass player, and record executive all rolled into one. "The men in my life have come and gone," she told *Fashion*. "I didn't get married and have children because I wanted to make a career for myself. You can't say I wish I had or I wish I could have. All you can do is look to what's going on now and fight hard to do better and be better."

Daptone cofounder Neil Sugarman has another concise definition of the creative and business intentions that solidified his and Roth's creative interests. "We proved that what we're doing has a place in modern times," he explained. "We were never thinking about whether that sound is old, we know what we're going for and it's focused: the songwriting and lyrical content all relates to Sharon." And it was always frustrating for the band to hear comments about whether they were "retro." "We're romantics!" Sugarman told Adrian Lee of *Maclean's* in 2014, clearly emphasizing the woman who would become their frontline singer, and also making the obvious distinction between themselves and the forces of nostalgia.

The fateful meeting between Roth, Sugarman, and Jones now seems like something that was designed in heaven—and, according to Jones, maybe it was. But sometimes heaven needs a little nudge to get things moving, and that's just what the dynamic soul singer provided. When she carefully crafted that solo arrival for the trio recording session her ex-beau had concocted, she was invited to sing all three of the vocals parts herself, and she so stunned the studio staff with her raw but accomplished vocal style and her equally rough, ready, and racy personality that they invited her to record another solo track, "Switchblade." A James Brown–infused homage delivered on her own, and which was subsequently included on an album called *Soul Tequila*, it also featured deep-funk legend Lee Fields and launched the basic nuts and bolts of a stellar new backup band, the Dap-Kings.

Jones would actively churn up the funk with them for the next twenty years, right up until the very day she passed away in November 2016. And it was Lee Fields himself, her early mentor, who would deliver the deeply moving eulogy at Brown Memorial Baptist Church for her memorial that December. Things had come full circle—maybe because she was the one who drew that circle—and Sharon Jones always had insisted that, yes, in true gospel music fashion, the circle would be unbroken.

EMBODIED SPIRIT
The Essence of Soul Music

"I feel like there is an angel inside of me that I am constantly shocking."
—JEAN COCTEAU in Francis Steegmuller, *Cocteau: A Biography*, 1970

In an interview with *Beyond Race Magazine* back in 2010, Jones offered up her most accurate assessment of what made soul music soul and what made her a soul singer. "Soul music to me? It comes from the heart. It comes from deep within. When we get up on that stage man, I'm feeding off the Dap-Kings, they're feeding off me, and we're *all* feeding off the audience. And we all have one *accord*, that's what we call it. Soul has nothin' to do with color at all, man."

Indeed, her stellar soul band is a wild racial mixture of white, black, Italian, South American, Jewish, south, north, east, and west. It is, in fact, the purest distillation of what America really is: not a cultural or a corporate merger but a spiritual merger. "These guys, they don't even realize what they do to me, or for me," she continued. "They write these songs for me. They tell a story, but then I get to put that story *down*, and send it out there." She certainly sends us, too, even though she had to wait a long, long time before assuming her rightful place in the spotlight. Much to our good fortune.

Obviously, waiting for success and fame to finally arrive in middle age might afford an artist a deeper perspective on their role as a performer and entertainer, while also providing a wealth of actual lived life experience to bring to bear in the expression of their craft. "Youth is wasted on the young" is another common adage that strikes most of us as true, especially when we try to understand the depth of human interaction a young person might bring to the creative table. Contrast that with Jones's exposure to a real world that didn't seem to want her, and you have the raw ingredients for an abiding self-confidence as she fought her way forward.

As usual, Dapette Starr Duncan Lowe offered an astute analysis of the emotional and professional dynamic at work with Jones when she told me, "Sharon was always a born leader. All of her personal experiences, ups and downs, culminated in the character and the person she was, even as a businessperson. Without all of her difficult experiences, she wouldn't have been who she was, the strongest person you ever met. She carried those experiences with her until it was her time to shine."

And, as well all know by now, she had to wait a long, long time before she got her chance to shine. On one of her visits to NPR in 2007, when she was just beginning to really break through the cosmetic gates of the music industry, Jones revealed how it had impacted on her self-esteem, but also how hard work bestowed a benevolent side as well. "I worked in corrections because they told me I wasn't going to make it in show business, and at the time I was past twenty-five . . . what the hell am I going to do? Singing is my life. . . . So I worked as a guard at Rikers Island from 1988 to 1990." It must have felt like she herself was also a prisoner, given that all she wanted to do in life was sing her heart out.

And as she told *Rolling Stone* later in her career, when new struggles had replaced the old ones, "One day I told the inmates that I also sang, and they wouldn't lock up until I did a verse of 'The Greatest Love of All,' then they refused to go into their cells until I sang the whole thing. I knew when I was there that I wasn't meant to be there. Even the inmates told me that. They said to me, 'Miss Jones, you aren't meant to be here. You're too nice.'" Luckily, for her and for us, she was just nice enough to suit the folks at Daptone. Yet this too-nice Miss Jones had lived almost half a century before her debut album was recorded and released, even if she'd been rehearsing for it her whole life and was more than ready to become a fervent missionary devoted to spreading the profane scripture of her deep funk.

In 2008, FaceCulture.com captured some of Jones's inherent sadness inadvertently when she shared her memories of struggling for some twenty years or so to *break into* the business, as if it was a big beautiful house she wasn't allowed to visit. "They told me I had to bleach my skin, my face was too dark, to be more pale," she said. Jones wasn't about to pretend to be some ersatz kind of Lena Horne clone, so her response was clear: "One day, people will accept me for what I *am*, what I sound like, not what I look like." It took a while, but eventually, they did. When it came to trying to explain what made she and her band unique, she was always able to pin it down. "What's unique? We're solid, man. When you're together as a group for ten or twenty years, you get *solid*. You sound together, because you are together. As in *together*."

There was a gratitude flowing back and forth between Jones and her band, and between the artist and her label, which is definitely palpable and substantial, and it clearly works both ways. Daptone was grateful for Jones's experience and spirit, and Jones was grateful that this group of young soul enthusiasts was willing to give her a chance to shine. And man, did they shine together immediately, as she expressed so well to *FaceCulture*. "Gabe saw something in me, heard something in me, and after doing a couple of songs, he called me back and said they were going to Europe. We went to London to open for Maceo Parker—that was my first time before a really big crowd."

First time? In footage of that concert she looked like she had just been born on that stage in front of that big crowd, she shook them to their bones. And her readiness for fame was obvious right from the beginning, especially in the way she plays the whole band like her own instrument. Like most great soul and funk artists, Jones is best known for losing herself in a song while at the same time listening carefully to her band and what they're playing. It's the classic equation: they're each giving each other fresh energy and sharing the flow.

Jones also explained to the *SoulZangers* show in 2010 how a depressing common storyline played out initially with her new band: they had to leave the country and go abroad in order to gain public recognition and some of the success they felt they were due. "European audiences really got us started early on. Everybody in the United States thought soul was *old*. Europe was different. Until Amy [Winehouse] and [Mark] Ronson started doin' their thing, dipping back into it. Then, *everybody* wanted to do it." Or at least try.

Jones also suddenly had many younger fellow devotees to help keep the faith alive. The late contemporary pop-soul artist Prince lifted up Jones's faith immensely when they met in 2011, after he'd earlier seen her perform at the SXSW Festival in Austin, Texas, and he asked her and the Dap-Kings to open for him at Madison Square Garden in New York City. According to a report in the *Daily Beast* by Matt Wilstein, after seeing Jones in action in Austin, Prince told her, "Girl, you took me to church!" Jones described the comment as her first "I don't know what to do with myself" moment. Backstage at the Garden concert, Prince declared her song "When I Get Home" "one of the funkiest songs I've heard in the last twenty-five years! I haven't heard a funk song that groovy!"

For Jones, Prince's acclaim was an obvious vindication of decades of hard work, as well as a validation for the funk groove she'd launched into with Roth. "The most valuable thing Prince taught me was to know my own worth, to trust in yourself, to believe in what you're doing and not to change for anyone." Clearly, both Jones and Roth knew that the special vibe they'd found together was the real thing—something you can't quite simulate or approximate, even in the manner accomplished so masterfully by the obviously brilliant Mark Ronson with Amy Winehouse.

In further pursuit of the soul music path as it relates to Jones and her label, Sarah Perry of *Atlas Society* offered a fine profile of Daptone's other cofounder, Neal Sugarman, in which she captured some of the wonky charm of their Brooklyn roots by vividly describing their base as a ramshackle red brick building with a cracked, dirt-stained window below an awkwardly hanging broken awning. But she also referenced what made it so special: rich R&B vocals pouring out into the street, with voices coming from a deep place—voices with the uncanny power to move us emotionally, to captivate and transform us. Sugarman's record company, as Perry described it, apparently liked to do things the hard way, embracing a sound shot directly from the '60s and captured straight to vinyl, all while its creators occasionally had to take on non-musical day jobs to pay the bills and still stay true to their shared dream.

Those at Daptone have clearly surprised, and maybe even shocked, many people in the record industry with both their devotion and their good fortune, promoting themselves (in the Stax tradition) as "the little label that could, would, and should." Perry noted that one of the secrets to their success might just be what they're *not*, as in *not* corporate, *not* slick, *not* greedy, *not* bloodthirsty, only *soulthirsty*. "We do better every year," Sugarman shared proudly, and they did so mostly by following a few simple, folksy, and family-oriented rules: no loans, no advances; if money is needed, simply work harder; and, above all, "stay true to the music." When you stop to think about it, that's rather radical in this jaded twenty-first century.

Neal Sugarman started his musical life in an intimate listening relationship with his father while growing up in Boston, where they devoted their time to close study of the soul classics together, and he inherited his father's appreciation for the finer points of rhythm. While studying at Berklee College of Music, listening to a lot of jazz and absorbing the giants of the saxophone, he began to focus his attention on the roots of the R&B sounds he and his father found so mesmerizing. Graduating in 1991, he moved to New York, where he parked cars and catered food during the day while playing gigs feverishly every night in the intense postgraduate soul programs offered by smoky clubs and bars.

In 1996 he met an organ player named Adam Scone and they formed the Sugarman Three. This was only a few months before he was introduced to Gabriel Roth, and just as short a time before he first encountered the sizzling Sharon Jones. In just two years, he'd have two albums under his belt, and he'd be ready for action when Roth called upon him to try out a new way of making music and doing business, which they defined, delightfully, as *having fun*.

Celebrating that success twenty years later, Perry faithfully chronicled Sugarman and his Daptone dynasty as the little label started to branch out with a new subsidiary imprint called Wick Records—one that would expand their reach beyond soul and into rock music, while still maintaining an allegiance to analog recording formats. For her *Atlas Society* profile in 2012, Perry described Wick as, "A label run by musicians for musicians, while continuing to subscribe to the same tried-and-true formula as its parent company. They maintain a drastically lean operation, from the low-key office space to the smallest staff possible, and that's been part of the consciously creative decision-making allowing *Daptone* to function on its own terms for so long, and at its own leisurely pace, without any unwanted influence being exerted from major label distributors."

Sugarman described himself as coming from the punk-rock era, and he believes its back-to-basics ethos has always stuck with him. Obviously it comes down to a basic value judgment as simple as finding big corporate labels to have a sinister side, while independent labels have room for more integrity. It suited his taste for freedom that he seldom wanted to compromise: he didn't then and still doesn't to this day. From the very beginning, he and Daptone made creative choices based on gut instinct and intuition rather than the bottom line. They didn't even know where the bottom line was back then, so in 1996, when Roth was looking for three backup singers and Sharon Jones approached him with this lean and mean offer—"Why use three girls when I can do all three parts and save you some money?"—it was obviously a match made in heaven. She was spunk personified.

Sugarman also captured some of the charm of that early encounter between himself, Jones, and Roth in a way that explains a lot that's happened since. "Gabe was so impressed with Sharon's work that he also asked her to record her own song, much to her surprise. The Soul Providers needed a new vocalist, and now they had one. Sharon could do everything. She had smooth chocolate skin, big expressive eyes, and a megawatt smile. Everyone loved her."

Most importantly for Sugarman, and so personally rewarding for Jones, was that Roth liked her just the way she was, as "an experienced woman in her late forties with a sturdy handshake, a can-do attitude, and a little extra padding around the waist." She was finally being accepted on her own terms for the first time in a long time—make that forever. And yet she kept her day job as a corrections officer even while singing at weddings and going out on tour with the Soul Providers. It was always more about the music for her, not the money, just as it was for Roth and Sugarman.

When Roth split from defunct Desco Records, the natural move was to take the Providers, as well as Sugarman and Jones, and simply start all over again with Daptone as a label, the Dap-Kings as its house band, and Sharon Jones as its resident black Madonna. Their quest was as simple as basic logic, with Sugarman firmly believing that one ingredient was always essential for them: the call of rhythm and what makes it groove. Clearly, Sugarman adheres to his much-admired old-school roots, and his commitment to the idea of music needing to touch the senses in order to truly be considered soul music at all comes across on every track he lays down. Their sound always has a certain way of breathing—one our ears know instantly.

Interviewed on *The Colbert Report* in 2010, Sharon Jones was able to sum this up even more succinctly, with her usual disarmingly direct skill: "I'm not going anywhere but Daptone. Why do I need to go somewhere else when I've got everything coming from them?" She never did leave Daptone after her unexpected mid-life triumph, staying with the label right up until the very end, while Sugarman and Roth stuck with her with exactly the same sense of loyalty: This is the real deal, so why mess it up? Why indeed? If it isn't broken, as the saying goes, why fix it?

• • •

A brief comment on the origins of the word "dap" might help to clarify the subliminal message contained within the Daptone ethos. "Dap" is a friendly gesture of greeting, agreement, or solidarity between two people that has become popular in Western cultures since the 1970s, having originated from African American communities, where "giving dap" typically involves handshaking, hooking thumbs, fist pounding, or chest- and fist-bumping. "Giving dap" can refer to presenting many kinds of positive nonverbal communication, ranging from a brief moment of body contact to a complicated routine of hand slaps or snaps known only by the participants, thus giving it the aura of a secret society or cult of shared understanding.

This simpatico feeling is especially the case when the original production and management groove, or *tone*, was laid down so ideally by Sugarman and Roth right at the inception of their partnership. When Jeff Mao met Californian native Gabe Roth for a live audience interview at the Red Bull Academy in 2010, he characterized the musician and producer, in a dramatic yet accurate assessment, as having soul flowing freely from every pore of his body. He also accurately depicted Daptone itself as being "a vitally active and artistic studio that provides analog relief from the rest of the pop sphere's relentless digital din."

Roth himself seems to have had an ironic success in the music industry, not *despite* the fact that he's often declared his reluctance to be part of the industry at all but *because* of his ability to do so without swallowing its business mythologies uncritically. He and Sugarman have held steadfast to a basic philosophy of making the records that they themselves would like to listen to, rather than the ones that might sell in big numbers to strangers.

Roth's ethos is rooted in the simple realization that if you wanted something to sound rough and raw like the live recordings he loved, that had to be your approach to making the record: doing it *live* in the studio. "A lot of people are really into vintage equipment," he told Mao, "And I've got some stuff like that, but the key was, especially on the first records I was making, to use a lot of microphones from a cheap electronics store like RadioShack, to buy a microphone for like $5.00 . . . to use whatever you have and just rely on the performance of the musicians and on your own ears."

This was an experimental approach—a kind of guerilla strategy to recording in search of really raw sonic environments that more money just can't buy. We could call it the "money can't buy you sound" school of thought. This approach is encapsulated in the game plan of a producer who, as Roth himself says, can be *outside* of the record and *inside* of it at the same time. He's inside it when listening to the arrangement and all the core engineering details, such as whether the mic preamp is distorting, but he's also far enough outside of it to be able to listen carefully, not as a producer or a musician, but, as he put it so well, "as someone who works in a coffee shop, and it's their favorite record while going home." In other words, he views this radical kind of engineer/producer skill as one of being able to listen like a human being.

As such, Roth tends to avoid the acres of super specialized high-tech electronic or equipment magazines in favor of what he describes as "blind listening" in the studio. He'll have two or three mics plugged in, but he won't know where or to what. The result is that he then goes back to the control room to find that there is, perhaps, a $3,000 RCA ribbon microphone from the '50s on the horns, but he might also have his cheap RadioShack mic, or an SM57, or a condenser, aimed at other instruments without knowing which is where. This makes him listen differently—really differently—and extra carefully, using only instinct and intuition.

As a result of this hyper-organic and almost meditative method, Roth is quite hesitant when people approach him, as they so often do, with questions about how he gets the "magic" into his sound or what kind of gear or tape machine he's using for this or that particular groove. To Roth, this fetishistic aspect of the business is very distracting, and is almost as inconsequential as someone asking Picasso what kind of brushes he used. (Smart enough to be humble, Roth will clarify that he's not saying he *is* a Picasso, only that it's the musicians who are playing the music, not the engineer or the equipment, and it's certainly not the arranger.)

A key component for Roth in capturing the slippery essence of a Sharon Jones hurricane of energy has been to utilize a 4- or 8-track machine, as opposed to the digital approach of having unlimited numbers of tracks and hence limitless but dizzying options. For him, all technology remains exactly as it is—technics, a tool—and there's often something misguided in the process of multiplying one's production controls out to infinity. When he talks about this to rapt listeners searching for his holy grail, they're often mystified when he explains that there isn't one. Instead, it's just the best way that highly creative people came up with in the old days (by which he usually means the glory days of Stax Records, that other legendary little label) to do the job at hand, and that, if anything, the real holy grail is simply a matter of classical craftsmanship.

The best embodiment of Roth's streamlining of that old-school craftsmanship is the personal and professional commitment of the musicians, the engineers, and the arrangers. A good example of this notion in action would be, while making a Sharon Jones record, taping the entire orchestra section on one track, in one day, for the whole album. Radical simplicity, perhaps, but it came after he had toiled for weeks over the arrangements to get them just right, altering overly busy details prior to ever even entering the studio. As indicated, it's a very small studio—the same size as the living room in an average family home—so that intimacy was part of the natural environment of the space itself, which was then enhanced by Roth's deft engineering touch.

Prior to shifting into action, Roth might suddenly choose to delete a highly favorable part of the string orchestra arrangement, not because it was subpar but because it might collide too much with a part of the song where Jones was delivering a supernatural vocal, and he wouldn't want to take away from what she was doing. This is emblematic of the kind of producer, engineer, and arranger he is: serving as a sonic architect, designing the overall aural building, but also as an interior designer, moving around pieces of sonic furniture if they happen to get in the way of the key occupant—the singer.

"Making all the decisions, listening while you do it," was how he described it to Mao at Red Bull. "It takes a kind of commitment—you have to know what you're doing and you have to listen to it and know it right then and there. This is what I want the record to sound like. It hits the tape and that's it." Others may call this method flying by the seat of your pants; Roth calls it entering the state of flow and accepting all the aleatory outcomes in advance. Even if he occasionally makes mistakes, like having the trumpet mic'd too loud, he approaches it in a very Zen-like manner, accepting the imperfections as part of the process. He even declares, through using this flow method, that there will always be imbalances and imperfections; but it shouldn't even be perfect at all, he seems to be telling us, because it's a *record*. It's a living record of what actually happened.

Part of that subtle feel he's going for is certainly evident on the old Stax records he and Jones both loved, and to some extent their other Memphis counterpart, the even lesser known Hi Records style of Willie Mitchell. In both cases it's a live feel containing a multitude of spontaneous moments, all utterly unplanned and maybe even unplannable, as I'll discuss shortly. Nowadays, as Roth's comparable technique reveals to us, all the "weird" parts are often absent, and all the records sound exactly the same, because they are: perfect and pristine, but also somewhat lifeless, and certainly not live. Roth's method, by contrast, provides far more freedom and flexibility, allowing him to do anything he wants to a record without a moment of hesitation or doubt.

Although he concedes that most contemporary producers might think using 4- or 8-track systems are limiting because they now lean so heavily on computers to select individual fragments and collage them together, Roth still believes that the historic analog method enhances the recording process for the musicians. Only a creative artist would give a damn about the kind of experience the other artists who are actually *making* the music come to life are having and sharing in the studio. He does stipulate, though, that he still might want to insert something into a recording or superimpose something over it, but because he's working with tape, he makes these interventions in an artisanal fashion, with a razor blade!

One of the keys to Daptone's success—both its creative acclaim and its more recent commercial recognition—is the simple fact that Roth and his collaborators always wanted and have fiercely guarded their personal control over their own destiny. They decided early on to place themselves in the role of flexible masters of their own independent domain. This enviable position really has only three core hinges: freedom of choice and expression, not owing any corporate overlords any money or contractual obligations, and not having anybody who can pull the plug on a project or tell them what to do.

To cap it off, they have lately been branching out into far-ranging styles and pursuing whatever sound strikes them as exciting at the moment—something that arises from the fact that they're also not limited to any particular genre. Musical borders mean nothing to this label because the only reason its founders make any specific record at all is because it has a sound they happen to love.

Love: that's not a word one hears much in the music industry these days, if ever. That word is also the reason why so many followers of the label and its frontline band and singer have formed a deeply personal and intimate relationship with both. They trust the label, trust the producers, trust the band and its singer, and, most importantly, they know the music: they're smart listeners who end up being the most loyal kind. This kind of grassroots loyalty doesn't even really require that big a promotional budget or expensively created video to sell the product. When it comes to recording the actual analog artifact, Roth's philosophy is even more esoteric. "It sounds crazy, but if you listen to it and it feels good, then there's no reason not to do it," he told Red Bull. "The only reason not to do it is if you're trying to get signed to Sony." Which is precisely why he's never been very interested in getting signed to Sony.

This same sort of flexible flow state also played into Roth's storied special creative and professional relationship with Sharon Jones, with whom he had a rather unusual constellation of relationships: fellow musician (as the bass player), engineer, arranger, songwriter, producer, and record label executive. One of the many reasons he got along so well with her, he would reveal, apart from being on such close terms for so many years, was that the two of them were completely opposite in their approach to crafting the finished artwork. He considered this the classic Apollonian/Dionysian balance, wherein the complementary harmony of oppositional attitudes and approaches merged into a transformative collaboration.

Roth characterized Jones, in the most charitable and affectionate terms imaginable, as crazy, passionate, singing from her gut; someone who wouldn't do what you told her, wouldn't do it the same way twice, wouldn't do two takes, and so on. While he, though flexible and a big fan of the flow state, knew what he wanted and recognized it once it came along, but not always right away. Roth has a mathematical and analytical mind—his first career choice actually was mathematics—which works best when he surrounds himself with incredibly talented musicians who are also deeply soulful people. When this harmonious union of interactive opposites happens in action, what you ended up with was often a brilliant Sharon Jones and the Dap-Kings album.

• • •

Like many multitalented individuals, Roth has more than his share of paradoxes at the heart of his operating systems. While eschewing the obsessive technicalities inherent in the most fetishistic of musical audiophiles and preferring to concentrate his attention on the flow state, he's still more than capable of getting into the most esoteric discussions about equipment and the technology of making music. He's clearly not immune to a good nerd-fest on the subject, and some of the more entertaining moments of his public interview with Jeff Mao were his interactions with participants who wanted to turn the proceedings into an engineering seminar. He was game for that, too.

He explained that a great drummer—for instance, someone like Dap-King Homer Steinweiss—makes you feel good when they hit the hi-hat, and doubly good when they thump on the snare, because certain drummers have a *tone*. They have a *feel* on the drum set going in, and that's 90 percent of the battle. His second fixation (in a good way) is the quality of the set and its ability to sustain the tone of the player, which requires him to stand in the room and tune the snare, then take a pillow out of the bass drum or put another pillow in (thickening the sound, à la Ringo Starr or Charlie Watts, for instance). Then he tapes up the tom, or puts it in a different room, experimenting until it sounds good to the ear, long before the mic even catches anything. Finally, the crucial thing for a drum is the placement of the mic once the tone sounds good to the human ear. There is, he confides, no secret placement, no holy grail.

Most importantly, Roth stresses, whether it's drum sounds or any sounds, he's listening to the *actual* playback of the tape machine, which is delayed, and he's very careful about how hard he's hitting the tape. But then, in a moment of consummate irony, the master producer costume fell away, and the musician underneath again rose to the surface as he modestly declared to the Red Bull audience that he didn't really have any more drum tips. A good drummer is always the best place to start. As for the rest of us mortals, whether we actually know what "crunchiness" really is, our ears know it when they hear it.

Roth is equally generous when talking with specialists about subjects he doesn't want to talk about, as when he shared with *Sound on Sound* magazine in 2008 some of the behind-the-scenes secrets that make Dap-tone recordings sound like Sharon Jones Daptone records. In a profile by Dan Daley called "Minimalist Engineering," he offered a crash course in how to arrive at maximalist sounds. While not being ideologically rigid when it comes to the job at hand, he demonstrated his outlier position in contemporary technology when he categorically stated, "Show me a computer that sounds as good as a tape machine and I'll use it." Needless to say, a decade later, that hasn't happened yet.

Identifying Roth quite properly as an audio architect, Daley's profile offers a wonderful glimpse beneath the wizard curtains of the booth he commands to masterfully manipulate the gifted Dap-King musicians, or behind a Jones song such as "Nobody's Baby," to pick just one that serves the purpose so well. It's totally true that such songs, and most of the albums Roth has played on, engineered, and produced for Jones and her crew, are veritable time machines of the most startling sort, transporting us back in history by evoking a crunch-drenched tone firmly rooted in the Memphis of circa 1962. Just don't mention the word "retro" too much around him.

"We're not doing a purposely 'retro' thing," he told Daley. "It's not about ideology. I'm not listening to old soul records and taking them apart clinically. It's more like a kind of informal schooling. You don't want to imitate, you want to let it influence you. One thing you learn is that sometimes mistakes are what makes a record sound great," he explained, returning to a favorite theme of his: that music should not be *perfect* or even correct.

Roth's personal belief is that if he and his musicians and their stellar singer were to find a sound that made them feel good when recording it, that flow or groove would translate without effort into making us feel good when we listen to it. Given the results of the last twenty years in his humble little studio, it's hard to disagree with whatever near-mystical techniques he might use to get them.

Still, the alchemy of sounds chased and captured in the studio is hauntingly similar to the transformation of base metals into gold, and some of Roth's arcane methodology obviously involves looking back to the analog past rather than forward into an ever-more-dizzying digital future. As Daley's piece demonstrates so well, since Daptone chose to celebrate 8-track recording rather than 16- or even 32-track, and to pay more attention to the music in its raw live state than to technological manipulations, there's very little likelihood of Roth calling up an Auto-Tune program in order to fix a flaw on one of its recordings.

This tape-only philosophy sometimes makes it seem like Roth and his collaborators are time-travelers seeking a distant innocence in the making of albums, with the Tascam 16-track deck in the control room being more of a sculptural artifact as they more frequently reach for the Otari MX5050 8-track, half-inch tape machine, a still-very-viable relic of bygone days. From the Trident Series 65 24-input desk, most of their mixes pulse through a restored 3M M23 quarter-inch 2-track deck or the Otari machine, both of which are called upon to manage authentic tape-slap and echo effects the old-school way by augmenting a pair of Orban spring reverbs and a Stocktonics plate reverb.

For Roth, this clearly gives "old school" a new meaning, without making it into a kind of vintage museum. His list of gear items runs the gamut from a relatively recent Rode NT1A large diaphragm condenser mic and an RCA DX77 to his precious collection of supposedly humble RadioShack mics and the Ampeg Gemini guitar amp he literally salvaged from a dumpster. In this most basic of approaches, nothing is in the studio just because it might be a cool collectible, even though many of these objects are quite rare. Everything at hand is where it is strictly because it sounds good, with *sounding good* being the operative strategy of any recording day. The only formula for success is the ironic commitment to not let anything become formulaic at all.

Even when speaking to an audiophile's magazine such as *Sound on Sound*, Roth had to admit that Daley's piece would unlikely be filled with granular descriptions of complex recording techniques when it came to detailing Daptone's magic touch. What Daley did enjoy declaring, however, was that the studio site proved that you can make a great deal happen out of very little in the techno razzle-dazzle department. Drums would generally get one or two mics of their own, being the foundation for every groove, with the RCA DX77 or the Shure 55 often strewn anti-strategically on the floor.

Roth is a master sound-builder. Other young digital wizards could learn a lot by attending the old-school curriculum of his production techniques, especially those super-modern engineers who rely so heavily on armies of microphones hyper-placed in a fetishistic fashion that they end up forgetting how to use their ears. Visiting musicians who finally see the secret behind his working methods (there is no magic formula, it's not how many mics you use but where you put them) often leave with raised eyebrows after discovering the simplicity of his technical attitude. Mostly, he just tells the musicians to go for it.

One result of this minimalist approach is, for instance, how there's a perfectly smooth decrease in the volume of tom-toms as they increase in density, with the fills appearing to move in a direction away from the lone microphone. The Akai MC 50 mic, produced in the '60s to interact with home tape recorders, is one that Roth has baptized the "Dictaphone mic" on the kick. These would be EQ'd and compressed together, with both mic channels sent to a single track. One visiting musician exclaimed that he hadn't heard that sound in a long time. Naturally: no one does it that way anymore, since many would have up to a hundred mics all esoterically channeled in every direction, simply because they can.

The same approach applies to the horn section, which along with rhythm has been the driving wheel of true soul music from the king of classical funk James Brown all the way to the contemporary funk of the Dap-Kings. Roth usually utilizes but a single microphone, more often than not his trusty Shure 315 (known as the "Elvis" microphone) to capture all three Dap-Kings horns, placing it on a stand about three or four feet in front of the players. He contends that you really want to let the horns "mix themselves," and that you should give them enough room for the sounds to blend together even before hitting the microphone. If this sounds like aural alchemy, that's exactly what it is.

Roth's way of describing this to *Sound on Sound* was typically understated and modest: "No tricks—just good guitars played by good guitar players through really good amps." All finesse, no force. Meanwhile, after doing duty as a superb bass player himself, back inside his control room he searches for and finds the classic soul-funk sound by rolling the low end off the tracks before they get to tape, explaining that the lowest frequencies have the most energy and can saturate the tape before the rest of the sound is able to benefit from the intentional distortion he wants in the mix.

For his main outboard rack, Roth has at his disposal a Tube-Tech compressor and EQ, two Purple Audio MC77 compressors, an Anthony Demaria Labs tube compressor, an API Lunchbox, and some vintage collectors items such as Orban spring reverbs and an Altec unit. For Sharon Jones's vocals, since she was actually another kind of musical instrument in human form, he tried to use anything that might catch her special lightning in a bottle—perhaps the RCA, or his Sennheiser 421, or a Shure SM58—with the first outing of her voice frequently being the one he ended up keeping.

For Jones's vocals he also liked to use spring reverbs and often tape slap, a surgical method that demands the kind of precise calculation that most others have abandoned in the digital age, since they so often let the computer do the thinking for them. With two inches of tape between the record and the repro heads running at fifteen inches per second, he takes one second and divides by seven, thus creating a delay of about 140 milliseconds—a duration maybe only Roth or a canary could detect and play with.

Roth's allegiance to analog history is not an attempt to merely simulate what it felt like to be working in 1965. While for many engineers the gold standard of sound might be a Steely Dan record (which is plenty perfect, by the way) Daptone might reach for the timeless records of Irma Thomas or Ann Peebles. Roth has also observed the irony of so many producers going through all kinds of gymnastics trying to make their records, especially the drums, sound like they were recorded on only one microphone. His secret: put only one microphone out there and massage everything through it lovingly and live, since this forces him to commit to decisions about sound and arrangements right there on the spot.

• • •

Much as a music journalist and historian such as myself loves to rhapsodize about a unique figure such as Sharon Jones, in the end the ones who really matter are the musicians, and specifically the Dap-Kings themselves. Two members in particular have offered deep insights into

Jones as a lead singer and artist: drummer Homer Steinweiss and Dave Guy, the trumpet player on the group's biggest records. Steinweiss is an incredibly gifted timekeeper, a player about whom *Drummers Resource Magazine*'s Nick Ruffini would rhapsodize on the publication's podcast Session 286: "If you're looking for vintage soul, Homer is your guy. He's a specialist by design and he likes it that way. There's an underground world of funk and soul that transcends time and makes you wonder if the music you're hearing is from 2017 or from 1977, and Homer is at the epicenter, honoring that tradition."

That's not all Steinweiss honors. He's never happier than when extolling the virtues of Jones, as he did on the Daptone site last year upon the release of her posthumous album, when he often remarked on how Sharon *shaped* him as a musician. The extent of her influence is hardly surprising when you consider the fact that he's been playing drums behind her since he was sixteen years old and readily acknowledges that she could teach him everything about how to play music. In fact, he has admitted quite frankly that he didn't really become a good musician until he was on the road with Jones for a few years and her vibe started to settle in. But it was her character that always impressed him the most. For the precocious teenager Steinweiss, one can only imagine how it felt to try and keep up with a dynamo older than his own mother, and especially so free-spirited a dame—one who just exuded that classic badass attitude that a young aspiring musician must have revered.

In this respect, and this sense of honoring her, Steinweiss was joined just as enthusiastically in remarks made by his fellow Dap-Kings percussion player, Fernando Velez, the sensitive percussion and conga master of the band, who was often stunned by the complete switch that would take place before and after Jones's performances, and by the shifting focus Jones was able to develop and utilize in her work. Like everyone else who knew her, he found her to be a regular person who was a lot of fun to be around when she wasn't performing. But once onstage, she transformed into a prizefighter, stalking the ring and reaching out intimately to the whole audience. For Velez, she was a life force, and the band had no choice but to follow her, to do justice to what she was offering up every night in every performance of every song.

After her passing, each and every band member recorded a self-produced and touchingly elegiac recollection of their beloved lead singer, placing them on the Daptone site as if they were personal postcards sent out to her fans. Time after time, they extolled her virtues as a musician, as a mother figure, as a soul artist, and as a consummate professional who helped groom them by sharing her wealth of life experience. Since they were all pretty much young enough to be her kids, or at least younger siblings, she also taught them what it meant to make real, authentic soul and funk music. She helped them to feel what it must have been like to be growing up in the golden analog age of vinyl bliss.

But Daptone Records isn't just about rewriting or recreating soul music history. It's not even really about homage, though that plays a legitimate role. It's all about giving and getting that shared feeling of *dap*. It's even more about learning the deep lessons embedded in these circular pieces of classic black vinyl and discovering how their '60s soul and '70s funk ancestors worked their magic. Based on the evidence amassed so far, one thing we can all be sure of is that their analog ancestors would probably approve.

Perhaps most tellingly, Starr Duncan Lowe told me that, for the Dap-Kings, "Sharon was the person who had solidified the emotional blueprint, the grammar of funk. She embodied, or personified, the period in history that they so loved to listen to: both the gospel side and the soul music side. So, like her, they also loved the influences of say, Shirley Caesar from South Carolina, or Albertina Walker from Chicago, or the great Ruth Brown from Virginia—she just loved Ruth Brown."

And just like the legendary southern farmer Shoutin' John, who may be an apocryphal figure but serves his real life purpose as a symbol, they shared his and Sharon's aptitude for the eminently churchy trait of celebrating and showing your gratitude *out loud*. Legend has it that when farmer John went to church and the other parishioners complained about how loudly he shouted to the rafters, he'd explain, "When I look at my fields with things growing, how can I not shout out to show my thanks to the Lord for what he's given me?" How indeed? And, just so, I sense that for the Dap-Kings in particular as a band, and for Daptone Records in general, Sharon Jones was their Shoutin' John. And they never tired of expressing their gratitude for her as a living reminder of the soul music they loved to play and to share with the world.

For Duncan Lowe, as a performing and recording collaborator, her soul sister Sharon Jones was a special case—someone who was fun, first and foremost, but also someone who was generous. "She was amazing, she allowed you your freedom, she'd step back and let you take your time in the light, she shared her space on the stage . . . but make no mistake . . . it was *her* stage, she *owned* it, every inch of it belonged to her, and she knew it. She was just kind about it."

QUEEN SURROUNDED BY KINGS
A Thing to Behold

"What makes us fit in is that we do it from the heart. When you do some-thing from the heart and soul, it's going to merge with everything around you, because music is a universal thing."
—LEE FIELDS to Neil Ferguson on *The Horn*, 2013

Sharon Jones often compared working with the Dap-Kings to being an athlete, and anyone who saw her perform can attest to the fact that she worked it all out in front of the world. Given how much funk energy she exuded, it sometimes surprises people to learn that she wasn't a songwriter and didn't personally pen any of the lyrics to the power-fully delivered songs that became so entwined with her persona. So what was the source of her magic?

Jones helped clarify some of that paradox to *Fresh Air*'s Terry Gross, who interviewed her in 2007. "I think I bring the songs that aren't about me, or related to my life," she said. "It's like, a song like 'How Do I Let a Good Man Down?' Let me tell you, I didn't write that song—because if I have a good man, I ain't gonna let him down!" But even though she excelled at being an intuitive medium and singing *other* people's thoughts and feelings, there were still some self-imposed limits for her. "I'm telling a story and if I can't tell the story, then I'm not going to sing it." She couldn't tell a story if she didn't agree with it in some way, shape, or form, or if she was expected to sing something that portrayed her as something she was not, such as begging someone in a weak way. "That's not me."

The best example of this discreetly selective process of singing only what she could personally identify with was her complete lack of interest even in singing a great song such as Aretha Franklin's "Chain of Fools." She just didn't want to relate to the sentiment in that song's style, so she didn't.

The mystery of how stylistic structures can remain constant in terms of intensity and energy output while their emotional and lyrical content is still modified by the time and circumstances of each singer is, of course, one of the joys of musical creative growth in the first place. The power of this storytelling muse is all the more evident in the case of an extreme empathy such as that practiced by Sharon Jones, yet still there lingers a prayerful and mournful expression of faith derailed—even belief betrayed—in an ode-like declamation of past hymns gone bad. It's sometimes a sour lament that embraces the style of lowdown soul at the expense of the genre of highborn scripture.

As a living embodiment of the soul style, with Sharon Jones we're dealing with a consummately gifted *empath*—an artist whose special skill is channeling the words of the songwriter almost like a séance medium, occupying the song and personifying its content through the awesome theatricality of her own persona. It's a theatrical mask that barely changed one iota in her travels from obscurity to celebrity over the course of forty years in the business, mostly because it wasn't really an *act*.

Her performing style was also the reflection of an innate ability to connect directly with her audience, from one soul to another: she was in fact the very personification of what the true soul sound is inherently all about. This is precisely why I believe that, when we listen to funk—especially funk of the Sharon Jones variety—we can still hear the recognizable echoes of gospel. Especially when Jones moans, in "Settling In," "Now my loneliness is what I'll never, ever feel again, yes I believe . . . I believe." She believes beyond belief.

Any change over time is never a complete change, since it's always got to be based on the development and synthesis of past models in the same idiom. Once gospel is incorporated into blues and rhythm is added to transform it into soul and funk, however, the message changes dramatically. Once bluesified by secular romance (sex) and rocked out by rhythm, it has already become soul in the blink of an eye, the beat of a heart. And then, once that heartbeat starts rising faster and faster to a fever pitch, it's already become funk. But for Jones, that inner yearning still remained a bold stance: hers was a long, jittery chain of faith under threat.

Funk still has a core message of liberation, however, and that's the crucial link. The other integral feature in the process is the communal structure of gospel music, in its call-and-response arrangements and its intense vocal harmonies. These continue unabated in soul and funk, which still symbolize the vibrant unity of a communal structure. Clearly, in terms of both perspective and its musical structure, gospel music was practically readymade for the upcoming secular needs of black musical emotions and their expression in both soul and funk. Like the African trance roots of gospel, it was also perfectly pre-adapted to turn into a different form of energy transport, the kind most associated with the transcendent frenzies of funk practiced by Brown and Jones.

Having traced the circuitous tracks of sacred trance music toward secular trance music, we're also at the location where the heart of the Sharon Jones paradox is beating, demonstrating her remarkable ability to reconcile the two sides of her character—the one needing the nourishment of prayer and the other one demanding the delights of funking it up. My main contention here is one we can easily hear if we listen carefully: gospel music is incredibly funky, and funk music is surprisingly spiritual.

There are, of course, as many flavors of funk as there are of its noble ancestors gospel, blues, R&B, and soul music. But one basic ingredient is shared in common by all of them: the heaviest of intricate and overlapping grooves. Funk is more or less what James Brown invented and what the Dap-Kings later perfected. It's been around officially since about 1966 and was largely promulgated and widely popularized by George Clinton, among others, especially in his various permutations of the Parliaments, Parliament, and P-Funk. The question "What is the funk?" is best answered with your ears, of course, by listening to some of its seminal '60s and '70s founders, but we can also traverse the historical territory for stylistic and conceptual clarity of expression.

It also helps to place Sharon Jones in a tangible and formal context. George Clinton took the serious thump and twitch embodied by James Brown and pushed it to new and deeper places that still reverberate today. Funk is obviously something one feels, and almost everybody has the potential ability to feel it, though as a caution to music critics, the more one thinks about it, the harder it is to get the feel of what it really is. It's just something that happens or doesn't. Jones would pick up that pure gauntlet or raw feeling short-circuiting the intellect, and she would run her own long-distance marathon with it.

The core ethos of Daptone, the basic style of the Dap-Kings, and the emotive spirit of Jones are all self-fulfilling prophecies in the secular scripture of holy funk. George Clinton, like Brown before him, was so far ahead of his time that record labels and listeners alike weren't quite sure what to call what he was doing, and his subsequent staying power has proven one of his foundational premises: the need for a proud appreciation of all that he generally calls "black music" represents. As he put it to so well to Rickey Vincent in his *Funk: The Music, the People, and the Rhythm of the One*, "Stripped to its bare roots, all of it is funk. It's the product we produce, and no one can do it like *we* do it."

What it is that they do—and what has remained embedded in the souls of the twenty-first century artists who inherited the history of a groove, bands like Sharon Jones and the Dap-Kings, for example—is to focus our attention on the throbbing physicality and transformational power of sound and beat. Considering the fact that funk and its heartfelt lyrics turn often-bleak urban realities upside down with distinctively danceable music, it is odd that until relatively recently the funk vibe had never been analyzed in the same way as, or received the critical attention that has been afforded to, jazz, rock, or blues. It's just as uniquely American as those genres, and as Clinton implied and my whole theme contends, it clearly emerged from the same roots, branching off the same sacred tree.

This provides another template through which to most fully appreciate Sharon Jones and her band: the notion that gospel music already *was* funk. So much so that it simply shifted from church to club to arena to stadium as it swept up more and more sinful believers in its romping wake. Funk is a many-splendored thing. Language breaks down at a certain point in its attempts to define or describe the core of funk, just as it does when we try to define those other exemplary inventions of the African American consciousness and culture, jazz, blues, and soul.

One of the other key joys of Vincent's early and useful study of funk (published in 1996, the same year Sharon Jones was being discovered by Gabe Roth) is that it offers up a valuable gradient for following this style (a word I prefer to genre) by constructing a series of funk dynasties. The fifth and most recent of these dynasties is the hip-hop nation of the '90s, one that also includes hybrids of funk/hip-hop like A Tribe Called Quest, as well as political rap like Public Enemy, "gangsta" rap like Tupac, and even funk-rock acts such as the Red Hot Chili Peppers.

Obviously, given the vibrancy of such essential folk music, there will be future funk dynasties yet to come. However, for our purposes, it's the earlier stages that provide the most telling link to groups such as Sharon Jones and the Dap-Kings and, indeed, the entire Daptone Records catalogue. I much appreciate Vincent's inclusion in his book of the nascent stages of funk growth, what he calls the pre-dynastics, and especially the fact that he offers a widely calibrated grasp of history that supports my basic theme here in these pages. In his pre-dynastic funk stage of the late '50s and early '60s, he includes the gospel music of James Cleveland, Mahalia Jackson, and the Soul Stirrers (the origin of Sam Cooke), to which I would also add the visionary Sister Rosetta Tharpe, who was practically the sacred godmother of Michael Jackson and Prince.

His pre-dynastic funk period (by which we mean funk before there was officially such a thing known as funk) also contains rhythm and blues and soul (before there was soul) like Ray Charles, Jackie Wilson, Booker T. and the MG's, the Isley Brothers, and of course all the artists recording at both Atlantic and Stax Records. Yet this pre-dynastic period should also contain blues and rock figures as well, such as Muddy Waters, Howlin' Wolf, Chuck Berry, Little Richard, Bo Diddley, and Johnny "Guitar" Watson. To some extent it can also include late-period Miles Davis and even John Coltrane, Sun Ra, Charles Mingus, and Art Blakey.

The unification period of soul-funk took place in the first fully actualized late '60s dynasty of James Brown, Aretha Franklin, Otis Redding, Wilson Pickett, Isaac Hayes, Parliaments, Joe Tex, and the Impressions. I would personally omit all Motown artists from the early dynasty of funk, as glorious as many of them were in their way, simply because they didn't carry forward the real ethos of the style. Perhaps weirdly, though, in the first funk dynasty one can also include black rock and rock/jazz/funk fusion, including Jimi Hendrix, Sly Stone, Buddy Miles, Electric Flag, Eric Burdon's War, and even Carlos Santana. At the edges of this first dynasty there even lurk such masters as Herbie Hancock, Donald Byrd, Jazz Crusaders, and, at the final borderline of everything, the Art Ensemble of Chicago.

The second funk dynasty in history occurred in the early-to-mid '70s and was what I call the "bright and shiny" period, which includes funky soul such as Stevie Wonder, Curtis Mayfield, Marvin Gaye, the O'Jays and Barry White; giant funk bands such as Brown's J.B.'s, Parliament, Funkadelic, Earth, Wind & Fire, and Tower of Power; and the too-poppy (for my taste) Commodores.

In the late '70s, the third funk dynasty started to get more serious again with artists such as Bootsy Collins's Rubber Band, the Bar-Kays, and Undisputed Truth, as well as even bigger funky-soul bands such as Rufus and Chaka Khan, Heatwave, and Maze, and of course dance-oriented funk bands such as Kool and the Gang, B.T. Express, the Fatback Band, and Chic (the beginnings of disco funk). In addition, jazz funk continued to push borderlines with George Duke, Grove Washington Jr., Roy Ayers, and Stanley Clarke.

The big boom occurred in the fourth funk dynasty of the '80s, with Rick James, Prince, Cameo, Gap Band, One Way, Living Color, Defunkt, Tackhead, and Afrika Bambaataa (who also, along with Gil Scott-Heron, provided the origins of rap), as well as the ongoing shine of lighter, funky pop (or pop-funk) by Michael Jackson and Janet Jackson, the SOS Band, Midnight Star, and Skyy.

A corner was definitely turned into a somewhat new stylistic territory during the fifth funk dynasty of the '90s, though it was clearly moving along a single continuum and creative spectrum from the very beginning. This was the domain of rap and hip-hop's borrowing of the groove from earlier funk as a frequent foundational structure over which to intone spoken word or urban poetry. As the most recent funk dynasty—though some might say it is barely recognizable as such—this mid-to-late-'90s style included Digital Underground, De La Soul, Digable Planets, Arrested Development, X-Clan, Ice Cube, Dr. Dre, Snoop Dogg, Ice-T, NWA, Easy E., the P-Funk All Stars, New Jack, New Rubber Band, O.G. Funk, and Meshell Ndegeocello, among others. Meanwhile, toward the end of the '90s, just as the crossover was occurring in which jazzy hip-hop went mainstream and began influencing white musicians for white audiences, such as Christina Aguilera and Amy Winehouse, there also started to be a backlash against the highly digital and slickly produced corporate sounds that had risen to the top of the industry hierarchy. That audience's digital weariness spawned an interest in revivalist funk and soul that followed more analog tastes and started a new wave of players who were not nostalgic or retro *per se* but who represented more of a fresh appetite for authenticity in style, sound, delivery, and production.

• • •

Just as soul was a mixture of gospel and blues, funk was a mixture of soul, R&B, and rock 'n' roll, with its most popular and pop-oriented version being the dance-tempo combination of all these roots into a complicated and steaming stew, with instrumentation and hot vocals emphasizing the extremely emotional rhythmic interplay between players. It's all about the tightness that erupts suddenly, moving the song forward before it dissolves back into another complex phase of rhythmic interplay leading to the next ultra-tight coda. The same could be said for West African possession music or Yoruba juju—the very word meaning to throw (the spirit) or something being thrown, generally via the talking drum.

In a 1992 interview with Lenny Henry for the BBC, one of the most legendary of funk arrangers from the classic second dynasty shared his secrets for isolating what makes funk funk. Fred Wesley worked with James Brown, George Clinton, and Bootsy Collins on many of their most memorable tunes. His recipe was simple but deep: "If you have a syncopated bass line, a strong heavy backbeat from the drummer, a counter line from the guitar or keyboard, and someone soul-singing on top of that in a gospel style, then you have funk. If you vary it in different ways you can write it down and you can construct the funk."

Performing "the funk" properly is *still* a vitally spiritual thing, and it takes a special type of artist to play it correctly. Rhythmic instruments often will deliver melodic lines while melodic instruments can throb with percussive power; they trade places back and forth in quite a complex architectural design. That's one of the reasons so many later-'90s producers sampled these early lines and reused them in their own song structures: they were able to digitally deconstruct the dense undergrowth and recycle them in more blandly computerized formats. The original funk grooves were *always* created interactively by the whole band together and worked out in a living breathing way that still can't be duplicated by modern computer equipment, mostly because wild human beings manifested it in *counterplay*.

There really isn't a single composer of any true funk tune, since the song that came out the other end of a session would usually be a one-of-a-kind conversation between the group as a whole structural unit, not unlike the way jazz or blues happens, on the spot. In *The Complete*

Book of Improvisation, Composition, and Funk Techniques, Howard Harris usefully and effectively captures the jazzy component of spontaneous funk: "Funk is a style of music in which elements of jazz, pop, rock, gospel and the blues are fused to create a rhythmic, soulful sound. Funk thrives on rhythm, and the art of it depends on the level of togetherness between the performers. It is, in its essence, togetherness in motion." That notion of togetherness in motion certainly describes the way a Sharon Jones and the Dap-Kings concert often felt like an Olympic team event: no one is in charge, but everyone is in command.

Added to that musical quality of the historic funk style that Daptone revived in the twenty-first century, and which they plan to continue mining after Jones's early departure in 2016, was the sense of liberation associated with '60s and '70s black culture, socially, politically, and culturally. Those years were memorable mostly as a time when a synthesis of previous black artistic traditions was in progress, fusing the sacred and secular, the celebratory and the confrontational. That time in history was unique in its amalgamation of authentic action and artistic urgency, and by the time the ultra-confident James Brown anointed himself (as he was often wont to do) "The Minister of New Super Heavy Funk" in 1974, there was indeed a brand-new musical bag on the scene.

Two and a half decades later, the Dap-Kings, with Sharon Jones throwing herself across the stage in true juju fashion, would pick up that bag and carry it furiously forward. They managed to do this for yet another two decades until she left us all, after succeeding precisely by paying careful attention to what was *in* Papa's brand-new bag, and maybe by declaring that now it was *Mama's* bag, too. For Roth and Jones, it was as simple as always wanting to make records that sounded to them like the records they both loved to listen to when they were coming up in the business. They were searching not just for the *sound* of '60s Memphis but for the *soul* of '60s Memphis, and they wanted to reincarnate its very essence.

One of the major indicators for soul-funk as practiced by the early '60s and '70s masters, and later by their inheritors, is the ability to swoop in and out of harmony, with a band cooking up a boiling mix of propulsive engines (and a hot vocalist soaring above the fray) while at the same time keeping the audience rooted in basic reality with a heavy, heavy bottom beat. The result can often be as heady as experimental jazz, with polyrhythmic structures superimposed over earthy foundations.

At the core of it all is syncopation, with multiple instruments propelled along a single groove but in different ways, with a melodic line from one player often becoming interchangeable with another's. A really fine musical structural unit such as James Brown's, George Clinton's, or the Dap-Kings can also provide a storm of different melodic lines delivered simultaneously, with bass and drums being the rhythmic blueprint, horns operating in a stratosphere of melody, rhythm also percussive in tone, and a ripping singer like Jones punctuating everything else with her own percussive yelp.

While there is a "jamming" aspect to funk of this kind—which further ties it to the complex organizational tones of free jazz—each individual player still has to make logical choices within the overall sonic building under construction. To this extent as well, collective improvisation, which is where funk arrives with a boom and a bang, was always already a huge part of the African music tradition. Whether it was part of trance-inducing looping juju in Senegal or Yoruba, or the interweaving of heartstrings in the slave-ship laments, or the cotton field–working beats of the oppressed, or the gospel chants in church, or the blues licks in urban clubs, or the soul bounce of dance floors, or the deep-funk groove of sweat-heavy arenas, most of this ongoing stream of music was written and arranged collectively and communally.

Funk definitely returns the musical content to the historic ideals of African ensemble composition, and as such it is certainly worth taking seriously enough to study simply because of its awesome role in popular culture. As Vincent puts it, "Black music has continued to innovate, from the first slave songs to the latest street-corner raps, the mission has been the same: to tell it like it is." That is perhaps the most crucial inheritance from African culture to have been absorbed so lovingly by both soul and funk music: the spiritual aspect inherent in music-making itself; the importance of bringing about a trance state and actually raising basic life rhythms up to a higher universal level. Looked at, and listened to, from this perspective, it seems obvious that African music in general—and gospel, blues, jazz, and rock music in particular—were handcrafted to accomplish this spirit arising; and that, with the funk, this ancient tradition was merely continued electrically and loudly. We've already seen how the original African musical traditions did not separate the sacred and the profane in everyday life, let alone arbitrarily designate some music as spiritual and other music as sinful. The only real sin was to be dead while you were still living. The same essential credo is true of all the most authentic forms of funk music.

Once we see that core cultural connection of music being *spirit embodied*—especially as exemplified by West African music's lack of interest in making melodies follow along the surface of rhythms and instead focusing all the attention on the rhythm itself—we can also see how the real key to funk is an obsession with letting go, of losing control, of submitting to a kind of pulsating oneness that leaves no choice but to start dancing without a shred of self-consciousness. Those who viewed Sharon Jones in action, or who have listened closely to her albums, will of course know exactly what I mean. It changes your nervous system forever.

It is also true that the very assumption early on that rhythm and blues music was a sinful surrender to the vulgar side of life would actually become one of the key cooking ingredients in the recipe for funk and for the menu of its preparation and delivery. And while the seemingly gentle, heartfelt energy of soul music became ever more popular after Ray Charles's first breakthrough, the biggest threshold for a new kind of music (which was actually, as stated, a very ancient kind) came about via the multiple breathtaking breakthroughs of Mr. Brown. His was the foot that kicked in the door that allowed funk to burst out into the popular culture, and that was the door the Dap-Kings breezed through once they were led by their dynamic dame.

A gorgeously rebellious demonstration of this grand soul continuity is heard with crystal clarity in a 7-inch single Jones released in 2007, "I'm Not Gonna Cry," on which she defiantly declares, "If you can't see what you doin' to me you must be blind, but I ain't gonna cry, no Lord." The tone and tenor of the message feels both church-bound and bedroom-bound at the same time: "Hey, sounds so nice, play it twice!"

One metaphor I'll offer up is a savory one, I think, at least with regard to the funky place where we've arrived: the notion of musical fermentation. Fermenting is the metabolic process by which sugar is converted to alcohol. This transformation has shadowed and paralleled the cultural experiences of the inventors of both gospel and soul music, and by the time it arrives at the fully fermented stage of James Brown, the new brew is dynamite. Once you notice the root connections, sometimes it feels like funk music is basically just gospel on steroids.

James Morthland described this phenomenon well in the liner notes to his 1994 CD compilation *The Roots of Funk*. "Essentially, James Brown demonstrated that it was possible to use the entire band as a drum kit, creating poly-rhythms that took the music back to Africa, leading to a pronounced sense of liberation. It's as though the musicians who had provided the dance tracks to the early '60s were now free to dance themselves." The shift I've followed and the continuity I've detected lies between what we could call the metaphysics of faith and the physics of love, and maybe even the quantum mechanics of lust and desire.

James Brown's main biographer, Cynthia Rose, expresses this continuity very well, too: "Funk is not a reconciliation of opposing rhythmic impulses, but the fusion and transcending of their essential conflict." That's the most accurate assessment of its mysterious allure I've heard so far. And, luckily for us, it's also an ongoing fusion and ever expanding transcendence that actively continues to this very day. At the tenth-anniversary party for Daptone, at the Nouveau Casino in Paris, *Full Power* asked the Dap-Kings about their intentions and what brought them together in the first place. "We're just a group of like-minded musicians that love playing together," Sugarman explained, "and we have a real taste for open sounding, authentic kind of music. Daptone is definitely a family of musicians who love each other."

That family, he clarified, came about from listening to music together, most crucially, and also from living together, traveling together, and playing live together. Every so often another new musician would come in and enter the fold. "Daptone is kind of like a college—people come to study and from there go out and start to do their own stuff. They graduate. We have an open-door policy, it's a group of people just trying to be creative and to reap the benefits from that attitude."

Actually, all of *us* are the true beneficiaries.

• • •

FUNKMASTERS: THE BOYS (AND GIRLS) IN THE BAND

With only very minor fluctuations over the years, the members of the Dap-Kings band cooking behind Sharon Jones remained almost constant. Not only do they feel like a tightly wound spring onstage, they also interrelate like a closely knit family commune in private.

Gabriel Roth (a.k.a. Bosco Mann): Cofounder / Bass / Bandleader / Producer

Roth was born in Riverside, California, and moved to New York in the early '90s, abandoning his early interest in mathematics in favor of music, though ironically he still approaches music in a very mathematical manner. He formed first Desco and then Daptone in order to freely pursue the kinds of sounds that mesmerized him in his youth. As a recording engineer and producer, he has won two Grammy Awards: in 2008 for Amy Winehouse's *Back to Black*, and in 2012 for the Booker T. Jones album *The Road from Memphis*.

As Rachel Khona observed empirically on *Simplemost*, "Bassists are the most important members of a band—according to science." Indeed, researchers have now determined that the bass is the backbone of any song, since it turns out that our brains can find a rhythm more easily when it's played in a lower, bassy tone. According to a National Academy of Sciences study using EEG test results, people are more perceptive to the changes in lower-pitched notes of bass than the higher-pitched notes of other instruments. As Khona put it, "The bass holds down a song, filling it with more depth and gravitas, and without it, music lacks structure."

Of course, anyone who's ever listened to the bassists in James Brown's fabled funk bands—Bootsy Collins, Bernard Odum, Charles Sherrell, Tim Drummond, and Fred Thomas—has already felt that from personal experience, deep down in their bones, where the bass resides. In the case of the multitalented and frenetic Gabe Roth, the bass thread weaves its way through a tightly crafted tapestry of heavy-bottomed time keeping with few equals.

Neal Sugarman: Cofounder / Tenor Saxophone

Sugarman, a native of the Boston area of Newton, Massachusetts, is also the cofounder and co-owner of Daptone with Roth, his longtime business partner and creative collaborator. He has been an active member of the Dap-Kings since 2001, and he is also still involved with his own soul-jazz project, the Sugarman Three, which predates his involvement with Sharon Jones and was the impetus for him and Roth to launch Daptone together. Perhaps as testament to their back-to-the-roots feel, the label's first and second releases, *Pure Cane Sugar* and *Dap-Dippin' with Sharon Jones and the Dap-Kings*, were both shipped from Sugarman's own kitchen table.

Sugarman started out playing sax for punk-rock bands such as Boy's Life and Black Cat Bone in the 1980s, before moving to New York in the '90s to pursue jazz. His fellow Sugarman Three players include drummer Rudy Albin, guitarist Al Street, and organist Adam Scone. In addition to his integral role with Daptone and the Dap-Kings, he has also amassed recording credits with Mark Ronson, Amy Winehouse, Eric Clapton, Sturgill Simpson, Charles Bradley, Al Green, and many others.

For Brad Faberman of *Village Voice*, "In an industry that rewards greed and egocentrism, tenor saxophonist, Neal Sugarman has made a career out of selflessness. On record and onstage, Sugarman plays only what is needed, and career-wise, he has done much the same. It's the journey that matters, a record is simply that: a document of the music-making experience."

Franklin Stribling (a.k.a. Binky Griptite): MC / Guitar
Who knows, perhaps Franklin Stribling wasn't a funky enough name, but Binky Griptite certainly is. Well aware of the difference between "retro" and "old school" (the former is a trend, the latter an attitude), Griptite is a brilliant guitarist and a suave master of ceremonies during live concerts. He is incredibly active as sideman and session master, with a credits list that includes performing on platinum records with Janet Jackson. But his primary claim to fame is as the electrifying guitarist for the Dap-Kings on all of their albums with Sharon Jones.

Thomas Brenneck: Guitar
Founder of the Menahan Street Band in 2007, Brenneck has been an active session musician, most frequently for Daptone on records by acts including Budos Band, El Michels Affair, and Antibalas. He also played guitar for Amy Winehouse and Christina Aguilera. He joined the Dap-Kings for the second, third, and fourth Sharon Jones albums, until departing and being replaced on guitar by Joseph Crispiano for their fifth and final studio release.

Joseph Crispiano: Guitar
Formerly a member of the Staten Island–based funk/soul event band the Bandulos, Crispiano joined the Dap-Kings after first appearing with them live at Bonnaroo in 2009. He contributed significantly to the Dap-Kings' final record with Sharon Jones, *Give the People What They Want*. He has also appeared on Sugarman Three and Lee Fields recordings, and on the 2015 Saun and Starr album *Look Closer*.

Homer "Funkyfoot" Steinweiss: Drums

The incredibly precocious Homer Steinweiss is a superb drummer, songwriter, composer, and producer best known for his work with Sharon and the Kings but also diversely active as an eclectic independent artist, having worked with the Arcs, Bruno Mars, Sheryl Crow, and the El Michels Affair, among many others. He was born into a musical family on March 25, 1982. His parents worked in the jewelry business and were very supportive of his early interest in music. He began playing in the early '90s after watching the conga player in the jazz band at his sister's high school in Manhattan. When his own conga teacher became unavailable, he switched to drums—luckily for us. Initially, he was interested in grunge, but an early drum teacher, Matt Paluto, guided him to the music of James Brown.

Steinweiss's career took off early when he was only sixteen after the Mighty Imperials released their first album, *Thunder Chicken*, on Daptone. The group's raw funk and soul sounds would lead into much collaboration, including with Jones and the Dap-Kings, as well as the Menahan Street Band. He has been the steady and stalwart other half of the Dap-Kings' masterful rhythm section ever since. Between 2001, when he was also still studying philosophy at SUNY Purchase, and 2017, when he played on the El Michels Affair album *Return to the 37th Chamber*, he appeared on over sixty-five recordings.

Fernando "Boogaloo" Velez: Percussion

A New Jersey–based percussionist and DJ, Velez was one of the founding members of the Dap-Kings and a critical component of their sound as the other half of a stellar rhythmic percussion section. He was also a founding member of Antibalas and toured and recorded with them until 2007. After providing percussion for six of the songs on Amy Winehouse's *Back to Black* in 2006, he was sought out by producer Mark Ronson to supply the beat and time for Daniel Merriweather's "War and Love" in 2009. He has also contributed to recordings by the Menahan Street Band, Lee Fields, Charles Bradley, and Theophilus

London, as well as rhythms for Jay-Z and Ariana Grande. He provided his superb drum stylings to the music for Martin Scorsese's film *The Wolf of Wall Street* and as part of the house band for HBO's *Night of Too Many Stars* and the 2012 edition of *VH1 Divas*.

Cochemea Gastelum: Baritone Saxophone

Born and raised in San Diego, California, "Cheme," as his friends and bandmates know him, is a Brooklyn-based multi-instrumentalist, composer, arranger, and improviser. In addition to delivering flute and sax playing that is crisp and adventurous, he is also a skillful music director with an uncanny ability to integrate disparate genres—a talent that held him in good stead for a band as stylistically layered as the Dap-Kings. He first gained notoriety while performing with Robert Walter's 20th Congress. He then established himself in the evolving Brooklyn Afrobeat and soul scenes, touring and recording with Antibalas, Budos, and the Dap-Kings.

Gastelum also branched out creatively in 2010 with a critically acclaimed and experimental solo album, *The Electric Sound of Johnny Arrow*, on which he overdubbed multiple instruments and directed an extensive entourage of twenty players through a carefully arranged polyrhythmic experience. He was also a featured soloist in the Tony Award–winning Broadway hit *Fela!*, and in 2011 he traveled to Africa with the cast for a run of historic performances in Lagos, Nigeria.

David Guy: Trumpet

After studying trumpet at La Guardia School of Performing Arts and the Manhattan School of Music and attaining a BA in performance from the New School for Contemporary Music, Guy immersed himself in touring and recording with the Sugarman Three, Budos Band, Menahan Street Band, Lee Fields, Charles Bradley, and of course the Dap-Kings. He also found himself in high demand as a studio musician, appearing on projects by Mark Ronson, Quincy Jones, Bebel Gilberto, and Eric Clapton, among others. His trumpet playing features on the 2016 Grammy Award–winning record "Uptown Funk" by Ronson and Bruno Mars.

Currently, Guy is a part owner of Sharon Jones and the Dap-Kings, an active studio musician, and trumpet player for the Roots in their role as house band on *The Tonight Show with Jimmy Fallon*.

Ian Hendrickson-Smith: Saxophone

New York City–based saxophonist and flutist Ian Hendrickson-Smith is mostly noted for his remarkable tone, soulful approach, and blues driven melodies, and is equally adept on all the saxophones. From 2004 to 2010, the versatile player maintained an intense recording and touring schedule as a member of Sharon Jones and the Dap-Kings. His extensive recording experience includes at least ten jazz records as bandleader, including releases with Lonnie Smith, Amy Winehouse, Mark Ronson, Bob Dylan, Al Green, Lady Gaga, Lee Fields, and of course Sharon Jones and the Dap-Kings. He is also the proprietor of an exciting independent jazz label, Rondette Jazz. Today, he plays on the road and on *The Tonight Show* with the Roots.

Saundra Williams and Starr Duncan Lowe (a.k.a. the Dapettes): Vocalists

Jones's crucial vocal partners—the emotional layers I prefer not to call *backup*. These powerful ladies were with Jones in her wilderness years. Williams and Duncan Lowe demonstrated a deep chemistry with Jones ever since their early days together circa 1987 as co-members of the wedding band the Good and Plenty Girls, also known as the Triple "S" Threat through the '90s. They kept in touch during the early 2000s, but it wasn't until the release of *I Learned the Hard Way* in 2008 that the three ladies joined forces again, with Williams and Duncan Lowe now officially known as the Dapettes. In 2015, they released their first post-Sharon effort, a superb duet album entitled *Look Closer*. It's time to take a closer look and a closer listen to these superfine vocalists in their own right.

Chris Davis: Trumpet / Brian Wolfe: Drums

Though not original members of the Dap-Kings, Davis and Wolfe became part of the touring band in 2016 and are also featured on the 2017 posthumous Jones album release *Soul of a Woman*.

Other Contributors

Other featured contributors to the Dap-Kings over the years include: Otis Youngblood (tenor sax), Jack Zapata (baritone sax), Earl Maxton (organ), Anda Szilagyi (trumpet), Leon El Michels (baritone sax), and Victor Axelrod (piano).

SOURCE OF THE SOUND
The Archival Studio

*"It was sad music. But it waved its sadness like a battle flag. It said the
universe had done all it could, but you were still alive."*
—TERRY PRATCHETT, *Soul Music*, 1994

S peaking to the *A.V. Club* in 2010, Sharon Jones was characteristically honest about how the music in her early days at Daptone used
to be more of a straightforward homage to a classic James Brown vibe,
but that it then began evolving rapidly, especially by the time of their
second outing, *Naturally.* "Yeah, we've grown," she said. "On the first
album, *Dap-Dippin'*, we were getting our push from the J.B.'s, that was
our thing. But as the years go on, our thing is just doing soul and R&B.
People said the *100 Days, 100 Nights* album had a Stax sound. But it's
all going to be Stax for us, everything we do."

It's all going to be Stax, and indeed it is. And that's precisely the
reason why Jones and her band wouldn't mind in the least if you favor-
ably compared the overlapping delivery styles and technical recording
aspects of a song such as "Tell Me," from that *100 Days* album, with
almost any slowly throbbing hurtful hymn to the mid-'60s Memphis
masters they so revere. That's exactly what they *want* you to recognize
and feel; in fact, they'd really be amazed if you *weren't* able to make the
deep connection they were offering up to you on a silver platter, or in

this case on a black vinyl platter. When you hear Jones pleading with her lover to look her in the eyes and urging him to tell her he loves her, this soul song feels so authentic you may not know what year you're living in.

In Andy Tennille's essay "The Return of Real Funk and Soul Music," included in *Best Music Writing 2008*, Gabe Roth explains, "Out of all the music I've been into over the years, Stax is the most inspiring. Stax was something that hadn't been done before or since. Motown was a factory but Stax was a family." After setting the scene by telling some of his own back-story to the rise and fall of Stax Records, Tennille confidently declared that the real renaissance of the Stax spirit had by then already been going on for almost a decade in a now-legendary dilapidated brownstone in Bushwick, Brooklyn. There, the small independent label that rose up with Sharon Jones at its forefront had been modestly creating an authentic soul and funk music that had not been seen or heard in America since Stax shut down almost three decades earlier.

Tennille was so right about the return of real soul and funk. "Everything's just gotten better," Roth confided to him, explaining that the musicianship was getter more sophisticated with each new release. "Sharon sounds better than she ever has, and everyone is just humming." And since these are classic R&B records in every sense, they also shared heartfelt messages of broken relationships and "appeals for affirmation and tales of unrequited love" (the basic raw material for the sprained heart). It is equally true that by moving forward they were also reaching back, with each new record sounding more and more like the Southern soul and funk of Stax every time. While it's true that it hasn't been done quite this way before, since the turn of the century, Daptone is exactly the same kind of creative and business operation—a soul family.

In characterizing Daptone's revivalist style, Michael Ayers of the *Village Voice* captured some of its paradoxical essence and how boogaloo-infused soul and archetypal R&B is the template for all the exuberance in Sharon Jones. "Onstage with the Dap-Kings, it's clear that she was born for performance. She conveys genuine heartbreak, gives a history lesson on dances like the Funky Chicken, and hauls ribald guys onstage to serenade, dance with and be jovially groped by. Her barely five foot frame gyrates in a spasm of ripples and shakes, she makes you feel like you're the only one in the room." What's also clear in her delivery is the presence not just of soul power but also of star power—the kind that can't be learned, imitated, or digitally simulated.

Luckily for those of us who aren't technically inclined but are mere mortals who love the music, what all those slightly esoteric (but nonetheless essential) audio recording ingredients that Roth references really mean is that we end up hearing an environment of tightly knit and precisely calibrated live sounds that closely evokes and channels the history treasured by Daptone, Roth, and Jones: the inimitable but inspiring, heavy sound of Stax Records. Its uplifting core of emotional power would move Sharon Jones far forward as a gutsy performer, and its gritty analog recording techniques would enhance Gabriel Roth's profile as a gifted producer.

Having established how important the sound of Stax was to the spirit of the Dap-Kings and the business ethos of Daptone, it might be useful to dip a little more into the label's history, to see exactly why it mattered so much and inspired our narrative so deeply. So a short trip down memory lane might be called for, perhaps to clarify why some of us so often appear to utter the name Stax in such hushed reverential tones. And it all started with a rather eccentric Southern white genius named Jim Stewart.

In the history of musical recordings, the perfect balance between a new hybrid blending of rural and urban spirits is often accomplished by the synthesis of two masterful production and marketing talents who harmonize their own opposite personalities in a similar manner. The best examples would be Ahmet Ertegun and Jerry Wexler riding the engineering genius of Tom Dowd at Atlantic Records, or, in the early days out of Philadelphia, Bert Berns, Kenneth Gamble, Leon Huff, and Thom Bell, working at Gamble/Huff. Meanwhile, in Memphis, there was the hyper-magical combination of David Porter and Isaac Hayes, while the uncannily prescient white executive and producer Jim Stewart guided a flock of brilliant black acts all the way through the almost mystical annals of Stax. White-owned but black-oriented, Stax Records would later become the historic soul dynasty fueling the dreams of both Gabe Roth and Sharon Jones. Its peak years, from 1961 to 1971, included a fruitful creative overlap with Atlantic, and that fertile ground provided the origins of the sound we hear warmly embraced so effectively in the twenty-first century by Daptone.

The visionary Stewart and his sister, Estelle Axton, had purchased the Capitol Cinema building on East McLemore Street, in the middle of a black neighborhood, in 1959. Originally calling their new venture Satellite Records, they renamed it Stax (short for Stewart and Axton) and ruled the roost from 1959 until 1975, when the label finally folded and entered the history books. In Gerri Hirshey's *Nowhere to Run*, gifted producer Steve Cropper characterized the Stax magic like this: "What we were doing was called the Stax sound or the Memphis sound, it wasn't Chicago, it wasn't New York, and it sure wasn't Detroit. It was a southern sound, a below the Bible belt sound. It was righteous and nasty. Which to our way of thinking was pretty close to life itself." It was also overwhelmingly tasty. As Hirshey aptly puts it, "The difference between Stax and Motown was written boldly on their studio buildings. Motown declared itself Hitsville U.S.A. in fat blue script. Stax, housed in its old movie theater, put its slogan on the marquee in worn black clamp-on lettering, Soulsville U.S.A."

Stax, Muscle Shoals (another white-managed black music label in Muscle Shoals, Alabama, run by Rick Hall, another genius who passed away last year), and, even in its own lesser way, Motown, all also offered clear evidence that new innovations in music such as R&B and soul (and, later on, hip-hop and rap) were always the by-products of independent producers and executives going their own way, often against the tide of the monopoly interests of major labels such as RCA, Capitol, Decca, or Columbia. By my definition, true soul would eventually be revealed to be Southern in its core origins, but not necessarily by mere

Sharon Jones studio portrait, Seattle, 2009. (Photo by Steven Dewall/Redferns/Getty Images)

Sister Rosetta
Tharpe, 1938.
(Photo by Michael
Ochs Archives/
Getty Images)

Mahalia Jackson at Newport
Jazz Festival, 1970. (Photo by
David Redfern/Getty Images)

James Brown at Newport Jazz Festival, 1968. (Photo by Hulton Archive/Getty Images)

Sharon Jones and the Dap-Kings portrait, Sasquatch! Music Festival, 2011.
(Photo by Steven Dewall/Redferns/Getty Images)

Sharon Jones reaching out to her audience, Sasquatch! Music Festival, 2011.
(Getty Images)

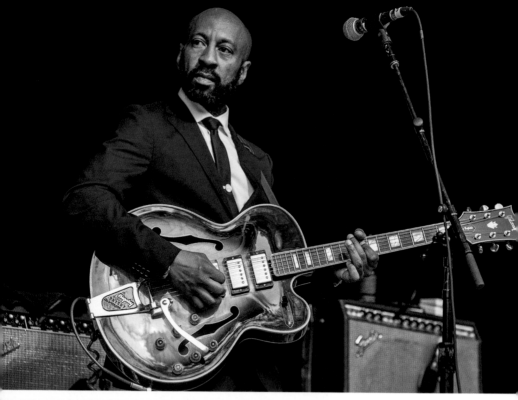

Binky Griptite, stellar MC and lead guitarist, Greek Theatre, 2015. (Photo by Harmony Gerber/Getty Images)

Saundra Williams and Starr Duncan Lowe, the Dapettes, two of the best supporting singers in the business of soul music, and the left- and right-hand women of Sharon Jones for many years. (Photo by Harmony Gerber/Getty Images)

Gabriel Roth, co-founder of Daptone Records and bassist/producer, with Homer Steinweiss on drums, Prospect Park, Brooklyn, 2016. (Photo by Al Pereira/WireImage/Getty Images)

Neal Sugarman, co-founder of Daptone Records and saxophone player, Austin 360, 2015. (Photo by Manuel Nauta/NurPhoto/Getty Images)

Sharon Jones and the Dap-Kings at the Apollo Theater, New York, 2010.
(Photo by Shahar Azran/WireImage/Getty Images)

Jones and her band in action, Big Chill Festival, Ledbury, UK, 2011.
(Getty Images)

Sharon waving to the world with her band on *The Tonight Show with Jay Leno*, 2010.
(Stacie McChesney/NBCU Photo Bank/Getty Images)

Sharon turns up the heat with her band at the Hudson Blues Festival, New York City, 2014.
(Getty Images)

Sharon Jones at North Sea Jazz Festival at Ahoy, Rotterdam, Netherlands, 2014.
(Photo by Greetsia Tent/WireImage/Getty Images)

Sharon Jones with Barbara Kopple, director of *Miss Sharon Jones!* (Photo by Gino DePinto for BUILD Series at the BUILD Studio)

Dap-Kings manager Alex Kadvan attends the screening of *Miss Sharon Jones!* at the SXSW Music Festival in Austin, Texas, 2016. (Photo by Mike Windle/Getty Images)

Sharon Jones at Forecastle Festival, 2014. (Joshua N. Timmermans/ZUMA Wire/Alamy Live News)

geography alone, and the key ingredient to almost every great soul artist was the apparent, or perceived, turning of their backs on the musical formats of sacred scripture. Eventually, however, soul wouldn't even be limited by race, since it proved so profitable that its usurping by white pop was all but inevitable.

In one of its early publicity releases, the Stax label included an obscurely crafted piece of promotional copywriting, probably dashed off by Jim Stewart himself, that tells its own tale: "There's an old saying that goes like so, keep trying and you'll get where you want to go. You can conquer the world with your original sound. They knocked at the front door and couldn't get in. They heard a sound and went around to the back door, where the sound let them in." The sound let them in: that's the secret of the outsider status of Stax that quickly allowed them to rise to the top of the recording industry.

The great Isaac Hayes put it more succinctly, of course, when he hollered, "I'm a soul man, got what I got the hard way." That's the way the Stax sound developed: the label and its artists got there the hard way, through hard work, and, of course, by utilizing the talents of geniuses for arranging, singing, songwriting, and producing. Axton, who assumed a commanding business role, actually took out a second mortgage on her family home in 1958 so that she and Stewart could purchase professional Ampex monaural recording equipment—the very same kind of analog tape format which would become the holy grail for Daptone Records fifty years later.

For readers with an appetite for the deep backstory of what made this historic label so cherished, half a century later, and the miraculous birth of precious sounds by acts such as Booker T. and the M.G.'s, Wilson Pickett, Sam and Dave, Otis Redding, Isaac Hayes, the Staple Singers, Johnnie Taylor, Albert King, Rufus and Carla Thomas (a model for Sharon Jones), and the majesty of the Bar-Kays, I can heartily recommend the tome to turn to: *Soulsville U.S.A.: The Story of Stax Records* by Rob Bowman, which captures the label's lightning in a bottle.

Here was an energy field of magic Memphis noise so intense that it would still be inspiring Gabe Roth, Sharon Jones, and the Dap-Kings in the digital twenty-first century. Most crucially for our story, perhaps, Stax was one of the first truly integrated studios (another model for Daptone), with black and white musicians, songwriters, and executives working together to produce a unique sound. In addition to this book, Bowman also created a lengthy monograph that accompanied a ten-CD boxed set he co-produced, *The Complete Stax/Volt Soul Singles, 1972–1975*.

The importance of Memphis in musical history cannot be exaggerated. The songs and sounds that came from there are uniquely American. And, for many of us, Stax was the arterial pumping beat of the heart of the city—a city that practically lived and breathed music. After commencing as a white-owned business and shifting first to a half-white, half-black operation and then finally to an all-black enterprise, Stax also represented an innovative model for independence and freedom of expression. This despite the fact that it gradually unraveled due to over reaching ambition, government interference, the usurping of its content and product by CBS Records, and its ultimate bankruptcy demise at the hands of a local/national banking system.

But through its first two early creative periods of growth, Stax was clearly a special place to make music in the kind of family-oriented format that Daptone would effectively emulate in today's world. It's in its very DNA. Equally obvious were the spiritual/musical influences hovering over a city like Memphis, a city that claims more churches per person than any other in America. It was the home base for the Church of God in Christ, and even as a center for recording some of the most overwhelmingly emotional Pentecostal music ever created, it still somehow managed also to inspire and produce music in multiple other competing secular genres at the same time. In other words, it radiated both the sacred and the sinful.

After recording some forgettable 45s and albums in his early days as Satellite Records, which he made in his wife's uncle's two-car garage (giving new old meaning to the term garage-rock), Jim Stewart eventually made the shift to professional standards and to the gritty theater space he rented for $150 a month. This space had something unusual about it, a sense of "live" performance recording sonics resulting from reverberation effects that, though intimate, also paradoxically simulated the boom of a large concert hall. It was a feeling that Bowman cites as key to the evolution of what became known as the Stax sound—and it's the same husky hyper-physicality that would later inspire late '90s Daptone in its revivalist quest.

Ironically, with Stewart operating on such a meager budget that he couldn't afford to level the sloping theater floors, this limitation provided the accidental acoustic bonus of having no walls that were opposite each other. In addition to preparing the groundwork for unintentional *walls of sound*, the ceilings were twenty-five feet high, and a false partition cutting the space in half brought the highly personalized studio working environment to forty by forty-five feet in overall dimensions. That was its physical dimension; its emotional and spiritual dimensions were almost infinitely huge and still echo loud and clear today.

The first record issued by Satellite (as it was then still named, prior to the shift to Stax) was the Rufus and Carla Thomas number "'Cause I Love You," backed with "Deep Down Inside," which became the label's first big success. It also marked a change in life and attitude for Stewart, who prior to this had focused on bland country or pop music, with this sudden hit plunging him into the much more vital and gripping domain of African American music. He must have felt like a blind man who'd regained his sight in a kind of miracle: he didn't want to go back, he didn't even want to look back, only forward to the future of Satellite/Stax as strictly a rhythm-and-blues label. At that point in 1960, remember, there was barely a name for soul music. It was only a glimmer in the ears of competing Memphis natives like Stewart and his chief competitor, Willie "Pops" Mitchell of Hi Records.

Another business bonus was the Satellite Record Store, operated by Stewart's sister, Estelle Axton, which provided an obvious outlet for their new product and was located smack in the heart of the black community, becoming a local cultural mecca as well. David Porter, who would eventually pair with Isaac Hayes in a hit-making songwriting machine, worked at the grocery store across the street from the studio. Booker T. Jones, the force behind the M.G.'s, and the group's stellar white players, Duck Dunn and Steve Cropper, all hung out at the store. Indeed, several of Stax's future notable employees—including Deanie Parker, Homer Banks, James Cross, William Brown, Johnny Keyes, and Henry Bush—all started out as counter help at Estelle's record store. The ambitious siblings quickly quit their day jobs and rented the empty barbershop next door to the store as the first site of Satellite Records until it morphed into Stax in 1968, a golden year for soul music in America.

In those early days, as Bowman chronicles so well, the record industry operated much like a food chain, with larger companies picking up the distribution of potential hit releases from small local businesses like Stewart and Axton's. Atlantic Records was particularly adept and successful at finding future gems and acquiring first the songs and eventually the distribution of the entire business concern. Once the Thomas song became popular, Satellite signed the first of many contracts with Atlantic (and others) in order to reach a wider audience, which it did immediately by selling ten times the number of copies it had managed to move previously.

This would be the beginning of the Satellite/Stax saga, and the evolutionary leap that gained the label the oft-referenced descriptor, "The little label that could." That feeling of ultra-potent energy would be paid homage to some thirty years later when Daptone Records reverentially referred to itself as "the little label that could, should, and would." At that stage, Stax was also breaking serious new social ground, confounding other white Memphis-based businesses that were equally as baffled by the label's equalized engagement with black Americans as by its commercial success.

Quite without realizing it, Stewart and Axton had also invented the core concept for what might respectfully be called a mom-and-pop operation—another business model adopted cheerily by Daptone in its own do-it-yourself philosophy, and one that appeared somewhat nostalgic at the turn of the twenty-first century. Bowman also rightly characterizes it as "a case study in how black and white could intersect and interact," since Estelle defined it as never *seeing* color, only *hearing* talent. That was certainly one of the label's claims to fame, the other one being its sound—a sonic technique that still serves as a daily vitamin for free-form outfits such as Daptone and for gifted producers such as Gabe Roth. (Luckily for us, Roth and Sugarman have yet to make the mistake of cutting a big distribution deal with a major label.)

After several releases in 1961 that were either all-white or all-black in their basic musicianship and personnel, it was the Mar-Keys' "Last Night"—a record cut by an integrated band consisting of the white Steve Cropper and Duck Dunn and Estelle's son Charles Axton playing with youthful chums such as Don Nix and Wayne Jackson, Jerry Smith, and vocalist Ronnie Angel—that ignited Stax's crucial mixed-race message. This also appears to have been the initial historic recording on which what we now identify as the Stax sound began to emerge and evolve.

"Last Night" would be the first of many rough-and-tumble instrumental hits to come, the most important of which were those crafted by the amazing Booker T. and the M.G.'s, the half-white, half-black band (Jones, Al Jackson, Cropper, and Dunn) that Bowman has anointed (quite correctly, I think), "The greatest instrumental soul group in the world." "Last Night" also has the honor of being the song that not only delivered the company its first chart hit but also brought it to the attention of another record company: one already named Satellite, this one based in California. This chance realization necessitated the shift in name to the now-famous combination of Stewart and Axton's surnames to craft the curious neologism St-ax.

Just then, as Booker T.'s contagious instrumental hit "Green Onions" was climbing the charts, Stewart and Axton would encounter a part-time preacher and powerhouse singer who would change the soul- and pop-music scenes forever: Otis Redding. Yet the operation at this stage in 1963 was still very much mom-and-pop in tone and structure, with Estelle running the record shop, Jim still working part-time at a bank, Cropper running the studio, and the crew releasing a couple of singles per month, with an album maybe every three months.

By 1964, with the label just about to enter its golden age, thirty-two 45s were released by Stax via Atlantic and Volt, as well as on its own imprint, with twelve of these being by the label's mainstays of proven performers, Rufus and Carla Thomas and Booker T. and the M.G.'s, and their newest diamond cutter, Redding. Stax's chief competitor, Motown, which represented more of the northern urban branch of soul (as well as the crossover pop varieties), was busy breaking the bank, of course, while the more Southern, rural spirit of sibling sonic visionaries Jim Stewart and Estelle Axton was following a somewhat slower but much more (to some) earthy approach.

One of Stewart's chief obsessions—curiously, given his own heritage—was to keep the Stax sound as *black* as possible, declaring that even if pots of gold awaited from the crossover pop-soul boom, he just wasn't interested if that meant compromising or betraying what he'd come to appreciate as the special sound he'd accidentally created. Though he admitted to grudgingly envying Motown's popular success, he still claimed it just wasn't "their thing." This even though in a few short years Stax would have its own mainstream success with the issuing of Isaac Hayes's classic 1969 album *Hot Buttered Soul*.

After penning such soul gems as "Hold On I'm Coming" and "Soul Man," Hayes was more than ready to break out of the confines of a songwriting role and assume his true mantle as a performing superstar—one that almost rivaled the popularity of Mr. Brown himself at one point. But as big as Hayes was in the '70s—a decade during which he practically re-invented the groove that would lead to the more accessible Marvin Gaye, Stevie Wonder, Funkadelic, and Curtis Mayfield—he was also a road sign pointing to the internal changes and outward creative decline already afoot at Stax.

Commercially, however, it was still then a studio bonanza—one heralded by the astonishing brilliance and energy of Otis Redding and Wilson Pickett, both of whom had breathtaking but brief lives and careers, while also dramatically revolutionizing soul and pop at the same time and memorializing what came to be known as the Memphis Sound, which has so impacted music history. Booker T. once affirmed that of course you're going to have an identifiable sound if all the records emerge from the same studio using the same approach and practically the same players. Part of its magic, though, also relied on a distinctive but microscopic rhythmic delay of two and four—a rhythm recognizable on most up-tempo Stax albums. Another part of it was also due (as Gabe Roth would later attest) to the minimalist mic placement, confined quarters, and the quirky room's inherent acoustic bounce.

The vocalists at Stax also employed a slight and instinctual delay as well, which as Bowman points out was likely the result of standing about ten feet or so from the drummer, behind a sound baffle, while wearing no headphones, and hearing what came over the top of the baffle as it bounced off the ceiling and hit them in the head. Apart from this unique sound, Stax's rise was propelled by the hiring of one Al Bell, a dynamic promoter, public relations wiz, and radio specialist, to help spread the soul gospel. According to some historians, Stax didn't really start until Bell got there because apparently the Stewart-Axton team and their musicians had tons of talent but absolutely no marketing skills whatsoever. (Bell would eventually be engaged in some production as well as management, and even became a co-owner of the label at one stage.)

Within weeks of Bell's arrival at the company, Isaac Hayes and David Porter crafted a seminal masterpiece for Sam (Moore) and Dave (Prater) that proved to be their breakout hit: "You Don't Know Like I Know." Once again, it is clear that much of the form and content of soul music came directly from the call-and-response techniques and lyrical forms of gospel. Hayes provided the kernel of the song, simply adapting the melody, chords, and the first four lines from a sacred hymn, while admitting comfortably that most of his ideas and titles came from the church. The title references a gospel song called "You Don't Know Like I Know What the Lord Has Done for Me," and Hayes openly declared that if "the Lord can make you feel so good and do things for you, why couldn't a woman do the same things, too?" Thus the lyric, "You don't know like I know what this woman has done for me." Such a genre-morphing sentiment could easily be compared with the feminine devotion to troublesome partners so often referenced by Sharon Jones in her own Dap-King songs.

The same core philosophy of adaptation can also be interpreted in other Stax masterpieces such as "In the Midnight Hour" or "Knock on Wood." Fervor is fervor, wherever or whoever it comes from, whether scripture or sex. Porter had divined (no pun intended) that all the best songs followed a certain formula: they all had an opening that introduced a scenario that led to some sort of action, followed by a kind of denouement, though he probably didn't use that fancy word. They were mostly in the first person, too, and very few if any of them ended with a formal resolution of their dilemma. The first song to utilize this stated formula, and result in a phenomenal effect, was the classic "Hold On, I'm Coming" in 1966. Believe it or not, the song's timeless lyrics originated from Hayes being impatient while waiting in the studio and calling out gruffly to Porter, who was in the washroom, to hurry up and get out here . . . to which Porter responded with those golden "hold on" tag lines. Apparently, chance really *does* favor the well prepared.

• • •

Noel Murray of the *A.V. Club* once asked Sharon Jones if the music on her albums would sound as good if they had been recorded digitally rather than in the old-school analog format. "I don't really know," she replied. "It doesn't matter. Gabe Roth always says, it isn't even really the equipment, it's the musicians!" As we've also heard Roth suggest many times, however, the musicians sound a certain way because of the machinery they're interacting with in their recording tango. As the brilliant Homer Steinweiss once explained to *Modern Drummer*, "At Daptone, the gear is all analog. For the most part, only one mic is all we ever need." Of course, that slightly belies the fact that they're also in the hands of Roth, a sheer engineering genius, even if he is as modest as he appears to be on the Daptone site, where he states, "It's all about the band, and the little room they play in. They know each other well and they know the little room very well."

Their small cramped quarters have acquired a legendary status over the years, however, due to how huge and lush the sounds are that they can coax out of it. In fact, their ability to just go ahead and make the music that sounds good to them personally by collaborating with fellow fetish-istic vintage-audio lovers is about all there is to their so-called marketing plan. As a result of keeping company with other players who are as deeply into the genre as they are, they've been blessed with an uncanny ability to create a kind of brand recognition that few other labels can boast these days. This is of course exactly the strategy that Stax applied: when you picked up a record and saw the label's logo, you just knew there was going to be a specific vibe when the needle hit the groove. And that feeling is just what they're hoping their Daptone label provokes in people today.

One thing we do know for sure, however, is that among the key differences in recording techniques during this Stax golden age was a rapid search for perfect *feeling* rather than perfection in the sound, *per se*—unlike today's world of perpetual Auto-Tuning and computer/digital toying and tinkering. Rapid, because they often recorded several tracks from different bands in one day, one right after the other, with the rhythm section generally working out the foundation while the horn players might be out to lunch or for a smoke. Then, once the rhythm section had worked out the map of the song, the horn players would work out their parts, and finally everyone would cut the record "live" in the studio together, as if they were performing in a club, which in a sense is exactly what they were doing.

Stax never worried about the occasional audio mistake, or tempo flaw, or delayed action or reaction, especially not if the song had real soul power that couldn't ever be duplicated. At Stax, as Bowman writes, "It was of little consequence. If a given take had that gospel-infused sanctified feeling, it was a keeper." With Al Bell choreographing the radio stations, Jim Stewart or Steve Cropper playing the mixing board, and Isaac Hayes and Dave Porter starting to rip it up as songwriters, the formula and its execution started to hit high gear.

Production-wise, the efforts were similarly communal and family oriented, with ace promoter Bell initiating the policy of song credits stating, "Produced by staff," though there was an equal amount of deferment to the acknowledged masters of the groove in the persons of Steve Cropper and Wayne Jackson. By 1967, Stax had become so hot that Stewart could no longer handle all the production and engineering duties on his own, so he brought in Ron Capone to assist. Capone was somewhat amazed at how primitive the studio's technical setup still was, given that the end result was so often stellar. He found a studio that had been designed with a Scully 4-track recording machine and overdubbing capability, but where headphones were still not used at all. When recording an overdub, the studio speakers were used for monitors, which meant that the sound coming from the speakers bled into the microphones.

He also found that Stewart wasn't at all interested in stereo effects, with all the 45s the label created having been made in monaural. In this regard, of course, Stewart was actually a visionary, not a reactionary, since today's audiophiles, all the way up to a genius such as Brian Wilson, regularly express and extol the superior virtues of a mono mix. As the new in-house engineer Capone recalled it, Stewart would put the Voice of the Theater speaker in front of you with an 18-inch woofer, then put that in front of the mono machine and order Capone not to listen to the 4-track. He declared that he didn't care what went to the 4-track, even if for a technical specialist like Capone some of the levels that went into it were "outrageous." When the original mixing board was installed by in-house master engineer Welton Jetton, he had padded it down so severely that if Stewart had opened the sound up huge, with the meters cranked up all the way, there was still no way he would ever get any distortion from the board.

For reverb, there were two live chambers at the back of the studio, one of which was so humid it filled with water, and Capone recalled that crickets would often set up homes in the other chamber. On top of all those surreal features, the chambers were outfitted originally with the cheapest speakers money could buy, which Stewart had replaced with the tiny speakers you find in drive-in movies. The microphones in the chambers were also of similarly low-grade quality. And yet the sound that resulted from this weird mix was a kind of blissful sonic utopia—one that again calls back to mind Gabe Roth's contemporary preference for the kind of cheap RadioShack mics he likes to use at Daptone today. Then, as now, it's all about music first, and mechanics, if ever, a distant second.

Later on in the Stax saga, during the Atlantic distribution years, the Warner Bros. period, and then the rough era of CBS Records, the recognizable aura of Stax's sound and spirit started to alter, even if the technology was actually supposedly superior. And as Bowman effectively points out in his book, once the use of strings and background vocalists from Detroit, and then different rhythm sections, entered the nebulous alchemical mix that was the secret Stewart domain in 1967–1970, followed by the looming social and cultural shift toward the new disco aesthetic, "The idea of a readily identifiable Stax sound was beginning to fade into history."

After the label folded in 1975, the Stax family went through a number of last-gasp convulsions. A series of events led the company to become a victim of a number of forces, especially overexpansion and an ill-fitting distribution deal with CBS, doomed by a clash of corporate cultures beyond repair, greed, poor decisions, and the mismanagement of its local bank. The storied history of this innovative record company is a sad saga of creativity colliding with commerce at the same time as a glorious achievement in music, especially soul and funk music. Unfortunately, Jim Stewart did not fare well after the collapse of his intensely personal creation, despite an attempt by Fantasy Records to revive Stax in 1977. Having never drawn up a contract that specified his role as a producer on the recordings made by his own company during its first seven years of life, he still to this day (at eighty-nine years of age) receives no royalty payments at all for the remarkable music he helped manifest. When he was inducted into the Rock and Roll Hall of Fame in 2002, he sent his granddaughter to the ceremony to accept the award on his behalf.

In 1980, the Union Bank passed on the legendary Stax Records studio building it had commandeered to Memphis's Southside Church of God Christ for the princely sum of ten dollars, after it was claimed the church wanted to renovate it as a community center. It already was one, of course. Even though many offers were made to the church to preserve the building for heritage, it refused to sell it, apparently to prevent anyone from turning the building into a monument to what it still perceived as "devil's music," instead of what it really was—a historic site of a living popular culture. Oddly, in retrospect the church's rigorous control now feels like a temporary triumph of gospel music over Satan's sound, at least in that final round.

That much is the sad part of the Soulsville saga; the glorious side is the quirky fact that the Stax master tapes and the East Memphis catalogue have evolved into a revered national treasure of sorts and have undergone significant reissuing to the tune of three annotated boxed sets containing every A-side of every R&B single ever created by the studio. These songs comprise some twenty-eight discs and contain just about three full days of solid musical magic. In the late 1990s (the very period when Daptone was starting out), the studio's contributions to soul culture went through a kind of renaissance, resulting in a born-again and fervent neo-soul music movement, of which the Dap-Kings represent a major portion. As Bowman states emotionally, "It's a legacy that makes the world just a little bit richer place to live." Amen, brother.

• • •

The studio ethos of Stewart and Axton is one whose vibrant can-do spirit obviously still lives on in certain quarters, most notably in a tiny house of soul in the Bushwick district of Brooklyn, New York. I'm once again pleased to say that occasionally those old folk adages we all heard do seem to ring true. Here's another one: "history never actually repeats itself, however it often rhymes." Having mentioned the *aura* of the Stax sound, I can guarantee that the spirit created in late-'60s and early-'70s Memphis at both Stax and Hi Records can easily be heard echoing clearly in the little Daptone empire of Brooklyn. In fact, let's just be plain and call it an *aura echo*. The folks at Daptone won't mind being referenced as musicians and producers who memorialized that Memphis analog sound; indeed, that was their game plan from Daptone's birth at the very beginning of the twenty-first century. But far from the anxiety of influence, in this case it's more like the bountiful blessings of inspiration.

It's easy enough to conduct a taste test yourself to confirm this obvious fact. Listening in this order to two songs recorded three or four decades apart by two distinctly different but inherently linked creative outfits will quickly demonstrate what the term *aura echo* might mean. Listen to the instrumental track "Mr. Kesselman" by the Soul Providers (the Desco progenitor of the Dap-Kings, prior to the inception of Daptone) from the album *Soul Tequila* in 1996, followed by the classic instrumental Stax tune "Green Onions" by Booker T. and The M.G.'s from 1962. Now play "Damn It's Hot, Pt. 1 and 2" by Sharon Jones, from *Spike's Choice Desco 45 Collection*, released in 1998, or Sharon's "Hook and Sling Meets the Superfly" or "Double Cross" by the Sugarman Three on the same record, followed by the Stax aura echo of "Walking the Dog" by Rufus Thomas from 1963 or "Mr. Big Stuff" by Jean Knight from 1971. Try out "Talking About a Good Thing" or "Catapult" by Naomi Davis (before she became Shelton), and "Toothpick" by the Mighty Imperials from *Spike's Choice 2: Desco 45 Collection* from 2000, followed by the Stax aura echo of "Tramp" by Carla Thomas and Otis Redding from 1967, or the iconic "I'll Take You There" by Staple Singers in 1971.

Tune in to the long bump-and-grinding instrumental by the Dap-Kings called "Casella Walk" from *Dap-Dippin'* in 2002, followed by the Stax echo of Booker T.'s incredible gem "Time Is Tight," from 1968. Try jumping from "100 Days, 100 Nights" on the album of the same title in

2007 and Sharon's moaning croon of "Let Them Knock," followed by the Stax aura echo of "The Life I Live" and "Wait a Minute," both by Barbara Stevens in 1962. And, just for good measure, slip into the groove of Sharon's "The Game Gets Old" from 2010's *I Learned the Hard Way*, followed by "Who's Making Love?" by Johnnie Taylor in 1968.

You get the general idea. I'd also suggest doing this in reverse chronological order, with the Daptone tunes coming before their stylistic inspirations, because I think your ears will enjoy it most that way. However you choose to do this little taste test, though, the results will be the same, and the evidence will be obvious: Daptone is not a matter of copying, imitating, evoking, or duplicating something, it's simply a matter of making soul and funk music the way it was meant to be made.

There are no ifs ands or buts about it: in a very true and really touching way, apart from listening to the many vintage records released by the above-mentioned pantheon of soul stars, if anyone wants to know what the historic analog majesty of both the Stax and Hi labels really sounded like, all they have to do is pick up any of the Desco/Daptone albums by Lee Fields and Neal Sugarman, among others, or any of the seven superb albums recorded by Daptone featuring Sharon Jones and the Dap-Kings. Their authentic soul inheritance, and the first will and the testament of funk—it's right there waiting for you.

PERSONAL DELIVERY
Directly from My Heart to You

"My heart is carrying so much pain, hurt, love . . . if I could put all this into one word . . . it's impossible . . . so that's what soul is."
—CHARLES BRADLEY, in the video for the song "Victim of Love," from the album *Victim of Love*, featuring the Menahan Street Band, 2014

Sharon Jones and her band, the Dap-Kings, have now surpassed sales of several million records worldwide and set a new high standard for soul music and its passionate live performance. Creative collaborations with artists such as Prince, John Legend, and Lou Reed have cultivated a fan base to which few can compare and forged an insurmountable respect from artists and musicians alike. As a trailblazer, Sharon Jones was incredibly impactful, and the reason is simple: she was real, and she wrapped the whole world in her arms.

Jones may not have been the most well-read or educated person, not the most sophisticated or articulate, even, but her tale was spoken directly from the heart. She had that certain nebulous *something* that ordinary cultural sophistication just couldn't match, that special ability as a mediumistic storyteller that requires a novel sort of genius, not to live her life only for herself but to transform her personality into a kind of human mirror in which we can see our own hopes, desires, and dreams reflected back to us. I'm reminded of a remark that is often misattributed to Motown's Berry Gordy, but which he actually borrowed from the great painter of everyday life, Paul Cezanne: "Genius is the ability to renew one's emotions in daily experience."

To the extent that this observation contains a deep insight, which I suspect it does, Jones was a very special genius indeed, and she too was a painter of everyday life, using her voice as the brush. We can only wonder what her own authorial voice would have told us about her life story. But I'm also struck by the fact that her real and actual autobiography can more readily be found in the seven records she released on Daptone, made with the musicians who clearly adored her. And now that she's gone, *that* is the place we'll have to look for her true life story: the passionate and funky soul music she loved to make more than anything else in the world, the music that in fact *was* her world.

STILL LIFE WITH SOUL: A PORTRAIT OF THE MUSIC

Although Jones appeared on multiple 45-rpm releases and two full-length compilation albums on Desco commencing in 1996, she emerged as a headlining feature artist with Daptone in 2002, as the lead singer of the Dap-Kings. Prior to that debut, however, she gave stellar performances on these early ventures, which have since become collector's items:

**The Soul Providers featuring Lee Fields, *Soul Tequila*
(Pure Records/C&S Records CS-#8535-2)**
Released 1996
Produced by the Soul Providers
Recorded and mixed at Dare Studios, New York
Duration: 44:25

***Spike's Choice: The Desco '45 Collection* (Pure Records)**
Released November 10, 1998
Duration: 1:13:48

Dap-Dippin' with Sharon Jones and the Dap-Kings (DAP-001)
Released May 14, 2002
Produced by Gabriel Roth
Duration: 45:24
Personnel: Sharon Jones: vocals / Gabriel Roth: bandleader, bass /
Leon Michels: tenor saxophone / Jack Zapata (a.k.a. Martin Perna):
baritone saxophone / Binky Griptite: guitar, emcee / Fernando
Velez: congas / Earl Maxton (a.k.a. Victor Axelrod): organs / Homer
Steinweiss: drums / Anda Szilagyi: trumpet.

1. "Introduction" (Bosco Mann) 1:30
2. "Got a Thing on My Mind" (Bosco Mann) 2:58
3. "What Have You Done for Me Lately?" (Janet Jackson /
   Terry Lewis / James Harris) 3:16
4. "The Dap Dip" (Bosco Mann) 4:01
5. "Give Me a Chance" (Bosco Mann) 3:10
6. "Got to Be the Way It Is" (Bosco Mann) 3:28
7. "Make It Good to Me" (Bosco Mann) 3:25
8. "Ain't It Hard" (Bosco Mann) 4:52
9. "Pick It Up, Lay It in the Cut" (Bosco Mann) 4:30
10. "Casella Walk" (Bosco Mann) 4:07
11. Untitled Hidden Track (The Dap-Kings and Sharon Jones) 10:02

It is with the initial album release by the newly minted Daptone
Records label that Jones's legend truly begins. Originally classified as
a funk/soul record, *Dap-Dippin'* is also forty-five minutes and twenty-
four seconds of emotional intensity from start to finish—a suitable
debut for the forty-six-year-old vocalist and her new band, and also as
the premiere full-length album release of the brand new Daptone label.
Its eccentric reinterpretation of a Janet Jackson song, "What Have You
Done For Me Lately?," still manages to succeed due to Sharon's incom-
parable authenticity. Produced by Bosco Mann (the mercurial Gabriel
Roth's studio persona), who also wrote most of the songs, it spawned a

hot single, the stellar "Make It Good to Me," demonstrating instantly that Jones was a force to be reckoned with. The single's B-side was an instrumental, "Casella Walk," featuring the Dap-Kings in a Booker T. groove that they would stay comfortably throbbing in for the next fourteen years.

In a profile by Andy Tennille, subsequently included in *Best Music Writing 2008*, Jones recalled thinking, "What the hell does this little white boy know about funk? But Gabe knew what he was doing, and I remember thinking that boy was reincarnated—he was a fifty-five-year-old black man in a little Jewish boy's body!" Suddenly, she was part of the Super Soul Revue group along with Lee Fields, Joseph Henry, and gospel singer Naomi Davis, which led rapidly to Roth supersonically gestating a raft of tunes and shifting into high gear with *Dap-Dippin'*, invented as a vehicle for the little prison guard with the big heart. This now-classic soul gem was followed in quick succession by the Sugarman Three's *Pure Cane Sugar* and the Mighty Imperials' *Thunder Chicken*.

With multiple bands alternating in the family-oriented revue, including Roth's other group, Antibalas, the choice was eventually made to focus all Daptone's energies on the Kings. Roth characterized what they were up to for Tennille: "It was real interesting because our music was some raw take your pants off shit. We got into the dumpy Lee Dorsey grooves." At that crossover point, the Antibalas record *Who Is This America* emerged first from the label's new/old Brooklyn studio, followed by *Dippin'*.

"Make It Good to Me," is one of the classics on Jones's debut that firmly entrenches the heartache that's present in most of the songs that would follow, a slow bump-and-grind tune that doesn't hide what she's aching for, what's she's dying to have. The vocalist doesn't really want to know where her lover has been, and no words can make her feel any better about his betrayal. But if he holds her, she can more easily forget all the harm he's done to her, since if he doesn't have the right words to make her feel better, then he may as well do it the old-fashioned way.

Naturally (DAP-004)
Released January 25, 2005
Duration: 40:15
Produced by Gabriel Roth (listed as Bosco Mann)
Personnel: Sharon Jones: vocals / Ed Michels: baritone saxophone
/ Neal Sugarman: tenor saxophone / Dave Guy: trumpet / Homer
Steinweiss: drums / Binky Griptite: guitar, back up vocals, emcee /
Boogaloo Velez: congas / Thomas Brenneck: guitar, piano / Gabriel
Roth: bass, piano, vibes, tambourine, bandleader. *Also featuring*: Alex
Kadvan: cello / Antoine Silverman, Entcho Todorov: violin / Stuart
Bogie: jaw harp / Earl Maxton (a.k.a. Victor Axelrod): organ.

1. "How Do I Let a Good Man Down?" (Bosco Mann) 3:02
2. "Natural Born Lover" (Bosco Mann) 3:04
3. "Stranded in Your Love" featuring Lee Fields (Bosco Mann) 5:37
4. "My Man Is a Mean Man" (Bosco Mann) 3:16
5. "You're Gonna Get It" (Bosco Mann) 4:59
6. "How Long Do I Have to Wait for You?" (Bosco Mann) 4:03
7. "This Land Is Your Land" (Woody Guthrie) 4:31
8. "Your Thing Is a Drag" (Bosco Mann) 3:33
9. "Fish in the Dish" (Bosco Mann) 3:18
10. "All Over Again" (Bosco Mann) 4:43

By the time Jones and the Dap-Kings' second outing, *Naturally*, was released, the in-house technology at Daptone had grown serious, and audiences had started listening. The band had played on Conan O'Brien's TV show and begun touring big festivals in Europe and across the States. *Naturally* was a brilliant follow-up effort on which Jones and Roth began to assemble the permanent wrecking-crew personnel of her band, including the stalwart Neal Sugarman on tenor, Dave Guy on trumpet, and Tommy Brenneck on guitar and piano. It also features great backup vocals by the legendary Lee Fields, the artist for whom Sharon was originally tapped to provide backup vocals in her initial encounter with Roth back in 1996. The quirky inclusion of Woody Guthrie's 1944 "This Land Is Your Land" ended up creating a cult audience for Jones's uniquely funked-out version of a classic piece of American folk music. Even more timely today is the refrain from the original: "There was a big high wall there that tried to stop me, the sign was painted private property but on the backside it didn't say nothin'."

When performing "How Do I Let a Good Man Down," Jones liked to bring up stunned guys from the audience and let them bump and grind against her sturdy frame, after explaining that she always thought about Tina Turner when she sang the song. She also liked to enjoy herself in a charmingly self-deprecating way, as she did at the Beat Club in March of 2005, when she purred this ad-lib: "I may not have those long legs like Tina, but hey, Dap-Kings, help me let these short little legs strut across this stage. Let me strut around for a while." She announces in this tune that even though her lover has never hurt her or treated her badly, she still had to find somebody else, not to harm him but only to do right for herself. As she explains it, one man makes her happy, but the other gives her chills. "I can't have my cake and eat it too, so I gonna get up and walk out on you." The song moves along like a rocking freight train, with Jones chirping away like a blissed-out conductor announcing her next love stop, half remorseful about leaving some good guy, half ecstatic about clutching onto her new bad boy. "I gotta let him down, I gotta let him down, I gotta let him down."

"Stranded" is a true gem, and with its soaring duet with Lee Fields situates call-and-response motifs in a dramatically new mode. Jones's rendition of "You're Gonna Get It" also leaves no doubt as to the deep command she had over a soul lyric about the different kinds of love she's familiar with (the kind that makes you helpless or strong, makes you do right or do wrong). "I got the kind of love that's gonna make you higher baby than what you're dreaming of. And I'm gonna give it to you."

It was around the time of this album's release that Roth got the fateful call from a young producer, Mark Ronson, who had sampled one of Jones's songs for his earlier record, *Here Comes the Fuzz*, and wanted to collaborate on some production, engineering, and recording projects, the first one being by some kid called Amy. The original rough-and-tumble, live-in-the-studio sound of Daptone proved so popular that Roth and Ronson also worked together on Lily Allen's *Alright, Still*, and on several tracks from Ronson's album of covers, *Version*. Working on other people's projects started to get draining quickly, however, especially since Roth was ready to move forward with Sharon Jones in a big way on their third outing together, *100 Days, 100 Nights*.

100 Days, 100 Nights (DAP-012)
Released October 2, 2007
Produced and engineered by Gabriel Roth
Mastered by Scott Hull
Duration: 33:48
Personnel: Sharon Jones: vocals / Homer Steinweiss: drums / Binky Griptite: guitar, emcee / Dave Guy: trumpet / Fernando Velez: congas, bongos, tambourine / Gabe Roth: bass, bandleader / Neal Sugarman: tenor saxophone / Thomas Brenneck: guitar / Ian Hendrickson-Smith: baritone saxophone. *Also featuring*: Toby Pazner: vibraphone / Aaron Johnson: trombones / Bushwick Philharmonic: strings / The Voices of Thunder: backup vocals / Cliff Driver: piano / Earl Maxton: organ, clavinet, piano / the Dapettes: backup vocals / the Gospel Queens: backup vocals.

    1. "100 Days, 100 Nights" (Bosco Mann) 3:45
    2. "Nobody's Baby" (Homer Steinweiss) 2:27
    3. "Tell Me" (Neal Sugarman / Sharon Jones) 2:46
    4. "Be Easy" (Bosco Mann) 3:03
    5. "When the Other Foots Drops, Uncle" (Bosco Mann) 3:15
    6. "Let Them Knock" (Bosco Mann) 4:29

7. "Something's Changed" (Bosco Mann) 2:56
8. "Humble Me" (Bosco Mann) 4:05
9. "Keep On Looking" (Bosco Mann) 2:49
10. "Answer Me" (Bosco Mann) 4:08

The third studio album by Jones and the Dap-Kings, *100 Days, 100 Nights*, was released right in the middle of the global mania surrounding the doomed singer/songwriter who shot to the stratosphere after Mark Ronson borrowed Jones's band to record his protégé's award-winning second record. That singer, Amy Winehouse, would in turn borrow Jones's band to go on a global concert tour. For a time, it was natural enough for Jones to feel slightly sidelined, to say the least, as she watched Winehouse gain massive fame, win five Grammys, and then feverishly embark on a path to self-destruction.

Again, the album features vintage sounds recorded on vintage sound equipment, human emotion captured by mechanical engineering in the old-school manner. It was also once again recorded in Daptone's tiny Brooklyn studio home, using analog equipment direct to two-inch tape, as well as utilizing the vinyl format that most delighted revivalist tastes for authentic '60s funk. Ian Hendrickson-Smith joined the crew at this stage on baritone, and would remain an anchor until relatively recently (he's now in the *Tonight Show* band, along with David Guy). Additional spice is provided by the Bushwick Philharmonic Choir and the impeccable Gospel Queens.

The album's title refers to the time it takes, in Jones's estimation, for a man to reveal his true feelings and unfold his heart, and the vibe also again contains a nod of respect to precursors like James Brown, with a song called "For the Godfather." The CD pressing of the album also included a bonus disc framed around a mock radio station presenting an imaginary show improbably called *Binky Griptite's Ghettofunkpowerhour*, as a vehicle for releasing almost an hour more of free music, comprising twenty-seven additional tracks selected from Daptone's extensive back catalogue.

The online music service Rhapsody ranked the album at #9 on its list of the best albums of the decade, declaring, "Maybe there's something anachronistic about a band that plays funk music in the twenty-first century as if hip-hop never happened. But when the music's this good, those concerns fly out the window. Jones pours everything she's got into this album, and her gruff, passionate, brassy style grabs you by the collar and doesn't let go until the end. The Dap-Kings restrain themselves behind her, shuffling and jangling but leaving her plenty of space to maneuver a clutch of good songs."

"Let Them Knock" is another little hot hymn to Him, in which the vocalist declaims her intention to answer her door to no one, no way, no matter how hard they bang, until she and her man are through. Clearly, when she's making love, the world has got nothing to offer her, since, as she puts it perfectly, "I don't answer to nobody but you." The song is crooned in a joyful yelp under a wave of synchronized brass from the horn section, and all yanked along perfectly, as usual, by one of the finest rhythm sections in the business.

After a concert in Chicago around the time of *100 Days, 100 Nights*, *Time Out Chicago* declared that even though Jones was only four feet eleven, her spectacular stage presence was huge. The magazine then decided to sum up her performing phenomenon by making pointed and sarcastic remarks aimed at *all* young white exponents of "blue-eyed" soul everywhere, while targeting one famous name in particular as a kind of stylistic dartboard: "Hey, Duffy! *This* is what soul really sounds like: tribal, earthy, hip shakin', swerve throwin' . . . it sounds like Sharon Jones." To me, that says it all.

Daptone Gold (DAP 018)
Released December 2009

1. "Introduction" (Franklin Stribling) Binky Griptite 0:51
2. "I'm Not Gonna Cry" (Thomas Brenneck/Bosco Mann) Sharon Jones and the Dap-Kings 3:22

3. "Up from the South" (Thomas Brenneck/Daniel Foder) The Budos Band 3:28

4. "What Have You Done?" (Bosco Mann) Naomi Shelton and the Gospel Queens 3:29

5. "How Long Do I Have to Wait?" (Bosco Mann) Sharon Jones and the Dap-Kings 4:05

6. "Could Have Been" (Bosco Mann) Lee Fields 3:31

7. "Che Che Cole Makossa" (Victor Axelrod/Bosco Mann) Antibalas with Mayra Vega 4:09

8. "Budos Rising" (John Carbonella/Daniel Foder) The Budos Band 4:49

9. "Got a Thing on My Mind" (Bosco Mann) Sharon Jones and the Dap-Kings 2:53

10. "The World Is Going Up in Flames" (Charles Bradley/Thomas Brenneck) Charles Bradley and Menahan Street Band 3:22

11. "Make It Good to Me" (Bosco Mann) Sharon Jones and the Dap-Kings 4:39

12. "Stand Up" (Neal Sugarman) Lee Fields and Sugarman Co. 3:54

13. "What Is This?" (Rev. Willie Morganfield) Naomi Shelton and the Gospel Queens 3:13

14. "A Lover Like Me" (Bosco Mann/Neal Sugarman) Binky Griptite with the Sugarman Three 2:38

15. "Make the Road by Walking" (Bosco Mann/Thomas Brenneck/ Homer Steinweiss) Menahan Street Band 3:03

16. "Tell Me" (Sharon Jones/Neal Sugarman) Sharon Jones and the Dap-Kings 2:46

17. "Down to It" (Bosco Mann/Neal Sugarman) Sugarman and Co. 4:13

18. "Nervous Like Me" (Bosco Mann) The Dap-Kings 3:07

19. "Giving Up" (V. McCoy/F. Norman) Sharon Jones and the Dap-Kings 3:09

20. "Ghostwalk" (Bosco Mann/Thomas Brenneck) The Budos Band 2:11

21. "I Need You to Hold My Hand" (F. Williams) Cynthia Langston and the Gospel Queens 3:21
22. "The Stroll Pt. 2" (Binky Griptite) Binky Griptite and the Mellomatics 2:11
23. "Stranded in Your Love" (Bosco Mann) Sharon Jones and Lee Fields 5:48

This assortment of gems is a certified Daptone confection, with all of the label's signature high-quality sonics intact. Reviewing the album, *AllMusic*'s Hal Horowitz rightly called Daptone "one of the world's most dependable sources of soul and R&B with extensions into gospel and world music," and this special compilation of twenty-three tunes from the label's first decade clearly demonstrates how and why. Horowitz also correctly claimed that this little label had earned the right to be considered the musical match for both Stax and Motown—creatively if not quite yet commercially—and especially because of its totally identifiable and distinctive analog sound.

This collection is far from a best-of selection and is more of a gift to collectors, since many of the tracks were previously only available on rare 45-rpm singles, including the label's superfine debut release, "Got a Thing on My Mind," as well as six other tunes by Queen Jones and her Kings. Of note is Jones's uniquely Sharon-drenched version of a Gladys Knight song, "Giving Up." An early incarnation of the Kings, Antibalas, is also featured on the album, along with the Budos Band, both of whom pull off a lively fusion of horn-based R&B mashed together with world music vibes. The Kings also contribute early instrumental tracks that summon the ghost of Booker T. and the M.G.'s in a most reverential manner, while Elmer "Lee" Fields offers his own finest Wilson Pickett séance via the bump and grind of "Stand Up."

From the perspective of my current study, the most revealing inclusion is of three gospel songs that position both the label and Jones squarely halfway between the church and the tavern. Naomi Shelton and the Gospel Queens (also fronted here by Cynthia Langston for one track) are exactly that: majestic old-school gospel testifying at its finest. Some of these singers also had the distinction of having worked with Jones in her early days as a struggling wedding-band performer—an irony that always makes me wonder how hot and wicked such marital receptions must have been, with these dames cooking away in front of family and friends.

One has to concur with the *AllMusic* critic who declared that this album "reaffirms your hope that someone is still crafting music as raw, rootsy and furiously funky as this for the contemporary market. That makes this an indispensible addition to any soul lover's collection, regardless of age or demographic." I would also add that any listener seeking an overall and comprehensive introduction to the extended Daptone family of artists couldn't hope for a better sampling than this goldmine. It's a great aerial view of what Daptone is all about. The song "Giving Up" is a grand indication of Jones's respect for some of her roots, a 1964 Gladys Knight tune by Van McCoy here given a royal treatment, sped up almost imperceptibly and honored by the preserved-in-amber Daptone touch, resulting in sheer emotive magic.

I Learned the Hard Way (DAP-019)

Released April 6, 2010
Produced by Bosco Mann
Duration: 39:30
Personnel: Sharon Jones: vocals / Thomas Brenneck: guitars, piano / Dave Guy: trumpet / Ian Hendrickson-Smith: baritone saxophone, flute / Gabriel Roth: bass / Homer Steinweiss: drums / Neal Sugarman: tenor saxophone / Fernando Velez: bongos, congas, tambourine. *Also featuring*: Victor Axelrod: piano, organ / Moon Bancs: marching snare / Cosmo Bann: guitars / AnGee Blake: background vocals / Sam Boncon: piano, clavinet / Chris Cardona: violin / Nydia Dávila: soul claps / El Deuvo: cabasa / Brian Floody: timpani / Cochemea Gastelum: alto saxophone, tenor saxophone / Jimmy Hill: organ / Aaron Jonson: trombones / Alex Kadvan:

cello / Leon Michels: tenor saxophone / Toby Pazner: vibraphone, glockenspiel / Boom Boom Romero: drums / Antoine Silverman: violin / Daisy Sugarman: flute / Entcho Todorov: violin / Saundra Williams: background vocals / Anja Wood: cello / the Bushwick Callers: background vocals.

1. "The Game Gets Old" (Dave Guy, Homer Steinweiss, Tommy Brenneck) 3:55
2. "I Learned the Hard Way" (Bosco Mann) 3:47
3. "Better Things" (Homer Steinweiss) 3:38
4. "Give It Back" (Dave Guy) 3:22
5. "Money" (Bosco Mann) 3:22
6. "The Reason" (Neal Sugarman) 2:20
7. "Window Shopping" (Wayne Gordon, Lawrence Gordon, Derek Nievergelt) 4:35
8. "She Ain't a Child No More" (Bosco Mann) 2:35
9. "I'll Still Be True" (Thomas Brenneck) 3:48
10. "Without a Heart" (Bosco Mann) 2:45
11. "If You Call" (Bosco Mann) 3:00
12. "Mama Don't Like My Man" (Bosco Mann) 2:31

Perhaps the most ironic record title in history, given how long she'd been struggling to reach for the brass ring in the music industry, and how swiftly younger and perhaps more conventionally cute singers were elevated to pop superstardom, Jones's fourth outing was also by far her strongest yet. *I Learned the Hard Way* shows her returning to form after regaining some personal and professional balance, post-Amy, with her band back in action where they belonged—with her. Released on April 6, 2010, having been recorded at House of Soul Studios during 2009, this one indicated that Jones was finally getting her due after paying her dues for so long, debuting at #15 on the *Billboard* 200 and selling 23,000 copies during the first week—a possible indicator also of the increased profile provided by the band's association with Winehouse. It also received consistently positive reviews from critics who were beginning to recognize how special Jones really was.

I Learned the Hard Way was released on CD and vinyl, and in MP3 and FLAC formats, with the vinyl edition also containing a code for a free MP3 download of the whole album from the Daptone website. The digital version included an exclusive bonus track, "When I Come Home," that was later also made available as a 7-inch single. Daptone, true to its tradition, still believed not only in vinyl records but also in the copious release of singles, an echo of bygone industry days that happily creatively competes with the monolithic world of online streaming and single-song access generated electronically in a youth-obsessed era.

Listeners as well as critics were praising Jones's maturing voice (ironic, considering she was now fifty-four years of age) as well as the usual soulful technical mastery of the Dap-Kings, their incorporation of regional soul music styles, and the ability to both swagger and stir the spirit by fitting in with tradition without being beholden to it. In general, the public and the music industry had come to realize that when Jones sang of infidelity, hard times, and tough lessons, she was doing so out of personal experience and with complete authority, not impersonating existential damage in the youthful and theatrical Taylor Swift or Katy Perry mode of operation.

Boston Phoenix critic Jeff Tamarkin praised Jones and the band's commitment to retro soul (though technically it was really more revival soul) and noted that they never leave the impression that they're trying to recapture past glory because their music just felt "right," and therefore also quite contemporary. This take was echoed widely, especially in the *Washington Post*, where Sarah Godfrey applauded the band's vintage sound by declaring it so entrenched in retro soul that it "creates" rather than emulates those '60s sounds. She was seconded by critic Bryan Sanchez, who called the album "a beautiful representation of what real, honest and true soul music really is." Hear, hear!

For me, the most accurate assessment came from Nate Chinen of the *New York Times*, who found a sustained "plaintive air" in its songs about eroded trust, exasperated patience, and wounded indignation. The album also upped the ante on the instrumentation and arrangement aspect of the Kings and the solid foundation they erected for Jones to stomp on, with the usual lineup here complemented by an additional twenty-eight musicians, including strings, flutes, clavinet, and timpani. The sonic results are astronomically deep. Try a taste for yourself.

The song "Mama Don't Like My Man" is a sustained plea for parental understanding, and the choral unison gives this gem a '60s girl-group sheen straight from the golden Spector era. It would have perfectly suited the Ronettes or the Shangri-Las. Even more satisfying, though, is the way it also ideally suits the ragged emotional power of Sharon Jones.

Soul Time (DAP-024)

Released November 1, 2011 (UK)
Sharon Jones: vocals / Thomas Brenneck: guitars, piano / Dave Guy: trumpet / Ian Hendrickson-Smith: baritone saxophone, flute / Gabriel Roth: bass / Homer Steinweiss: drums / Neal Sugarman: tenor saxophone / Fernando Velez: bongos, congas, tambourine.

1. "Genuine, Pt. 1" (Bosco Mann) 3:58
2. "Genuine, Pt. 2" (Bosco Mann) 3:04
3. "Longer and Stronger" (Bosco Mann) 3:40
4. "He Said I Can" (Bosco Mann) 2:49
5. "I'm Not Gonna Cry" (Thomas Brenneck, Bosco Mann) 3:24
6. "When I Come Home" (Bosco Mann) 2:54
7. "What If We All Stopped Paying Taxes?" (Bosco Mann) 4:40
8. "Settling In" (Bosco Mann) 2:48
9. "Ain't No Chimneys in the Projects" (Sharon Jones) 2:21
10. "New Shoes" (Binky Griptite) 2:16
11. "Without a Trace" (Thomas Brenneck) 3:51
12. "Inspiration Information" (Shuggie Otis) 4:21

I enjoy the way the online magazine *Soul Tracks* characterized the fifth album by Jones and the Kings, observing that by now we were all used to her toying with James Brown grooves in her work, but this time, "The Daptone superstar does the full monty on Brown's legacy and cranks up the J.B. horn power, the profuse funk and raw nostalgia spawning from Bosco Mann's production." Nevertheless, *Soul Time* was a bit of a breather for the band and singer: a compilation of previously released rarities and B-sides such as the singles "Ain't No Chimneys in the Projects," "Genuine," and "I'm Not Gonna Cry." It once again fully explores the painful side of personal relationships in the tearful ballads "Longer and Stronger" and "Without a Trace," but it also examines social issues in a Gil Scott-Heron–like motif of wry commentary, "What If We All Stop Paying Taxes?," which purrs under a heavy, Sly Stone–style groove. By the way, the revolution isn't going to be televised, but you can still listen to it.

Although this was not a record of fresh new songs *per se*, *Soul Time* is nonetheless a useful chronicle of how far Jones and her band had traveled and the trajectory they used to cover that funky ground. Some of the early tunes even hark back to the long shadow cast by the Soul Providers, the original group formed by then-partners Roth and Philip Lehman back in the mid-'90s. Another deep-funk echo appears with the reverberating presence of the great Lee Fields over the years, since it was the mercurial Fields who actually prompted or perhaps provoked the initial evolution of Roth from Soul Provider to Dap-King visionary.

Some of the material on *Soul Time* seems to maintain the essential rough-and-tumble quality of those early days, and as such it's a valuable document that maps the fresh territory that would eventually be ruled over exclusively and majestically by Queen Jones. Desco Records had provided an invaluable service to both artists and audiences alike by hosting a popular series of revue-style live shows with local talent and also releasing a steady stream of steaming funk 45-rpm singles, all in an age and era when the music industry had gone corporate in a big way, business-wise, and fully embraced digital electronic dance music.

These early, now legendary releases and shows started to create a high degree of street intrigue among serious soul and funk aficionados and collectors, whom perhaps it's more accurate to call by their real name: cultists. Quite a few people who started collecting the records actually thought they'd been produced in the 1960s or '70s—an intentional mystery element enhanced by the fact that the label often deliberately omitted the recording dates to foster an even greater appetite for their obvious authenticity.

This UK-released compilation of non-album tracks is also a good initiation ritual for folks who want to know what all the hubbub's about. The songs "Longer and Stronger" and "Inspiration Information" (an inspired version of the classic Shuggie Otis tune) are the standouts on this stellar selection. The big surprise is what Jones and her boys do with Otis's wistfully mournful tune, twisting it like a pretzel into a delightful soul jump: "Jump, laugh, smile, and having fun, smile, love, and burn and get on down." They certainly do burn, and they seriously get on down.

Give the People What They Want (DAP-032)

Released January 14, 2014
Duration: 33:38
Personnel: Sharon Jones: vocals / Homer Steinweiss: Drums: / Binky Griptite: guitars / Joseph Crispiano: guitar / Gabriel Roth: bass / Neal Sugarman: tenor saxophone, piano / Cochemea Gastelum: baritone saxophone / Dave Guy: trumpet / Fernando Velez: tambourine, congas. *Also featuring*: Aaron Johnson: trombone / Victor Axelrod: Farfisa organ, chimes, glockenspiel, Wurlitzer electric piano / Jimi Ashes: timpani / Jordan McLean: trumpet / the Dapettes: background vocals.

1. "Retreat" (Bosco Mann) 3:31
2. "Stranger to My Happiness" (Bosco Mann) 3:31
3. "We Get Along" (Joe Crispiano, Homer Steinweiss) 3:03
4. "You'll Be Lonely" (Cochemea Gastelum) 3:45
5. "Now I See" (Homer Steinweiss) 3:10
6. "Making Up and Breaking Up" (Bosco Mann) 2:23

7. "Get Up and Get Out" (Homer Steinweiss) 3:27
8. "Long Time, Wrong Time" (Cochemea Gastelum) 3:21
9. "People Don't Get What They Deserve" (Bosco Mann) 3:25
10. "Slow Down, Love" (Bosco Mann) 4:02

Delayed due to Jones's health issues, her last studio album, recorded in 2012, was finally released on January 14, 2014, to the acclaim of *Rolling Stone* magazine, whose Will Hermes declared that it not only extended and preserved traditions in the soul and funk genre but that it resulted in "a national treasure and an instant soul party." The CD package also included a secret code for a free download that included a bonus fifty-eight-minute Daptone Records sampler selection.

The song "Stranger to My Happiness" is a serious standout with a message as uplifting as it is despairing, booming along with a chunky baritone sax pumping out the rhythm as Jones warbles her truth: that considering how many lovers she's had, it's been a challenge to maintain her balance, especially since she's only been able to call very few of them a real friend. "But it's a mystery just how you came in and stole my heart away and left me there again." The song sizzles and soars and almost makes you forget that what it's about is not just that evil men do harm but also that almost every man is capable of imagining that he has a plan to settle down yet can't quite pull it off. The end result is always the same: Jones feels like a stranger to her own happiness.

Daptone Gold 2: Daptone Does It Again (DAP 036)
Released September 18, 2015
Executive-produced by Gabriel Roth and Neal Sugarman
Mastered by J. J. Golden

1. "Better Things" (Homer Steinweiss) Sharon Jones and the Dap-Kings 3:38
2. "Strictly Reserved" (Charles Bradley/Thomas Brenneck) Charles Bradley 3:42

3. "Sinner" (Max Shrager) Naomi Shelton and the Gospel Queens 2:51

4. "Hot Shot" (Cheme Gastelum/Bosco Mann) Saun and Starr 3:31

5. "Dirty Money" (Luke O'Malley) Antibalas 6:14

6. "Inspiration Information" (Shuggie Otis) Sharon Jones and the Dap-Kings 4:07

7. "The Traitor" (Thomas Brenneck/Dave Guy/Leon Michels) Menahan Street Band 2:42

8. "Heartaches and Pain" (Charles Bradley/Thomas Brenneck) Charles Bradley 2:54

9. "Unbroken Unshaven" (Thomas Brenneck/Jared Tankel) The Budos Band 2:57

10. "Retreat!" (Bosco Mann) Sharon Jones and the Dap-Kings 3:35

11. "Witches Boogaloo" (Joe Crispiano/Dave Guy/Bosco Mann/ Neal Sugarman/Adam Scone/Rudy Petschauer) The Sugarman Three 4:02

12. "Look Closer (Can't You See the Signs?)" (Joe Crispiano/Cheme Gastelum/Wayne Gordon/Bosco Mann/Homer Steinweiss) Saun and Starr 3:43

13. "Keep Coming Back" (Menahan Street Band) Menahan Street Band 3:14

14. "I Learned the Hard Way" (Bosco Mann) Sharon Jones and the Dap-Kings 3:46

15. "Got to Get Back to My Baby" (Thomas Brenneck/Daniel Foder/Jared Tankel) The Sugarman Three 4:40

16. "Aphasia" (Thomas Brenneck/Daniel Foder/Mike Deller) The Budos Band 4:17

17. "Out of the Wilderness" (traditional) The Como Mamas 4:10

18. "Little Boys with Shiny Toys" (Homer Steinweiss) Sharon Jones and the Dap-Kings 3:58

19. "You Gotta Move" (Mississippi Fred McDowell) Naomi Shelton and the Gospel Queens 3:01

20. "Luv Jones" (Thomas Brenneck/Dave Guy/LaRose Jackson/
    Leon Michels) Charles Bradley and LaRose Jackson 3:50
21. "Thunderclap" (The Dap-Kings) Sharon Jones and the
    Dap-Kings 2:56

There's no business like soul business, and with casual but informa-
tive liner notes penned by soul DJ extraordinaire Mr. Fine Wine from
WFMU's *Downtown Soulville*, that special Daptone spirit is celebrated
again on this second collection of 45-rpm gems. I'm especially fond of
a descriptive phrase Mr. Wine coined to capture some of Jones's paradoxical riffing about having better things to do than remember her old
flame, with an instrumental party simmering in the background of her
mid-tempo moaning. He calls it "an instant classic of the ambiguous-
breakup-song subgenre of soul." It suddenly struck me that this is precisely what so much of the Dap-Kings music featuring Sharon really is
about: breakups that don't quite stay broken but get carried around with
us, day by day.

Mr. Wine's other declaration is equally right on target: "This is the
label, a family of musicians, at the top of its game. Do you know how
lucky we are to witness Daptone in its prime? Not because they 'sound
old,' that's not the point, what they sound is heartfelt and damn good!
And that's the highest compliment I can give." Indeed, the Daptone crew
was rightfully proud of building its studio from the ground up, adding
down-home finishing touches such as installing old clothing under the
floorboards of the isolation booth where singers and soloists record their
parts to give vibrancy and warmth to the sound. All such attention to
historical analog detail provides ample evidence of what makes them so
special in the tenderhearted business of *straight-to-the-gut soul*.

As a result, some of the label's signature sound references great singers like Wendy Rene (Mary Frierson), who first recorded with the Dra-
pels from 1962 to 1967 and then went solo with such gems as "Give You
What I Got," "The Same Guy," and her magnificent "After Laughter
Comes the Tears" in 1964. The best parallels between Rene and Jones

are found in early Daptone singles such as "Got a Thing on My Mind" from 2001, which speeds along at a supersonic rate, its lyrics rippling and almost overlapping: "Sure 'nuff gonna find it, don't let nobody tell me my thing it won't come true."

The song "Better Things" from *I Learned the Hard Way* is perhaps the ideal Jones tune in this great sequel singles mix, which also features a ton of other superb Daptone label superstars. It rocks and rolls its way along a jagged dance of freedom, furiously declaring, "I got better things to do, better things to do than remember you."

It's a Holiday Soul Party (DAP-037)
Released October 30, 2015
Duration: 33:42
Personnel: Sharon Jones: vocals / Thomas Brenneck: guitars, piano / Dave Guy: trumpet / Ian Hendrickson-Smith: baritone saxophone, flute / Gabriel Roth: bass / Homer Steinweiss: drums / Neal Sugarman: tenor saxophone / Fernando Velez: bongos, congas, tambourine.

1. "8 Days (of Hanukkah)" (The Dap-Kings) 3:42
2. "Ain't No Chimneys in the Projects" (Sharon Jones) 2:22
3. "White Christmas" (Irving Berlin) 2:17
4. "Just Another Christmas Song" (Homer Steinweiss) 3:08
5. "Silent Night" (traditional) 4:16
6. "Big Bulbs" (The Dap-Kings) 2:56
7. "Please Come Home for Christmas" (Gene Redd) 2:58
8. "Funky Little Drummer Boy" (The Dap-Kings) 3:18
9. "Silver Bells" (Ray Evans/Jay Livingston) 3:19
10. "World of Love" (Binky Griptite) 3:19
11. "God Rest Ye Merry Gents" (The Dap-Kings) 2:17

It's a hot *Holiday Soul Party*. This pleasant little 2015 romp is exactly what the title suggests: a raunchy ride through seasonal classics dragged up and down the church pews into a deep-funk groove, while the musicians party ferociously and breathe passionate new life into the tradition of roasting chestnuts, both the real kind and the kind made of our shared song history. The word "celebration" takes on a hot new meaning in the hands of Jones and her boys.

This album also contains one of Jones's earliest and most heartfelt songs, reflecting on the meaning of Christmas growing up in the poor urban neighborhoods of public housing. Another song, "Funky Little Drummer Boy," is almost impossible to describe: it's a living love affair between bass, horns, and drums—and, of course, that voice. What they do to this hoary old chestnut is simply divine, and even though an army of other pop stars has played around with it, too, but either devotionally or deviantly, their versions all fade away next to hers.

Miss Sharon Jones!: The Soundtrack (DAP-043)
Released August 19, 2016
Duration: 57:04
Personnel: Sharon Jones: vocals / Homer Steinweiss: drums: / Binky Griptite: guitars / Joseph Crispiano: guitar / Gabriel Roth: bass / Neal Sugarman: tenor saxophone, piano / Cochemea Gastelum: baritone saxophone / Dave Guy: trumpet / Fernando Velez: tambourine, congas.

1. "Tell Me" (Sharon Jones, Neal Sugarman) 2:47
2. "Retreat!" (Bosco Mann) 3:34
3. "Genuine, Pt. 1" (Bosco Mann) 3:58
4. "Longer and Stronger" (Bosco Mann) 3:42
5. "If You Call" (Bosco Mann) 2:59
6. "100 Days, 100 Nights" (Bosco Mann) 3:45
7. "People Don't Get What They Deserve" (Bosco Mann) 3:24
8. "Humble Me" (Bosco Mann) 4:05
9. "I'll Still Be True" (Thomas Brenneck, Homer Steinweiss) 3:47
10. "Let Them Knock" (Bosco Mann) 4:28

11. "Stranger to My Happiness" (Bosco Mann) 3:31

12. "Keep On Looking" (Thomas Brenneck, Homer Steinweiss) 2:49

13. "Mama Don't Like My Man" (Bosco Mann) 2:30

14. "I Learned the Hard Way" (Bosco Mann) 3:46

15. "Slow Down, Love" (Bosco Mann) 4:01

16. "I'm Still Here" (Sharon Jones and the Dap-Kings) 3:58

As *AllMusic*'s Mark Deming aptly put it, as "a solid introduction to Jones's music, or a convenient overview of her career to date, this album does it well, and shows why she's made it into the big leagues against all the odds."

The song "People Don't Get What They Deserve" is not only a rollicking soul romp—and it is that—it is also a kind of backstory for Jones in general. "Money don't follow sweat, money don't follow brains, money don't follow deeds of reason." It's a plaintive wail, not a complaint so much as a statement of how unfair life can often be. After growing up believing that each person gets rewarded in direct relation to what they deserve and how hard they've worked, eventually the more grown-up realization is a more sorrowful one. She never got what she deserved for the simple reason that no one ever really does.

This sad song from her *I Learned the Hard Way* album feels like a constant reminder of her own life story: something inside her always lets her know when things are going wrong in a love affair. Jones learned the hard way, from personal experience, and now she knows: this seems to have been the perennial human lament in almost every blues, soul, or funk song, and is especially present at the core of so many great Sharon Jones songs: the realization that home is where the heart was, even if it is also broken.

Nominated for an Academy Award for "Best Original Song in a Documentary," "I'm Still Here" was a collective composition by Sharon and the band while they were together in the studio, contemplating their next album. Cochemea Gastelum has described how he happened to be sitting next to Jones with a notepad when she told him that she wanted to tell her personal story in a song. She had begun to narrate the tale of how she had left North Augusta with her mother in the '60s and arrived in New York, and then the whole band started "bashing the story into lyrics" together, communally.

The song is quite a heart-tugger, whether or not you know the particulars of Jones's personal narrative. The *Hollywood Reporter* noted, "The right song can help create a mood that sums up the spirit of a film. 'I'm Still Here,' which, like many of these contenders, plays over the film's end credits, became a battle cry for Jones in the face of her fight against pancreatic cancer. . . . The song, credited to the full band, has taken on an extra dimension following Jones's death, says Gastelum. 'Now that she's gone, I hear the song, and it's like the meaning is, she's still here . . . her energy is still here.'"

Listeners to the song itself—during the film's closing moments or on the movie soundtrack album—can easily attest to how moving it is in its deceptive simplicity. Jones sings with an almost brutal honesty likely gleaned from playing so many tiny drinking holes around the world prior to her late blooming fame. "Sometimes you just got to let those little things go." Perhaps, but it was much harder for us to let *her* go.

Soul of a Woman (DAP-004)

Released November 17, 2017
Duration: 35:38
Produced by Bosco Mann
Personnel: Sharon Jones: vocals / Joseph Crispiano: guitar / Homer Steinweiss: drums / Cochemea Gastelum: saxophone / Binky Griptite: guitar / Dave Guy: trumpet / Bosco Mann: bass / Neal Sugarman: saxophone / Fernando Velez: percussion / Saun and Starr: background vocals. *Also featuring*: the Universal Church of God Choir: background vocals ("Call on God") / Chris Davis: trumpet ("Sail On!") / Brian Wolfe: drums / Victor Axelrod: organ ("Pass Me By" and "Call on God") / Thomas Brenneck: guitar ("Call on God") / Ian Hendrickson-Smith: tenor sax ("Sail On!").

1. "Matter of Time" (Binky Griptite) 3:22
2. "Sail On!" (Cochemea Gastelum) 3:00
3. "Just Give Me Your Time" (Gabe Roth) 2:29
4. "Come and Be a Winner" (Joseph Crispiano) 2:56
5. "Rumors" (Homer Steinweiss, Fernando Velez) 2:33
6. "Pass Me By" (Binky Griptite) 3:20
7. "Searching for a New Day" (Joseph Crispiano, Homer Steinweiss) 3:14
8. "These Tears (No Longer for You)" (Wayne Gordon) 3:35
9. "When I Saw Your Face" (Dave Guy) 3:23
10. "Girl! (You Got to Forgive Him)" (Gabe Roth) 4:09
11. "Call on God" (Sharon Jones) 3:37

As the folks at Daptone Records put it so succinctly in the media release for the album on their label's website, "We told you we had something special for you. Though we'll never again see her electric form shimmy across the stage, Sharon Jones continues to give us her soul and her music. Before she passed away in November of 2016, she was working in the studio with the Dap-Kings recording what would become the final studio album from the band. We are proud to present it, a true testament to the life and career of Daptone's fearless leader and one of the world's greatest performers." Hear, hear. That's not even remotely promotional hyperbole folks, it's just a scientific fact, and one that emphatically illustrates just how much Jones's contagious energy continues to live on.

Listening to this record, which was released one day before the one-year anniversary of her passing, is of course both wistful and elegiac. The LP was recorded to 8-track tape at the House of Soul in Bushwick, New York, during the times when Jones was between medical treatments. "When she was strongest, that's when we go into the studio," bass player and producer Gabe Roth said in his press statement. "Sharon couldn't phone it in, so she would only work when she was really feeling it." And this final album demonstrates just how much she was really feeling it, while the final video release that accompanied it, for the song "Matter of Time," visually captures the intimate grace of those special studio moments with what Roth accurately called "one of the most influential rhythm-and-blues voices of the twenty-first century."

Jon Pareles summed it up well, as he usually does, for the *New York Times*: "Sharon Jones sounds anything but fragile on *Soul of a Woman*: she wails, she shouts, she rasps, she exhorts, she fills phrases with teasing curlicues and holds pure tones endlessly aloft. Her voice and songs stay bold, gutsy and down-to-earth." And as per usual with the Dap-Kings and their gloriously analog label, the record sounds like it was recorded live in the studio, because that's exactly what happened, with each instrument frozen perfectly in space and located in the center of our heads and hearts.

This is definitely a tribute to an entire genre of diverse soul stylings: jumping in place and rumba-like bump-and-grinds on "Sail On"; hand-clapped joyous exuberance on "Rumors"; a sultry girl-group dance-athon in "When I Saw Your Face"; a hopeful and optimistic hymn to justice prevailing (even if it takes forever) in "Matter of Time"; a survivor's anthem of moving beyond a broken heart in "These Tears (No Longer for You)"; and, most impressively, a return to form for a gospel queen on "Call on God," a spiritual tune she wrote way back in the 1970s for the Gospel Wonders at the Universal Church of God. The closing song is a promise of blissful comfort after harrowing sorrow, a lofty emanation celebrating God's support in times of distress—one that strongly states her belief that there'll come a time when she (and, by extension, all of us) will share His love for eternity. With this closing track, Sharon Jones goes back home to where her music first began to take shape: back to church.

Writing for *Bandcamp Daily*, Max Levenson made several astute observations upon the release of this sporadically recorded final venture, most notably the fact that, though struggling, Jones sounds ready to take on the world the way she always did. "In the end, there is no defeat to be found on Jones's final recording. Instead it's a testament to her faith in music and in the power of love. Jones sings her heart out with the same commanding power that has defined her career; you'd be forgiven for thinking this was her first album, not her last." Perhaps most crucially, unlike the recent final albums from David Bowie and Leonard Cohen, both of whom bravely confronted their own mortality head on, the songs Jones delivers celebrate life in "both its highs and its lows," as Levenson observed. "At times Jones is burning brightly in the throes of love, and in other moments, she's stewing in the pits of heartbreak." That paradox is, of course, the ultimate essence of soul music.

I find it impossible not to concur with another equally deep listener from the *New York Times*, Simon Vozick-Levinson, who described the gift of a final album after her loss: "Fans were devastated. One year later her absence is still deeply felt but some solace arrives. It's a remarkable work with highlights that range from anti-war barnburners, recorded in a first take, to orchestral Sturm and Drang." I also agree that for listeners unfamiliar with the late star, if they came across the album in a record store without knowing her history, it'd be easy to mistake it for some lost masterwork from the mid-'70s, since that, after all, was the whole charming point of the Dap-Kings in the first place: revivalist fervor that was real. But as Vozick-Levinson emphasized, that was only part of her importance. "At its best, this album is a reminder that hers was a singular voice, hard to ignore in any era."

Indeed, the final song, "Call on God," can even be considered a bridge between two distant eras in itself, since Jones wrote it for her church choir thirty years earlier, while after her memorial service some of her gospel sisters joined the band in the studio and overdubbed their own choral parts onto the old track. As Roth put it so wistfully to Vozick-Levinson, "They got to sing with her one last time with her in their headphones. It is a beautiful way to complete the album, with something very personal that connected what she'd done her whole life, something that connected the Dap-Kings with the church people to honor her together."

As Daptone cofounder and Dap-Kings saxophonist Neal Sugarman told *Rolling Stone*, "The first time people hear *Soul of a Woman*—especially the hardcore Sharon fans—people are going to get real down, and then it's going to take them back up. From my perspective, it's one more nail in the annals of classic soul records because Sharon has proven through her catalogue and live shows that she is one of the greats. Hopefully these are classic records, which means they'll live on forever."

At the memorial service for Jones, Sugarman declared that when seeing and hearing the musical sisters from her old sacred sound days waft in and out of several classic spiritual melodies, especially Sharon's hymn-like "Call on God," "We were floored!" There was no somber tone to be heard either when they all convened to overlay the choral backing onto a solo hymn that Jones had cut alone in the studio. Suddenly the tune started to soar skyward, carrying some of the implicit message of all things saturated with the Sharon spirit. She took a bite out of everything and just lit everything on fire, in Roth's summary characterization. Indeed, that may as well have been another part of her job description here on earth.

Meanwhile, Sugarman told *Billboard* that it was the very aspect of impending absence that made recording the songs for her posthumous album so riveting, and it's the same internal sense of the temporary that fuels all gospel sounds as well—that sense that our true aspirational home is elsewhere. "I felt she was, at the end, singing better than she had in a long time," he said. "She was grasping her mortality—singing her heart out as much as she could, knowing that it may not go on forever. The recording process was exactly the same, the same group of people, but there was also this sense of, 'What can we play that's going to make it great for Sharon?' If the groove wasn't right, she would tell you."

Roth added that Daptone's analog recording process was also uniquely creative in another way, especially for this posthumous release. An 8-track setup tends to force all the players to step up the intensity level of their delivery, since with tape formats it's harder to hide imperfections or fake someone's performance. This forces the producer to realize the significance of what's happening in the moment, more like a live-concert performance. As Roth put it, with characteristic bluntness, "These records sound great because everyone's playing their asses off."

This has got to be connected with the fact that there's something, if not more *real*, then certainly much more visceral and more transient about what the ear is hearing. It's likely because we are hearing a moment that actually just happened in the studio, maybe even accidentally, as if it were an intimate club setting—or, indeed, even a sacred church setting. If so, it's a special church that has a cherished place for the returning sinners who may have taken a temporary vacation outside the fold.

Jones's posthumous album also has the feel of two very different kinds of records. It could even have been a double-album release, due to the mix of gritty bluesy content with more lush orchestrated string pieces. Its compression into one disc, however, just enhances the multiple facets of the singer and her band all the more, especially the spiritual aspects of its several gospel-tinged pieces. It is in those, of course, that one gets the feeling she had come full circle and was going back to church after straying so far out into the secular world.

Being without Jones has proven poignant but inspiring to her band, who had quickly become like younger brothers and sisters to her through her career, and that's exactly how she treated them. Now, her absence has proven to be a little haunting, as Sugarman explained: "It continues to come in and out in these weird waves of the reality that we're not going to be able to play this music with Sharon anymore."

GET ON UP!
Luck Be a Lady

"Whether it was gospel or soul, it was always about the words for me. Didn't matter if it was 'Please, Please, Please' or 'If I Can Touch the Hem of His Garment.' It was all about reaching the people."
—Naomi Shelton to the *New York Times*, 2009

A bsolutely live! There's nothing else quite like it, especially if it's Sharon Jones in full-throated and full-figured action. In 2014, the suddenly famous soul star confirmed to Oliver Wang of the *Guardian* the vital importance, for her, of appearing live and being up in front of people in order to get the most rewarding return on her vocal artistry. "People buy my albums, and I love my albums too, because when we do them we try to record live with that same energy . . . but I can never get the energy on an album that I have when I'm live on stage." Jones affirmed that she was "hard-giving" in her music, and that's why her personal passion comes out while she's on any stage: all her energy comes pouring out of her and, as she put it, "I'm giving everything back!" She would frequently state a preference for smaller venues—mostly clubs, rather than big theaters, arenas, or stadiums—an understandable preference in her case, since, in large venues, people can't get up to dance. And, in the end, making people *get on up* was at the very core of her missionary function.

This notion of "giving everything back" was probably something she learned from one of her idols, James Brown, and it was a performing trait that came just as naturally to her. In fact, standing on the same stage he once graced at the Apollo Theater, perhaps the sacred temple of secular soul, she came to fully understood what it meant to deliver more hard-working entertainment to her audiences than the average artist would even dream of. She always gave 110 percent of her 110 pounds.

It took a lot to stop Jones from offering this kind of live personal delivery to her fans in concert, but then, while preparing to complete *Give the People What They Want* ahead of its slated release, she was diagnosed with cancer, and both the much-anticipated project and her subsequent tour had to be delayed. This period in Jones's life and career is well-documented in *Miss Sharon Jones!*, the heart-stirring film by Academy Award–winning filmmaker Barbara Kopple (director of *Harlan County, USA*, and *American Dream*). Few documentaries on musicians manage to capture and convey raw dedication and tenacity as well as this one. It often seems in the film that the only thing she is ever actually dying from is her forced absence from the stage.

Eventually, after a hiatus, Jones's sixth studio recording arrived on January 14, 2014. It would be nominated for a Grammy for "Best R&B Album" the following year. Jones often rued the fact that she was placed in the R&B category, not Soul, where she belongs, although weirdly there is no Soul category at the Grammys. Once again, though, it was clear to critics and listening audiences alike that this album and Jones's music in general were preserving a soul tradition while also exploding and amplifying it at the same time—no mean feat. Which meant that it was time for Jones and her instant soul party to go out on the road once again. The road was where music *really* happened: live.

For *Spin* magazine's Anupa Mistry, Jones's concerts proved that "music from another time can still thrill us in this one because of its practically tyrannical insistence on bliss." This telling theme, the tyrannical insistence on bliss, is both the key to her style and also the reason for her personal survival. And the best snapshot of that bliss in action would always have to be a survey of her copious live performances. Most poignantly, Abbey Simmons, the band's assistant tour manager and Sharon's closest nurturer and caretaker, told Jacob Blickenstaff (the gifted photographer who captured the incendiary live image on the cover of this book) of the *New York Times*, "Basically, Sharon wants to die on stage."

After Jones's passing, Nina Corcoran of *Nerdist* compiled a very good list of what she considered the singer's finest concert performances, a personal favorite combination of songs making up a kind of utopian Sharon Jones night out. Corcoran's purpose was to demonstrate "just how contagious her vibrant positivity was," and she succeeded in doing so. "Let's cherish the life that Sharon Jones lived because one thing is certain, she's still singing her heart out on a different plane and giving it to all of us from above," she concluded.

I can easily concur with Corcoran's choice of peak performances, which are definitely among the most memorable of Jones's dervish-like whirls across our global stages. In particular, Jones's 2009 rendition of "Let Them Knock" in Sydney, Australia, was a glory to behold; having just come off the high of recording and releasing *100 Days, 100 Nights*, she took the band, the stage, and the audience to incredible heights with her heavy-duty delivery. "Watching her command the stage with unbridled spirit, she is invincible," Corcoran observed. "You're tempted to take a sip of water just watching her shake it."

I would also definitely agree that Jones and her rock-steady band seemed to start a humble flame and pour more and more soul fuel onto it until it became a raging bonfire. The sheer intensity and heat was especially evident when one saw them live and heard what Jones was capable of once she was unleashed and reached her emotional peak. Geoffrey Himes of *Paste* magazine conveyed this well in his own 2016 tribute to Jones's otherworldly empathic skills. "It was only when you saw Sharon Jones and the Dap-Kings live onstage that you understood their immense appeal. Like her role model James Brown, she created a performance that linked the sound of her voice to the movements of her body to the mood of the moment. That created an experience that could only be approximated by recordings or even by videos. The sheer physicality of being in the same space with her was transformative."

This force field was further evidence of the primary distinction between the elder trouper and the many younger stars that could be spectacular in the studio but so often wilted in front of an audience. Jones was the opposite: a wildflower that only fully bloomed once it was in front of a live crowd urging her on. It's certainly true that the archival documents of her recordings are carefully crafted and perfectly produced sonic diagrams of something that had to be seen and heard to be believed. And yet even then one couldn't believe it, any more than your eyes and ears could fully register the sizzling live and embodied experience of Mr. Brown in his prime. David Ma of the *Guardian* was even more precise in conveying what her physical presence really meant: "If you were lucky enough to see her perform live, you felt as if you had underpaid. The band backing her up and letting her float over their deep groove worked equally hard, though like all the most gifted artists, they had a special knack for making it look effortless."

Several of Jones's signature concert performances capture her distinct *joie de vivre* and what I'd identify as her volatile combination of vim, vigor, and verve. They illustrate what Ma meant by that curious feeling of having felt like you've had an experience for which you hadn't paid nearly enough. There's also a pleasant growth curve in the scale of these appearances as Jones and her band go from relatively small clubs to medium size theatres and finally to large stadiums as more and more people became acquainted with the magic of her mojo.

A few of the Dap-Kings' earliest tours, for instance, took in venues in the Netherlands holding a couple of hundred attendees—roughly the same size as the Phoenix Club in Toronto, where music critic John Corcelli was bowled over by Jones and her boys. These halls may have been the most ideal for allowing the proper level of intimacy in order to most effectively absorb what Jones was putting out. But of course, as Dapette Saundra Williams pointed out to me most emphatically about the power of those Sharon Jones vocal chords, "Sharon could take the largest arena or stadium and just shrink it down to the size of your own living room at home. She made you feel at home. Sometimes it was an intimacy so profound it was scary."

The *Hollywood Reporter*, in assessing a Daptone Soul Revue appearance by Jones and Charles Bradley, among other label favorites, at the fabled Apollo Theater in 2014, suitably referenced her early inspiration, James Brown. "The hardest working man in show business may have set a high standard in this concert room back in 1962, but Jones had little trouble keeping the stage warm in his absence." That critical take alone must have made Jones, the woman whose name had practically become synonymous with challenges, feel that all her struggles had been worthwhile.

In an *Under the Radar* interview that same year, Matt Fink lauded Jones, noting how her music had been a comfort to so many people in hard times and asking if music in general had served the same purpose for *her* through her own tough struggles, and how such challenges changed her outlook on life. "You realize you can be gone any minute," she responded, with typical Sharon Jones candor. "Life is precious. . . . While you are here, you have to follow your heart and your dream . . . and that's what I'm doing, putting out this music. We're trying to keep that Motown, Stax soul music alive, and I think that's what we're accomplishing with what we're doing." Indeed they were, especially in the live shows that became identified so deeply with her personal connection with her audience. The following concert cross-section of Jones and the Dap-Kings' ascent provides a snapshot of how they thrived best, live onstage, in front of mesmerized human beings.

THE DOLHUIS, DORDRECHT, THE NETHERLANDS, DECEMBER 24, 2003

Fittingly, given the back-to-the-roots aesthetic of Jones and the Dap-Kings and the whole Daptone operation, one of their earliest and most intense performances was at this noble heritage building. Originally a monastery erected in the year 1463 (talk about back to the roots!), in the twenty-first century it rapidly developed a reputation as a cultural and musical center devoted to new and emerging artists and offering a phenomenally hospitable acoustic environment highly attuned to the vibe of blues and soul artists.

Since they only released one album, *Dap-Dippin'*, at this point, the set lists at these early concerts—ostensibly the Daptone version of a promotion tour—were naturally somewhat limited, though there was also a flock of steaming singles and standard soul classics to choose from as well. In a sense, Sharon and her boys were getting their sea legs with these early gigs.

This concert opened, as most later appearances also would, with the band entering into a devout love affair with Booker T. and laying down an instrumental carpet in preparation for their singer. The horn section in particular provided a hot, swinging groove lifted up by the sweltering time signature of bass and drums until Queen Jones arrives, in her crouching stance, to implore the tiny crowd, "Do you feel all right, are you feelin' all right?" before shifting into a perfect grab bag of James Brown gems and improvised soul worship at the altar of funk.

THE BEAT CLUB, DORDRECHT, THE NETHERLANDS, MARCH 29, 2005

Beat Club is an important Dutch outlet for what has come quaintly to be called "vintage" music, with a steady and growing following locally and globally. Founded in 2003 to remedy a perceived lack of vital live music clubs, it started at first as an organic range of small ultra-underground venues, closer to private parties than formal concerts, but over the years, word of mouth and the Dutch appetite for vintage sounds has allowed these venues to grow exponentially along with their audiences.

Across their 2005 tour, Jones and her band would fold into their menu additional new songs from their second album release, *Naturally*, and start to expand upon the raunchy repertoire they were beginning to hone down to a finely tuned soul machine. This performance was recorded and mixed for broadcast by Ben Mendes of NPO Radio. The Dap-Kings open with instrumental sparklers called "Nervous Like Me" and "Razor Blade" before sliding into their customary introduction of the woman everyone has come to see as she stalks the stage and flings her stocky frame around in a commanding ritual of losing it. Their four minute and twenty-three second introduction had by now become a template, but a really fine one. They welcome the crowd to their Desco Soul Revue (as it was then called): "Are you are ready to get funked up? Do you know who you came here to see?"

Jones comes dancing onstage, her shiny silver dress looking like it had been spray painted on her, already in high gear (she only had one gear really), and slips into "How Do I Let a Good Man Down?" from *Naturally*. At this point she really lets loose, calling out, "Band! It's time for me to get a little wet up here!" And that's just what she does, grinding out "Got to Be the Way It Is" before slowing things down a bit with "How Long Do I Have to Wait for You?"

By the time she arrives at "Your Thing Is a Drag," Jones is covered in sweat and just beginning to let go totally with her unbridled sex appeal—the kind that Beyoncé couldn't ever hope to even approximate, let alone equal. She flails around a handkerchief, like Louis Armstrong: "I know you think you've got your own new bag, but your thing . . . is a drag." But then it's "time for me to get a little serious, gotta get a little political up in here" as she launches into a message to then-president George W. Bush about visiting him "with attitude" (and the same damp, silvery dress) and demanding to know how he would fund all his guns and bombs and warfare "if we all stopped paying taxes."

Jones's taxation lament is also the perfect segue into a true national anthem originally penned by folk activist Woody Guthrie but utterly reinvented from the ground up by Jones and her boys, "This Land Is Your Land." What she does to this folk classic is a spectacle to behold and hear—a living marvel. Then, as she slides into "Fish in the Dish," Jones channels the pure sexy raunch of Bessie Smith or Big Mama Thornton, before announcing, "Well, Janet Jackson's got her version of this song but this here's my version. Let's go." With that, she delivers a version of "What Have You Done for Me Lately?" that would leave Janet's jaw dropping. Then it's time for her to revisit the ghost of James

Brown again on "Things Got to Get Better" . . . before it's too late.

The Dutch host and radio broadcaster Ben Mendes put it most succinctly: "No matter where Sharon Jones is or what kind of music she's singing, the strength of her gospel roots enables her to pour her soul into every note she sings and lets anyone who hears her know that Jones is Soul Sister #1."

SYDNEY FESTIVAL, SYDNEY, AUSTRALIA, JANUARY 11, 2009

Set list: Intro / "Mellomatic Mood" / "I'm Not Gonna Cry" / "How Do I Let a Good Man Down?" / "Miss Jones's History Lesson" / "Keep on Looking" / "You're Gonna Get It" / "Be Easy" / "What Have You Done for Me Lately?" / "There Was a Time" / "Let Them Knock" / "Tell Me" / "Road of Broken Hearted Men" / "Are You Going to Give It Back?" / "Got to Be the Way It Is" / "A Change Is Gonna Come" / "100 Days, 100 Nights" / Encore: "My Man Is a Mean Man"

In between the release of *100 Days, 100 Nights* and *I Learned the Hard Way*, with a steaming-hot and fresh assortment of ever expanding material, Jones and the Dap-Kings seemed to really enjoy their reception from fans way down under, and they went back as often as possible. At the Sydney Festival in 2009, they treated the Aussie audience to their special brand of soul-infused funk, with Jones delivering her usual stunningly personal and acrobatic style of bluesy bounce.

By now, the crew had gotten the ritual down to a fine art—including, of course, the hothouse intro evoking the famous James Brown's frenzied preparation of yore: "Ladies and gentlemen there are seven acknowledged wonders of the world, you are about to meet the eighth!" As usual, Jones is in fine form, and after delivering the opening dishes on the menu she launches into something called "Miss Jones's History Lesson," a rappy little confection in which she explains "a few things about Sharon Jones and the Dap-Kings," including the fact that they've been around for about thirteen years but "y'all may not have heard of us . . . until along came Amy Winehouse and she snatched them away and took the Dap-Kings on a little adventure." She then thanks Amy and Mark Ronson for that little adventure and shares some of what she was doing while she waited for the Amy merry-go-round to end, as end it must.

Now she wants to show y'all where she comes from, so she begins her conversation with the group: "Band—hey, Dap-Kings!" "Yeah!" "Time to let Sharon Jones work it out." What that means is diving into a rap about two hundred years of her ancestry, which of course also requires that she take off her shoes, an inevitable part of every show that would get the crowd hollering as much as when some pretty young things start stripping off their clothes. Then the history lesson commences—West Africa, abduction, chains, boats; traveling involuntarily to America but still always dancing for hope—while Jones begins to shimmy in a way that's impossible to describe. It's a spirit dance, a Yoruba whirlwind that instantly helps the audience understand where gospel music, soul, and funk all came from.

Jones then starts a trip back through time, back to her hometown and to Mr. Brown's hometown, Augusta, Georgia, and collides with a J.B. classic, "There Was a Time." Even through the humble lens of the Moshcam, a rough-and-tumble video shot from inside the crowd, it's obvious that we're all in another dimension by now. Jones is in a trance of sorts; the audience is lifted up on her throbbing little worker's body as she tells us all about "The Road of Broken Hearted Men," and we're stunned: is this soul, is it funk, or is this gospel? The answer is yes!

By the time Jones and the band arrive at their encore of "My Man Is a Mean Man," the ultimate anti-torch song, those in the audience look as though they have been competing in the Olympics of Pain and Joy. Their faces are transported, transcendent, mystified, testified, and re-fried. Yes, it's been a religious experience, but no one knows exactly what faith has been celebrated. All they know is that they've just witnessed something from beyond descend down among them before lifting off and leaving them breathlessly hopeful. They've just all been given an intravenous transfusion from the custodian of hope: Sharon Jones.

STUBB'S, SXSW FESTIVAL, AUSTIN, TEXAS, MARCH 17, 2010 (BROADCAST ON NPR MUSIC) / AUSTIN MUSIC HALL, AUSTIN, TEXAS, MARCH 19, 2010

Set list: "I'll Still Be Here" / "I'm Not Gonna Cry" / "Road of Broken Hearted Men" / "This Land Is Your Land" / "Give It Back" / "She Ain't a Child No More" / "100 Days, 100 Nights"

Deep in the heart of the heart of Texas. The promotional material for these shows described Jones and the Dap-Kings as the kind of infectious, authentic soul and funk music that always inspires crowds to party like it's 1969, and I couldn't agree more. They *are* permanently grooving in 1969, yet in a way that will still be utterly fresh sounding in 2019. Stubb's was a tiny BBQ juke joint ideally situated to host an intimate Jones concert—the kind where you could be hit with the sweat bouncing off her flailing frame.

The Austin Music Hall, though a welcome addition to the city's venues and a good medium-sized theater location, had often encountered challenges since opening in 1995, including questionable acoustics and poor sightlines, and would eventually close down in 2016 to make way for new downtown office towers. In 2009, however, both of these venues rocked with the jittery Jones vibe during that year's edition of the storied South by Southwest Music Festival.

Jones comes out wiggling right away in her pale green sequined dress and launches into a session of superior *double entendre* and bottom-wagging while asking the crowd if they like her new dress and shoes (they did) and slithering her way into "I'll Still Be True" (from *I Learned the Hard Way*) and "I'm Not Gonna Cry" (a sultry single from *Daptone Gold*). Two covers follow: the Bobby Blue Bland tune "Road of Broken Hearted Men," which suited her perfectly, and her remarkable interpretation of Woody Guthrie's "This Land Is Your Land," which seems to improve with age every time they dish it out. "Give It Back" is a delightfully reverbed soul merger of Mary Wells blended with the Shangri-Las.

Jones then starts to grunt and sweat it out with the up-tempo "She Ain't a Child No More," which is incongruously about child mistreatment due to parental overindulging in alcohol but still comes across like a love affair gone bad. Few closing songs would ever be as climactic as the show-stopping "100 Days, 100 Nights" of Jones's farewell to the Music Hall. But it's the Stubb's show, which luckily was broadcast live by NPR, that really captured Jones's sense of urgency and joy as a performer. It's worth listening to the live recording and trying to imagine what it must have felt like to be sitting so close to her soul juice that your table would have been bombarded by bullets of goddess sweat.

CRYSTAL BALLROOM, PORTLAND, OREGON, JUNE 24, 2010

In the gorgeous heritage site of the Crystal Ballroom, Jones had the almost perfect venue, in terms of scale and ambience. Those who attend concerts at the Ballroom seem to be inspired by an energy emanating from the site itself—a phenomenon that social scientists refer to as "the power of place." The venue was originally built as Cotillion Hall in 1914; dance revivals were staged there throughout the Great Depression, and it has for over a century served as a premier location for live music and every other conceivable kind of cultural event. Its storied history has included police raids, visits by silent-screen idols and beat poets, psychedelic light shows in the '60s, narrow escapes from destruction by fire, demolition, and neglect, and finally its listing as a treasure in the National Register of Historic Places. Both James Brown and the Ike and Tina Turner Revue appeared there to great acclaim, as would Sharon Jones and the Dap-Kings, grooving to a crowd of about 1,500 standing (or twitching) patrons.

One reviewer who wrote about this event for the *Oregonian*, Kevin Friedman, delivered an amusing, tongue-in-cheek piece about his impossible attempt to play the part of an objective journalist when his listener's mind had been blown to pieces and melted into a pool of goo on the floor of the venue. While he admitted that such was the response to most Jones affairs, this one was better, hotter, and higher than anything he'd ever witnessed before or since. "I'm talking about an off the hook, can't help but move, standing is not an option, sweat from every pore kind of show."

Like the rest of us who have observed Jones in action, the 1,500 souls in the Crystal were amazed at the way this tiny fifty-four-year-old woman had so much energy oozing out of her that every single person felt like she was singing and dancing with *them*. But after whipping them into a frenzy and forcing them all to dance, she would outlast them all, all night long. "What fountain of youth she tapped into that she can do this," Friedman wondered, "not only on a given night, but apparently every night, boggles the already boggled mind!"

As per their usual ritual, the eleven-member Dap-King crew take to the stage first and deliver several original instrumentals, often impromptu jams, to start cooking the crowd in preparation for their apparition's arrival. The Kings' presentation has by this time been polished to a fine sheen, reflecting the classic soul revues of Mr. Dynamite in the '60s and '70s, and is designed to create a mood and increase the temperature of the room. Again echoing the style of Brown's keeper, Danny Ray, guitarist/MC Griptite booms out the names of the many hits of Miss Jones, with the band delivering ripping riffs from each song as he rapidly names the titles.

By the time Jones arrives onstage to plunge into the bluesy growl of "I Learned the Hard Way," the crowd's ovation almost feels like most performers' encore applause, the audience's emotions having been marinated to perfection by the band's setup. Each new song is featured in a kind of tapestry, allowing whole instrumental sections of the band to spare some equal time to show off their wares, though the entire enterprise is clearly designed to lift up, support, and showcase the vocalist and her yelping moans. They swiftly groove through "She Ain't a Child No More" and her funked-up version of Guthrie's "This Land Is Your Land," while "The Game Gets Old," for which she's supported by her girl backups, almost recalls the swinging of '60s girl groups such as the Ronettes or the Shirelles, but emotionally boosted up to a new dark majesty.

Again as usual, the band members stand stoically behind Jones in their cool sharkskin suits and let her deliver all the pathos and feeling on her own, without distracting with any flashy histrionics of their own, though they do emphasize their superior skills as instrumental drivers. It is Jones who commands the spotlight in her fringed flapper dress, sending off sparks from her heels as she click-clacks her way across the stage as if it were a soccer field, frequently rattling off bursts of staccato verbiage over the band in a patter crafted to tickle the crowd in places they never even knew they had. Particularly mesmerizing is her supersonic demonstration of certain dance crazes from about 1965—the boogaloo, the tighten-up, the hitchhiker, the swim—exactly as Brown used to do in his Apollo Theater appearances. But still it isn't nostalgic; it's just too real to feel contrived.

Eventually, Jones is left almost alone onstage, with only her backup babes and Binky alongside her, to deliver "Mama Don't Like My Man." Then, after a few more numbers from her early albums, she brings the house down with an encore of "100 Days, 100 Nights," a song that Friedman described as one that "fully transformed the Crystal Ballroom into a swampy, Chitlin' circuit juke-joint, the bodies in the audience writhing to an almost work-song style chant." This is what show business is all about.

NANCY PULSATIONS JAZZ FESTIVAL, NANCY, FRANCE, OCTOBER 6, 2010
Set list: "If You Call" / "Without a Heart" / "Give It Back" / "When I Get Home" / "The Game Gets Old" / "Money" / "She Ain't a Child No More" / "I Learned the Hard Way" / "I'm Not Gonna Cry" / "Window Shopping" / "Better Things" / "Mean Man" / "This Land Is Your Land" / "100 Days, 100 Nights"

Nancy Pulsations is a notable Gallic festival of jazz and multiple contemporary genres of related music, among them soul and funk, that takes place each year during the first two weeks in October. Launched in 1973 by local Nancy groups who wanted to organize a major jazz event in Lorraine, Pulsations has since established itself as a serious destination for festivalgoers. The lineup is eclectic in the extreme, with rock, pop, electro, soul, hip-hop, blues, reggae, folk, and jazz idioms all featured over fifteen feverish days. In 2010, among luminaries such as John Mayall, Eddie Gomez, and Marcus Miller, the still newish Sharon Jones and the Dap-Kings served up a huge dollop of the hot Sharon spice that would soon make them legendary.

To begin with, Pulsations is the ideal festival name to encapsulate what happens when Jones sidesteps onto the stage and demands to know if "everyone is feeling all right." But that's not good enough, because she's about to make them feel like they never felt anything before in their French lives. Maybe a little like Edith Piaf mixed with Josephine Baker, but on emotional steroids—the natural kind of supplement Jones specializes in prescribing for every spiritual illness. The doctor of delight is in the house.

This particular concert version of "If You Call" contains more blistering soul in a slow-motion mode than most complete albums by an army of young, ersatz synth-soul singers of today. Swaying and swooning, gliding like a melting glacier across the stage, this sorrowful song might have been a perfect vehicle for someone like the late Amy Winehouse, if she'd been better equipped to handle her stardom.

Bopping around in her low-cut dress, Jones runs through the full gamut of emotions and scales the heights with her Mary Wells–like crooning of "Window Shopping" and "Better Things," in which she proudly announces that she's a better woman than she's ever been, especially when not remembering what has been. She has "better things to do than remember you"—perhaps the ultimate anti-torch song.

At this stage, of course, Jones was in her prime, still two or three years away from her late struggles, full of gutsy laughter and parading the full impact of her pleasure at doing what she loved to do most: entertain the hell out of people and invite them into her private heaven.

STADE DE FRANCE, SAINT-DENIS, PARIS, FRANCE, JUNE 30, 2011

Yes, this was a Prince concert in a big, big outdoor stadium, but when Sharon Jones and the Dap-Kings opened for him during several of his stints in Paris, he was stunned by the grit of what she gave out.

Even though it's only nine minutes and eleven seconds long, Jones's version of "When I Come Home" is so hot, so dynamic, so filled with whoopee that it feels like a full concert. It also boasts a cameo appearance by His Purpleness himself, during which he unleashes a guitar solo that's at his usual sublime level but still doesn't approach the altitude at which Jones is flying when he enters the fray. It's worth watching the live footage, even though the audio was only roughly captured from the soundboard, in order to be reminded of what it meant to see Jones unleash her full fury. Though the vibe isn't quite the same as at the smaller clubs and theaters that suited her personality to a tee, it's still gratifying to see her so uplifted by the love of a huge crowd.

MADISON SQUARE GARDEN, NEW YORK CITY, FEBRUARY 19, 2016
Set list: Instrumental Intro / "Retreat!" / "If You Call" / "Stranger to My Happiness" / "She Ain't a Child No More" / "Long Time, Wrong Time" / "People Don't Get What They Deserve" / "Let Them Knock" / "I'm Not Gonna Cry" / "100 Days, 100 Nights"

Yes, the mortality clock had started ticking. Several of Jones's later shows—after her comeback celebrations, with her practically in the midst of knocking on heaven's door—showcased the indomitable spirit that fueled that little container of hers. Finally having arrived at big-league venues such as the Garden in New York, and having won the acclaim and admiration of a global audience, these last shows were bittersweet affairs. And yet, no matter how big the stadium was—as in this case, when she opened for the Hall and Oates tour—she still made the place shrink down in scale and the crowd feel that they were in her own living room at home.

Several things are notably different from the earlier live appearances by Jones and her band. The first is the most obvious one: Madison Square Garden is about twenty times the scale of some of their debut venues. The second is that, by the winter of 2016, their acclaim was such that most people in New York would have known that they might be witnessing her soul train pass by for one of the last times. The Dap-Kings' MC, the erstwhile Mr. Griptite, conveyed both aspects clearly when he closed out the set, after Jones's rendition of "100 Days, 100 Nights," by thanking both the crowd in "the greatest arena in the world" and the singer whose heart was so big she could easily fill that huge stadium with her love.

SEATTLE CENTER, SEATTLE, WASHINGTON, APRIL 16, 2016

The Seattle radio station KEXP presents free outdoor weekend concerts each August for a program called *Concerts at the Mural*, and this 2016 appearance was in celebration of the inauguration of the station's new home base at the Seattle Center, a civic, arts, social, and cultural gathering place devoted to creating exceptional urban experiences. This free concert was most certainly one of them. Presented only six months before Jones's passing, it already felt somewhat elegiac, almost as if a pre-mourning sentiment had settled over the sun-drenched outdoors crowd.

The band gave their usual sparkling opening intro, with MC Griptite bringing out Sharon in her gold lamé dress for a rousing version of what had become by then their own soul standard, "100 Days, 100 Nights." They started out ripping along, but at Jones's request began to slow it down to a kind of dirge-like rowing rhythm whose obvious gospel vibes couldn't be mistaken.

Jones teased the crowd at one point by saying that the next tune, a Gladys Knight and the Pips song, was recorded when Gladys was all of eighteen years old, but that "this fifty-nine-year-old woman up here gonna try to sound eighteen for y'all." And when she sang, "In every beat of my heart there's a beat for you, you're my inspiration and anything I do I'll do for you," pointing out to the swaying audience, they knew whereof she spoke. So did the band. In the footage filmed for this grand opening of the new KEXP broadcast station, every so often the camera lingers on the musicians who, while busy doing their thing, steal glances at their frontline singing star and can't disguise the combination of love, admiration, fear, and sadness they feel about the scope and depth of her struggle.

This band and their singer practically lived on the road, performing over 800 concerts given during their life as an active unit. The first was on August 9, 1999, at the Mercury Lounge in New York, also featuring the Soul Providers, Lee Fields, the Mighty Imperials, and the Sugarman Three, and came prior to their first album's release and indeed to the formation of Daptone Records. The second, on May 14, 2002, was given on the release date of their first album, *Dap-Dippin'*. Jones was involved in all of them apart from the last two in late 2016. These final two concerts were presented in the sad absence of Sharon Jones. On October 3, 2016, the band played on the South Lawn at the White House in Washington, D.C.; and on November 18, 2016 (the very day of her passing and in tribute to her spiritual presence), they were at the New Jersey Performing Arts Center in Newark, New Jersey.

By the time her final concerts rolled around, it was perfectly obvious to anyone with eyes and ears that Jones wasn't just singing soul music anymore—she was offering herself up as a living and breathing embodiment of the true dimensions of what her own gigantic soul tried every day to approximate: the faithful funk of gospel fury.

STILL TESTIFYING
The Way It Is

"Painless preaching is as good a term as any for what we do. If you're going to come away from a party singing the lyrics to a soul song, it's better that you sing of self-pride, like 'we're a winner,' instead of just 'do the boo-ga-loo.'"
—Curtis Mayfield, from Simon Frith, *Sociology of Rock*, 1978

Considering she could vamp it up and bump and grind with the best of them, Sharon Jones's music videos are rather restrained and old-fashioned affairs, at least in comparison to so many of the raunchy and sexually explicit examples of contemporary music films out there. And I mean that in the best possible way. Jones is still, of course, plenty raunchy, but it's all subtle and implied; it's simmering below the surface, but there's no in-your-face sex.

Jones let her feelings on this subject be known in a rather cranky but charming interview with the aptly named *Mother Jones* magazine in 2011. "I'm lookin' at these Disney characters, these young girls coming out looking like little whores. There ain't no way I'm gonna be droppin' nothing. If I was in my twenties, maybe. But I try to keep it looking decent. I don't want to expose too much of my bare ass." You don't have to be too much of a historian to know that she's probably referring to the likes of Britney Spears, Katy Perry, or Christina Aguilera.

Sometimes, "we're a winner" seems to be the key message of many Sharon Jones performances, and when her idiosyncratic song stylings are captured in the short documentary film form known as music video, it becomes all the more crystal clear. Naturally, these products are essential ingredients in the marketing machinery of the music industry, conveying individual songs to the listening audience and record-buying public for publicity purposes. However, when a video is produced well and edited cleverly enough, it also becomes an art form in its own right, elevating and enhancing a song into another dimension: a personal space in which we can share the feelings of this master empath as she let's us into her private world. In retrospect, videos are often the only remaining evidence of a great performing talent once he or she has moved on to more ethereal pastures, and as such Jones's do touch a tender nerve for those who love her work.

More often than not, the subtext of plot in a video for a song by Sharon Jones and her boys is an ironic twist on a famous maxim by the early existential philosopher Nietzsche, "That which does not kill me makes me stronger." It's not only in her later health struggles that we see and feel the impact of this message, it's all the way through her early struggles with a music industry more fixated on cutesy performers like Beyoncé, Rihanna, Aguilera, or Swift, at the expense of more earthy, unpolished, and natural creatures such as Jones. But sure enough, the struggles that didn't kill her did indeed make her stronger, even though the final struggle took her away from us way too soon, and her videos often convey some of the gritty reality she mirrored in her artistry, as a strong woman who comes out swinging.

I'm reminded of Michael Haralambos's observation in his study of the birth of a sound in black America that, "as with blues, a major function of soul music is catharsis. The expression of individual problems in songs is what makes them social." The same is certainly true of the finely finessed funk style of Jones and the Dap-Kings, and in most of their videos we see a cathartic narrative unfold that frequently focuses on the social vulnerability of a protagonist who rises to meet a challenge and triumphs over some adversity. Just as frequently, the threat being faced might come from within the protagonist herself, a strong-willed person who wrestles with her own private demons as well as outward public demands. Jones's life history contains more than enough encounters with indulgences of various kinds to qualify as an ongoing battle to overcome her own foibles, along with the obstacles the world placed in front of her.

Unlike a singer in possession of considerable vocal skills but much less equipped with life-mastering abilities such as Amy Winehouse, Sharon Jones at least overcame her own private struggles and prevailed against her early bad appetites. Suffice it to say, she encountered bumps in the road of life, including battles with poverty, bad love interests, and professional biases, all of which she faced with aplomb and pluck, but the main thing is she beat those demons, too, just as she beat the odds against her becoming a star in the first place. Of course, that final devil, the one in her pancreas, proved a little too much for even someone as tough as Jones to wrestle down, though she did a great job of keeping on with the fight right up until the bittersweet end.

As I've already suggested, I believe she was beyond being merely telegenic. Once you begin to feel the funky soul of this woman, you also start to see her video image in a new light—one that's truly sanctified and makes all the most prettified teen idols pale by comparison. I also suspect that it was her deep faith that gave her the strength to withstand any and all challenges, as well as to acquire a kind of beauty that's far more powerful than that created with makeup: a spiritual glow. But hers was also a deeply faithful persona still absolutely saturated with an unconventional brand of sex appeal.

Dapette Starr Duncan Lowe expressed this quite nicely when we spoke. "The videos for the songs are a good example of how good a storyteller she was. Every one has a story, and a story that makes sense, especially to her. If a story didn't make sense to her, she couldn't sing it. Her *machine* would just shut down. She *did not know how to pretend.* People might be surprised to find out that she was a shy person, but she was someone who also spoke her truth, no matter what." Indeed, the videos Jones and her band made to embody their songs are absolutely soaked and saturated with that same truth, and they all manage to visually capture that hard-to-define blissful energy of hers very well, in simple but compelling little films.

SHARON JONES AND THE DAP-KINGS: THE VIDEOS

Each of the videos produced to promote a song or album by Jones was a surprisingly low-key, low-tech, old-school narrative endeavor. In keeping with the artist's primary persona, they are all no-nonsense, engaging, and charming little movies for our ears.

"100 Days, 100 Nights"
Released October 29, 2007
Directed by Adam Elias Buncher

Using two authentic vintage cameras from the 1950s (which he purchased on eBay for fifty bucks apiece) and with production values reminiscent of *The Ed Sullivan Show*, Buncher manages to encapsulate the revivalist emotion and style sensibility of Jones and her band by reflecting and referencing historical television pop imagery. The results also evoke something of the early *Soul Train* television show, which not only embodied authentic black entertainment motifs but also exposed mainstream white audiences to those same performers for the first time in a mass medium. It's fuzzy, it's blurry, it's jerky, and it's just downright perfect. Cool grey tones capture Jones and the band on a minimal stage plinth that does the job at hand, paying homage but without nostalgia to the golden age of televised performances from long before the gilded age of music videos. Looking every bit as if it was made in 1962—and, given the vintage equipment, it practically was—the reel evokes the earnest yearning in the singer's attempt to understand what makes her man's heart so impenetrable.

For the singer, the reason is simple: it's because he's a man; it takes that long for her to know his feelings, and even longer before he figures out his own. Eventually his true self is unfolded, and regardless of how mellow or kind he might appear to be, he shows his true colors: there's something just beyond what he shows, she declares, in a voice that tells you she knows whereof she speaks.

The basic simplicity of this video is deceptive. The band cooks away on simmer behind Jones as the pale, watery visual texture brings you back to a soulful delivery that might also have been quite at home on the early Jack Parr or Steve Allen talk shows. The archival feel of this faux-historical footage is absolutely perfect for rendering both the song's narrative and the band's mission: keep it real.

Answer Me

Filmed originally by Matt Rogers in 2007 from the album *100 Days, 100 Nights*
Produced and directed by the Dap-Kings

While this is not exactly a "music video" in the technical or commercial sense of the term, how often do we get to see Sharon tickling the ivories in the Daptone House of Soul? Shot while she and the band were laying down the final track of this song from *100 Days, 100 Nights* and including a false start and some casually filmed idle banter, this clip's other joy is a testimony to the continuity of Jones's gospel roots through the soul and funk phases of her self-expression: "Answer me, sweet Jesus, can't you hear me calling you? . . . I need you Lord."

With Roth laying down his usual heavy bass line beside the piano, the singer softly croons, almost as if to a missing lover. She's run out of words to say; all she has left is this song. By the end of her plaintive wails, which build in intensity toward a mid-song climax prayer to the "son of the living god," she is not requesting or pleading but almost demanding an answer.

While we know that someone as faithful as Jones might never have demanded an answer from God in quite this way, we find ourselves urging her on as she gets more and more insistent. This woman deserves an answer, so go ahead and answer her.

"Tell Me"
Released February 5, 2008
Directed by Adam Elias Buncher

Another dreamy trip down memory lane that simulates a television program from the golden age of soul, this time with an announcer intoning a welcome to the Saturday afternoon dance party show of the mythical WDAP studios, "Tell Me" feels like a funkier version of *American Bandstand*. Flickering band shots and song titles lead us in to a multiscreen sequence of images merging the same gritty black-and-white performance with color versions of them, interspersed with live-actions shots of urban Brooklyn. Especially charming are the portrait-like shots of Jones's tried-and-true backup singers, two women who go way back with her—all the way back to the surreal period in her history before becoming a recording artist and eventually a renowned soul singer.

Without being at all derivative, this tune and its mini-movie accompaniment could also just as well have been created in 1962, emulating the sensual and earthy harmonies made famous by those legendary and revered Stax studios in Memphis. The band, their singer, and the video's director all manage to send a love letter back to that age, while at the same time forging a funky future that they themselves were in the process of building together at Daptone.

The storyline, as usual, is plain and simple: the singer has been away from her love for too long; she's been "searchin' Hell for you," but now that they're together at last, she's not asking for much really, since she's ready and willing to take him where he wants to go. There's only one thing she wants to hear from him: "Tell me you love, baby, tell me you care." It's hard to describe how heartbreaking such a plea can be, and hearing it at top volume while watching the video is the only way to demonstrate its emotional appeal.

"If You Call"
Released April 13, 2010
Directed by Philip Di Fiore

This one opens with the cinematic title "Part One." Another black-and-white gem, captured in stark and lonely tones, "If You Call" features Jones alone in a shadowy room, delivering a compelling torch song from *I Learned the Hard Way* as she looks forlornly at an old rotary telephone. Just in case she might need it, she takes a rather large butcher's knife and places it gently in her purse, while declaring that the doctor may as well cut her heart out, since it's of no use anymore.

One of the loneliest videos of all time, "If You Call" was created lovingly by the award-winning filmmaker Philip Di Fiore, perhaps best known for his remarkable documentary on the keyboard genius of Parliament and Funkadelic, *Stranger: Bernie Worrell on Earth.* His music videos can be accurately described as thrillingly cinematic and very cutting-edge, though they also maintain a gripping simplicity and eschew any special effects. His Sharon Jones films often creatively channel the 1970s street-cinema styles of *Across 110th Street* or *Mean Streets*. In short, they have true, old-school grit—especially in the imagery for this tune, which I've dubbed the second saddest song in music history (the first saddest song being whichever one each reader believes it to be).

"I Learned the Hard Way"
Released April 13, 2010
Directed by Philip Di Fiore

This one opens with the sequential title "Part Two," suggesting that it's a second scene from an ongoing "movie" first posited in the novelistic "If You Call" video by the same director. Using 35mm film to create this mini-drama was a brilliant choice, as it places the imagery in a warm frame of reference and also evokes the cinematic element so often missing from contemporary music videos, most of which are merely frenetic marketing tools designed to dazzle and seduce.

There's more trouble in paradise, it seems, as a lover's quarrel kicks off the footage with a gritty street encounter between Jones and her seemingly wandering beau. It's actually one of his pals, smoking in front of a bar (the sign on the window tongue-in-cheekily reading "Binky's Lounge" in reference to the Kings' guitarist), who tries to fend off a furious Sharon and dissuade her from confronting her man, who is inside, "just takin' care of some business." He sends her away and tells her to calm down, which she does by going off to a beach and starting to sing to us.

The all-too-familiar saga of betrayal begins to play out in a sequence of mostly happy encounters between the lovers that is paradoxically at odds with the song's content, and therefore all the more foreboding and melancholy. Jones is at her most vulnerable in this portrayal: "Now it hurts me inside, just to hear your name." The Dap-Kings also become part of the narrative, performing the song as a soundtrack to the melodrama unfolding onscreen. Jones has learned the hard way about her lover's true nature (which, as she's suggested earlier, takes one hundred days and nights to uncover), and she finally knows what she has to do.

The viewer is shifted back and forth between the frozen snowy beach where Jones sings, woefully alone, and the dark glow of the bar where the band is playing, while her man is hanging out and chatting with "friends" (that is, another woman, plus the dude who was standing watch for him outside). We're pulled from their past joys into his present infidelity, and are patiently waiting for the inevitable, when suddenly a disappointed Jones is standing stone-faced next to him. The smile melts from his face and the screen goes dark. Ouch!

"The Game Gets Old"
Released April 13, 2010
Directed by Philip Di Fiore

Also shot on 35mm film, this clip features Russell G. Jones, Lee Fields, Thomas Brenneck, and Charles Bradley. There's something majestic about Jones's lament about how many times she's played the game of love and how it always ends the same: in the blues. The game, at least as played by all her lovers, appears to always end in vain, and there's a sense of fatality to her acceptance of that familiar romance ending the same old way, once again. Maybe it's the pitch-black background and harsh spotlight, maybe it's the horn players booming their subtle support, maybe it's Jones's suddenly explosive bouffant hairdo and daffodil yellow dress; Di Fiore's repeated use of classic cinema stock not only gives the footage a dramatic old-school quality, it also emphasizes every hurtful detail and saturates the deep color tones seductively.

How many times can she lose this game of love? She had a love who played with her soul, and it hurt so bad . . . so bad she just has to share the pain with every other brokenhearted person on the planet. Jones is not claiming that love is a losing game, only that her choice of players always seems somehow doomed, delivering all of this in a bluesy format that suits her to a tee. In the midst of a filmed color performance, shot in the shadows, a black-and-white fragment of Sharon sitting and a large clock ticking from the "If You Call" video passes through the frame as a poignant reminder of this singer/character's ongoing troubles with men. An additional visual fragment from "I Learned the Hard Way" calls back to her former relationship, as she once again catches her old flame in the act of cheating on her. The flame gets cold.

"Retreat!"
Released October 9, 2013
Directed by Lizzi Akana

A good example of this ongoing Jones motif of never giving up or giving in but instead facing down the circumstances that threaten us would be the video for the song "Retreat!" from her final album, *Give the People What They Want*, in which the heroine is stalked and pursued by forces beyond her control. The visual premise, told in a deceptively simple, animated style, involves facing the fear of what's chasing you (here symbolized by wolf-like monsters in the woods) and finding a way to expand and enlarge yourself to the point where you're bigger that the forces aligned against you. You grow far beyond the size you thought you were, to a scale that can't be threatened by anything or anyone. Needless to say, Jones had accepted the metaphor of cancer being one of the monsters pursuing her, and she emphasized the notion of exploding up into a size way bigger than a mere disease as a means of communicating the art of survival she believed in so deeply. In short, the dame had guts beyond compare.

The Brooklyn-based Lizzi Akana's video for "Retreat!" is a more complicated piece of work than you might at first imagine—one that takes on a whole new layer of poignant meaning once the listener knows that it was only after writing and recording the song that Jones learned of her cancer diagnosis. It was subsequent to her treatment and upon returning to the concert stage, though, that Akana's quirky vision materialized—a vision that successfully blends a highly polished commercial format with an independent filmmaker's sense of experimental whimsy.

Speaking to Amid Amidi of *CartoonBrew* about her point of departure for the project, Akana said she was influenced by a number of intersecting sources, most notably the fact of Daptone's own drastically independent style and its evocation of classic '60s and '70s soul tones. "We started our research by pouring over classic psychedelic animation that popularized that era," she said. "We took notes from *Yellow Submarine*, *Fantastic Planet*, *The Point*, *The Wall*, and *Heavy Metal*, but we also looked to artists outside that sphere." Akana's extensive production and design team was especially inspired by the work of Alan Aldridge, the theatricality of Busby Berkeley, and the backgrounds of Eyvind Earle, particularly his big bold silhouettes, as featured in Disney's *Sleeping Beauty*. By deriving their inspiration from multiple sources, they succeeded in their objective of creating a "unique world that would ultimately strengthen Sharon's mythology."

Far from being an easygoing cartoon, this is a strange work of visual art that combines postmodern imagery with a funky and uplifting narrative. Opening with a fallen statue's hand holding a microphone, it then shows a figure who is clearly Jones but is costumed as Little Red Riding Hood, walking across a forest landscape that soon becomes menacingly filled with one wolf after another, stalking her while she intones her chirpily delivered warnings to anybody foolish enough to mess with her.

She announces that she sees those who would victimize her coming from a mile away, and even though they're all looking cocky and self-assured, they have no idea what they're in for when it comes to her own degree of independent survival skills. Her enemies foolishly think they can keep the sea at bay, but they'll soon find it's about to get real choppy. The key message is that anyone who plays with her, or tries to play her, is playing with fire. Hell hath no fury like a woman scorned. "I'll make you wish you was never born, what a fool you'd be to take me on."

As she is slowly surrounded by an army-scale pack of wolves, Jones drops her cloak to reveal her usual sequined stage sashay dress and declares that if they know what's good for them, they'll all retreat! While making these fierce declarations she also starts to grow larger and larger until she's attained a kind of comically surreal size reminiscent of the science-fiction film *Attack of the 50 Foot Woman*. She scatters the predatory pack while stomping her way across the landscape that used to menace her, picking up the microphone from the ancient statue's stone hand and starting to belt out the song we're hearing. Eventually we see her standing atop Planet Earth as it spins in space and transforms itself into an immense and glittery disco ball.

The most impactful and intense portions of the reel are those where Akana utilizes actual performance footage rendered in a twitchy stop-motion watercolor painting style that somehow captured the essence of the singer's robust, action-oriented presentation before returning to the original animated narrative. This hot and racy tune is clearly the absolute opposite of a torch song; in fact, it's an anti-torch song that replaces the usual "lover come back" message with a freedom-chant warning that she will literally incinerate you if you expect her to carry a torch. This dame carries a torch for no one; this dame *is* a torch.

"Stranger to My Happiness"
Released January 15, 2014
Directed by Rob Hatch-Miller and Puloma Basu

After the surreal and poppy animated imagery of "Retreat!," we return to a straight-ahead performance document on this video for a song from the delayed album *Give the People What They Want*. Presumably unavailable for actual personal involvement in "Retreat!" during her medical hiatus, Jones returns to deliver "Stranger to My Happiness," audaciously refusing to even consider putting on a wig for theatrical purposes. Her theater was real life.

Live performance as documentation was always a sure thing for this singer and her band, since her dynamic presence is all one needs to be mesmerized, and we forget about any special effects or hi-tech wizardry when we fall under her spell, which *Stereogum* described as "totally unbroken, a total badass and an absolute role model." Yes indeed, and to paraphrase Screamin' Jay, she definitely put a spell on us!

"Ain't No Chimneys in the Projects"
Released December 11, 2011
Directed by Ryan Louie

Ryan Louie bounces us back to an animated motif for a swinging track from Jones's *Soul Time!*, also featured on the later *It's a Holiday Soul Party* album. Again, Jones was sidelined from personal involvement due to her health challenges. Tom Breihan described this song as "new but old-school Christmas soul," and the accompanying video conveys some of the touching wonder of the plight of poor kids who want to have the fantasy of hope and happiness but are left sadly trying to string traditional decoration lights from the rooftop of their tenement building. What the child in the footage—obviously as a cipher for Sharon as a little girl—experiences is a dreamy attempt to transform all the stars in the snowy winter sky into her own personal decorations. It was also always her mother who reassured her that as soon as she fell asleep, a gift-giving chimney would magically appear, even there in their forlorn projects.

"8 Days of Hanukah"
Released December 7, 2015
Directed by Rich Terrana

Perhaps evoking Gabe Roth's own background, this is a pleasant animated confection filled with the symbols and objects of the Jewish holiday, cavorting across the screen and dancing to a soul beat laid down by Sharon and her boys. It's sheer seasonal silliness from start to finish, yet delivered with serious heart.

"White Christmas"
Released November 23, 2015
Directed by Robert Hatch-Miller and Puloma Basu

To paraphrase the late great Chuck Berry: roll over Berlin, and tell Crosby the news! Now we get to go to town with the great Irving Berlin's classic seasonal icon, normally delivered in hushed reverential tones, but here injected with enough soul power to drive it right through the rest of the year. The charmingly bald Jones is flanked by her whole crew and backup singers, all rocking their way into our hearts. Oddly reminiscent of the way their very first videos simulated *American Bandstand* or *Soul Train*, the set here is minimalist and compelling: a white background, empty but for a little riser platform, with the band cooking away behind Jones. They somehow speed up this gentle little croon-tune to an interpretive velocity no one could ever have imagined, until it settles you down into a groove that out-Tina's Ms. Turner. But instead of "Proud Mary" it's "Proud Sharon" that keeps on rolling. Bing Crosby was also rolling over, in his grave, while the rest of us were just content to be dreaming of a funky Black Christmas, and we were equally delighted to be left wondering . . . how the hell did they just manage to pull that off so smoothly? Some questions have no answers, they just point us back to the essence of all gospel, soul, and funk: a joyous celebration of wonderment personified.

"Please Come Home for Christmas"
Released December 20, 2016
Directed by Alex Howard and David Hatter

A somewhat elegiac production, released barely a month after Jones's passing, this classic seasonal soul gem is a cover of a song first done by the great Charles Brown in 1960 for a single on King Records, as drawn from Jones's *Holiday Soul Party* album from the year before. Jones takes on Brown's song with true verve and a little bit of homage to a gifted style precursor. The video suggests a theme of consolation, delivered in a charmingly wonky Claymation format, with band members doing cameos in a simple but touching tale of an old man going through a lonely holiday night without his late wife. It still contains a hopeful and happy ending, however; after all, in true soul music, hope was always in the cards.

Miss Sharon Jones!
Released September 11, 2015
Directed by Barbara Kopple

While it may not have been planned as a "music video" in the formal sense of the term but rather as a documentary glimpse into the life and lives behind the songs at a given point in time, this film still captures the visual vibe of the soul artistry of Sharon Jones and the Dap-Kings to such a joyous degree that it also delivers a huge whack of sheer musicality along the way. To my mind, the number of hot performances, both historical and contemporary, squeezed into its passionate ninety-five minutes qualifies it as an artifact that reminds us of what music videos might actually accomplish.

Videos, and by extension this biographical film about the intimate relationships between creative musicians, are archival in nature, and they remain with us as reliquaries. They archive something for posterity, especially for listeners who love the beautiful sound they explored but who never got the chance to see this band funking it up live onstage. Sadly, this is obviously even more the case when one of the artists in question leave us too soon, and rather than having her with us for an extended pleasure party we are left with only a handful of pieces of shiny metal on which their creative statement is magically compressed. It's alchemy of the highest order, then, to be able to watch this biographical film as a music video of sorts, one encapsulating *all* her music at once by taking us into the heart and soul of the woman who contributed so much to making it happen with her band.

In a very real sense, this documentary film is a montage of music videos interspersed with personal biographical detail. Barely one month after Jones's passing, while the loss was still surely only just sinking in, some of her band members shared with *Deadline Hollywood* their involvement in this emotional and cathartic film. "Alex, our manager had been wanting to get a documentary (as well as an autobiography) done for some time," Cochemea Gastelum recalled. "I don't know if he'd been actively looking for producers but VHS had come on board and they financed the project, then Barbara Kopple came into the picture as director. I don't think initially it was going to be planned as her cancer battle. That happened after the wheels were already in motion for the film."

Gabe Roth also observed that there were definitely times when Sharon was prone to feeling that the cameras were slightly intrusive, but

added that she had formed a deep connection with Kopple and understood what she wanted to do with the story. She was also clearly ready
to be "documented," so to speak. "She liked hamming it up and making
people laugh. She liked having people around she could perform for,
you know. When we all saw it for the first time together in Toronto she
seemed to really enjoy it."

Ironically, in many of the parts of the film that might provoke the
audience to seriously cry or remain very quiet, Jones is shown laugh-
ing to herself, or perhaps at herself. She was also undeniably satisfied
with all the work she had done over the years, and rightfully proud of
her recent fight, in addition to feeling legitimately honored that people
thought she was important enough to have her own documentary profile. Initially, though, there was considerable reluctance on the singer's
part. She balked at first. "You're gonna be all up in my face," she told
Kopple early on. "That's fake and phony, it's gonna be like those Kardashian girls." But once Kopple showed Jones her past films (among
them *Dixie Chicks: Shut Up and Sing*), Jones saw the potential for something quite different—as different, in fact, as she herself was from most
other soul singers or music stars. Her one proviso was a tongue-in-cheek
one: "You're not gonna catch me in my pajamas getting up out of bed!"
And, by the way, you can't get further away from the Kardashian girls
than Sharon Lafaye Jones.

Kopple was clearly impressed by every angle of her subject, especially
how open Jones was with her about her own life while staring mortality
in the face. She clearly didn't have a moment's hesitation about expressing complete honesty, which is hardly surprising, really, considering
that everyone I ever spoke to about the singer pretty much confirmed
that with Jones, what you saw was what you got. Most importantly, for
our purposes, the 2015 *Reporter* piece by Leslie Felperin stressed that
the most intensely affecting parts of the storyline were those in the more
intimate settings, such as when Jones sings in a small church in Queens
and appears to be transported by the joy of the Holy Spirit, dancing
with abandon, and in the closing segments during a rousing rendition

of the intensely inspiring hymn to endurance, "Longer and Stronger," in which the singer belts out the lines that might as well be her life's theme: "Fifty years of soul gone by and fifty more to come." If only. But it does also stress the welcome return to her deep gospel roots that was already underway toward the end of her too-short life.

Chris Willman of *Billboard* published a splendid piece on the film the day after the singer's passing, in which the director, Kopple, shared memories about the artist she had come to know quite intimately in a rather short time. She and Willman both reflected on what he called the indomitable and occasionally mischievous spirit captured by Kopple's shrewd lens. Kopple admitted that it had never even occurred to her during the four-year journey of the film's planning and production that it would end up serving as a eulogy and not what she had hoped it to be—a survival story. "When I was making the film I never thought for a minute than anything would happen to her. All the time I saw her it was done with such light and perseverance and energy that I thought someone with this kind of strength and courage and motivation *has* to make it."

The director had just left Jones in Cooperstown after a film screening at the Glimmerglass Festival and was driving back to Sharon Springs, where Jones was staying, when she heard that the singer had been rushed to the emergency room. Kopple quickly went to the hospital, where she was joined by all of the Dap-Kings and other close friends. They all strummed guitars and hummed along with her gentle singing right up to her final moments.

Kopple remembers Jones as a person who made you feel special and somehow at the center of her life, whoever you may be, whether famous or unknown. "My favorite moment in the film is when she's about to go on at the Beacon Theatre after battling back from not being able to perform," Kopple told *Billboard*. "She's about to arrive onstage in her sparkly dress, with her head sort of cocked to the side, and she looked to me like a boxer going into the ring."

Kopple was also most pleased that this stellar prizefighter was as least around long enough to learn that her final tune, "I'm Still Here," had won "Best Song" at the Critic's Choice Documentary Awards. It was a final tribute to her ongoing resilience. Indeed, the characteristically blunt and down-to-earth way that Jones described the ostensible subject of the film—her medical condition—was typically direct and to the point. Chris O'Falt of *IndieWire* would report that during his exchange with Jones about the film, she had growled fiercely, "Fuck cancer!"

In some ways, this film began as a glowing tribute to Jones's triumph, then shifted into a sad elegy on her art, and finally morphed into a moving requiem about her life among us. If absence makes the heart grow fonder, then, soon enough, lovers of soul music in general and admirers of courage in particular will be overflowing. This film remains as a stellar document about a unique kind of gift to the world in the shape of a little giant.

POSTHUMOUS VIDEOS

These two videos were released to accompany songs but were not strictly speaking created commercially. They were culled and collaged from existing footage of an archival nature but nonetheless managed to convey an effective narrative.

"Matter of Time

Released October 10, 2017
Produced and directed by Jeff Broadway and Cory Bailey

This video is practically a documentary on life on the road for a constantly traveling band whose members just lived to appear live onstage. Shot during Jones's final year on earth, it's a bonanza of short takes of Jones and her boys backstage, kibitzing and goofing around, meeting adoring fans, rehearsing, getting on and off endless buses and generally living life large, even with a final exit staring them all in the face. The song's closing lyric—"I can't wait too much longer for this world to get better"—takes on a special and touching meaning as Jones waves at us from an exit door sliding slowly closed forever.

Watching this video, perhaps especially when it was featured behind the Dap-Kings as they performed live on *The Tonight Show* on the night before the one-year anniversary of Jones passing, it feels spookily like a posthumous postcard from heaven, simultaneously happy and sad at the same time, with the sentiment "wish you were here" saturating every forlorn, flickering image.

"Call on God"
Produced and directed by the Dap-Kings

"Call on God," the song that closes *Soul of a Woman*, also received a video, produced in-house at Daptone, which while not polished and actually quite casual still manages to capture some of the embodiment of spirit that was the essence of Jones's soul music. It brings the churchy girl full circle from her earliest recorded outing with her choir.

Meanwhile, in a nice piece of parallel history, Daptone touchingly honored her memory with one more final recording, but ironically it was an old one. Accompanied by a charming portrait of Jones as a younger woman, in recognition of International Record Store Day 2017, four months after her death and forty years after its initial appearance, Daptone re-released Jones very first gospel/funk recording as a limited-edition, 7-inch single through its subsidiary, Ever-Soul Records. "Heaven Bound," to our ears today, represents a seminal watermark in the invention of a brand-new musical fusion, one that must have mystified listeners back then, without a clear-cut genre in which to locate and define it. But after the passage of four decades we can now recognize it as a unique hybrid that demonstrates just how far ahead of her time Jones really may have been.

LEGACY OF LOVE
She's Still Here

"When they say it can't be done, it's up to you to show them why they're wrong."
— MATT MULLINS, "Legacy," from the album *Challenger* by Memphis
May Fire, 2012

Her impact on my life?" Starr Duncan Lowe mused, when I asked her that sometimes-tricky question. She didn't skip a beat in delivering what I considered the perfect response. "She changed it. She stood out for me . . . as a tender, soft and gentle person. She was an excellent teacher. An example. Her life experience had made her into a great teacher, a teacher of how to live."

Some of our real teachers we just never forget, since what they taught us is something we carry around inside us, every day, especially if they taught us how to *be*. Perhaps the only true form of immortality we can really hope for is not living forever but rather leaving behind something that lingers on in the lives of others: a small monument to our short breath.

Strong sentiments were communicated in Brown Memorial Church in Brooklyn on December 14, 2016, for Sharon Jones's memorial service. The deep feelings conveyed a classic gospel vibe that Jones would have appreciated, since the choir was singing a favorite song of hers.

The moving memorial tune was first recorded by Sharon with E. L. Fields and the Gospel Wonders way back in 1978 with Brooklyn's own Universal Church of God Inc. They sang about holding their heads up high and being heaven-bound as they marched toward victory. Indeed, as I've suggested, she *must* have been heaven-bound, since she'd already been through hell right here on earth.

If there is one thing that the people I spoke to all agreed on, the ones who knew Sharon Jones the longest and the best, it was that she fought the good fight, and she did it *her way*. I'm pretty sure she would've been delighted to be compared to that other great fighter, the one who floated like a butterfly and stung like a bee. Whether it was her sister Willa, who knew her from the day she was born; or her pastor, Margo Fields, who knew her from the age of thirteen; or Saundra Williams and Starr Duncan Lowe, the vocalists who knew her from the age of thirty-four; or her manager, Alex Kadvan; or her fellow musicians; or filmmaker Barbara Kopple, who knew her right up to the end of her gutsy life-performance at sixty; they agreed that she fought like hell and lived a life that embraced both the sacred and the profane.

As Jones summed it up, proudly and rather wistfully, when speaking to Melissa Locker of her adopted hometown's magazine, *Brooklyn*, in the summer of her difficult but still triumphant final year of 2016, "I'm not really well known in everybody's household, but I got a documentary about me. I always felt my fans were a big part of what we did on stage. They were also a big part of me even in my sickness too." By then, partly as a result of the documentary that must have pleased her so much, maybe she even was a household name. If so, that name would be synonymous with soul power, persistence, perseverance, and paradox.

Why paradox? Well, Jones was tiny but towering, tender but tough, raunchy but religious. Her sister Willa described her to me a "tough cookie who never backed down from a fight," while Margo Fields described her to me as "a gentle soul who followed the way of the Lord." She was, in short, a total human being, with all of the consequences that being fully human entails, assuming you want to squeeze every last drop from being alive. I quickly learned that the secret to appreciating her essence was to accept both sides of her character with equal respect and to realize that some people are living reminders that opposites are not necessarily contradictions but rather components of a puzzle that everyone carries around inside.

As the trajectory of our soul music journey nears its conclusion, its circuitous route brings us by a joyful kind of recirculation, back to where it all began, to the secretly funky glories of gospel music and its bouncy celebration by this little giant, Sharon Jones. Full of both faith and fury in equal measure, she welcomed even the devil inside to make himself comfortable and enjoy the show. Jones was a great example of a savage sort of beauty and also of living the span of your allotted time on earth, especially its full depth and width, as a spiritual quest in search of an unknown country filled with unanswered questions. For all we know, she's merely moved on to the next phase of that quest—perhaps one that never ends at all, even if it appears to the rest of us to be interrupted by an unexpected mortality.

Another popularly held sentiment that can easily be shared in common with the memory of Sharon Jones is an insight often associated with the French author Victor Hugo, from his *Les Misérables*. This is the notion that music expresses what cannot be put into words but which cannot remain silent, perhaps especially in times of suffering and strife. To that extent, this observation also seems to confirm another intuition I have about Jones myself: that she was a living homeopathic remedy for what ails the rest of us. Words sometimes fail us when we try to express or describe the ineffable power of that kind of grace.

Two of the most frequently repeated words used to evoke the personal power of this performer who seems to have touched so many hearts across the planet were *soul* and *strength*. The first she had in truckloads, and the second she must have stored up in her own private reservoir. Speaking to the *Los Angeles Times* only two days after her passing, Gabe Roth described his fabulous singer and friend in the most unequivocal of ways: "She was the strongest person any of us had ever known, and she just kept singing. She didn't want to stop singing." He also noted, with some of the same sardonic irony that Jones herself had expressed, that she had suffered a stroke on November 8, US election night, while watching the startling voting returns.

When Roth joined her at her bedside in the hospital where she lay dying, she was in the process of telling all the people there that the new president had given her the stroke, keeping up the edgy humor that had sustained her for so long through early career struggles and later health issues. "She didn't seem anxious or scared or anything," Roth reported. "She just wanted to sing, you know, and every time there was a lull in the room she would start moaning some kind of gospel song." Turning her private hospice room into a kind of tiny theater stage of sorts, Binky Griptite would start strumming his guitar and Jones would alternate between humming, moaning, and actually vocalizing the words to classic reverence tunes such as "Nearer My God to Thee," "This Little Light of Mine," and, almost as if to cleverly preempt her own memorial service, "Amazing Grace."

For Roth and the eventually eleven band members in attendance, also joined by family and friends, it was a paradoxical combination of crazy, remarkable, and beautiful. "I've never seen anything like it," he concluded. That tenderness also reminds me of a pertinent insight that the great Lee Fields shared with Neil Ferguson of the *Horn*: "Sometimes the melancholy moments are the most cherishable moments that we have." Truth.

J. Kelly Nestruck of the *Globe and Mail* wryly observed, "If more artists are aware of their mortality and embracing it through their art, it may be because death, particularly for recording artists, has been complicated by the digital age. For artists, it's more important than ever to choose how your death is performed. Is the performance of dying new, or does it just seem so? A great deal of performance art has dealt with death as a risk or threat rather than an eventuality."

I am definitely struck by how differently we relate to an artist who we all know had a limited number of days left, as well as how they themselves relate to that dwindling number. It's a mortality naturally suffused with precisely that quality of precious melancholy during our most cherishable moments, as Lee Fields put it so well. In the case of Sharon Jones, she was always able to take her own early experiences with gospel fortitude and transform them into soul gratitude, thus multiplying her cherishable moments for all the rest of us exponentially. That transformative magic was one of her many gifts to us as a performer. She transformed our everyday lives by inviting us to participate so openly in her own.

It often seems to me that Sharon Jones's most splendid performance was in playing herself in her own life—a role that even in her darkest times she delivered with a joyous frenzy which was beyond reason. "Logic never really applied to Sharon," Gabe Roth told the *Los Angeles Times*. "She was a superhero. It never made sense where she got her strength from, she got on stage and connected with the audience and was able to transcend everything." Many others have also remarked, in agreement with her baritone sax player, Gastelum, that even in her later and weaker state she was somehow still a better performer. "I felt like she got stronger, not only as a performer-entertainer, but as a singer," Gastelum told the *Times*. "She just grew even bigger and more radiant, her voice opened up in a way I hadn't heard before."

All the tough times she ever went through only seemed to amplify her already ample supply of fearlessness and stamina. But Jones saw it all as just part of an ongoing narrative that became almost legendary after a while and also taught her not to get her hopes up very high because, as she told *Rolling Stone*, "Nothing comes easy for me. My life has a lot of letdowns." Amen to that.

For a person like Sharon, a boisterous soul music performance was a far better form of therapy than any medication, especially since seeing her live in concert almost felt like a special kind of radiation on its own. "When I walked out on stage," she explained to Jason Newman of the *New York Times*, "whatever pain there is, is gone. You forget about everything. There is no sickness. You're just floating, looking in their faces and hearing them scream. That's all it is to me." Surely that's what fully *being here* really means. Even though her life may have had a lot of letdowns, as she put it, at least she never once let *us* down.

Well, she's not here anymore, at least not in body, anyway. In a November 2016 profile piece for *FYI News*, Bill King attempted to assuage some of the swelling of emotions over her early departure. "Sixty is a terribly young age to exit this world, especially when you're an internationally admired and loved soul singer, someone who fought enormous odds to play and stay among the living. Photographing concerts for thirty-five years gives one an intimate view of performers and Jones for me ranks in the upper chambers of stage performers who truly understood their fans. They never slight or disappoint: Jones shows up! It's the full body/ music experience, a combination of James Brown soul and ceremonial African dance."

The angel and the devil inside her always seemed to be in perfect harmony, as if they'd worked out an agreement or bargain as to how to proceed with a unique and paradoxical specimen such as her. There's a well-titled chapter, "Sympathy for the Devil," in Gail Hirshey's excellent history of soul music, *Nowhere to Run*, which, though ostensibly about Screamin' Jay Hawkins, also sums up the deep affection we feel for the secular style of *sinful* music such as that of Sharon Jones. It was, after all, this exotic amalgam that coalesced both gospel and blues into soul and finally into funk and beyond. The devil, Hawkins felt, was lurking inside every person, and sometimes you just had to give him his due, perhaps hoping that maybe then he'd leave you alone. I'm fond of the sentiment behind the chapter title, quite apart from the great Rolling Stones song it obliquely references, because just as the phrase "giving the devil his due" implies, it's all about having sympathy for our own dark side, the side that makes us human. It also clarifies the deep essence of what soul music does so well.

Gospel music might perhaps be too optimistically hopeful in its vibe, allowing us to give up and give in, while the blues might be too forlorn a hopeless lament, permitting us to give in and give up, but when you combine the two, and then spice up the results with some hot funk rhythms, what you end up with is the perfect balance: the superlative delivery of Sharon Jones. What Jones was able to place at her disposal so artfully, then, was not just the energy of one or the other but the Janus-like *dinergy* of harmonizing both complementary opposites into a magical musical pattern. We should also remember that blues, well, blues was *still* just gospel music, a sacred sound that had been tempted to leave the church and dance down the profane street to the nearest juke joint.

In early 2014, Amanda Petrusich conducted a fine interview with Sharon Jones that was eventually published as a customarily elegant obituary for the *New Yorker* aptly titled "Postscript." In it, Petrusich recalled walking with the singer down 45th Street, looking for a suitably secluded and quiet sports bar for breakfast and a chat during which they discussed Jones's medical condition and treatments while she smoked weed from a blue vaporizer pen. She was a reporter's dream: loquacious, spontaneous, funny, and familiar, with a handshake both purposeful and strong, even though it was attached to a barely five-foot frame. Reflecting on that encounter posthumously allowed the journalist to give full expression to the deep impact the tiny soul star had made on her. She was, in the end, a little giant casting a huge spiritual shadow.

"I realize that in the flash of fresh mourning, it's easy to be hyperbolic about legacy," Petrusich wrote. "But I don't know how anyone could deny the potency of Jones's burly urging voice. She sang and moved in a way that seemed so pure and instinctive that it made every other performer in her orbit appear calculated and sluggish by comparison." Most impressive, perhaps, was her ability to have overcome so much and still to understand America as beautiful and inclusive and uniquely all our own. "This is a lesson that feels more important and more difficult to learn now than ever before," Petrusich concluded. "Jones, at least, made knowing it look effortless."

Like many other close observers of her compelling musical and spiritual legacy, I find it abundantly clear that the devil inside Miss Jones actually was an angel in disguise. In the end, one of the great ironies of gospel music is that perhaps its secret spiritual aroma *is* soul music, and that it also has a faith somehow mysteriously shared with funk. And it suddenly occurs to me now that *there* is an ideal requiem for the Sunday of her life. But it isn't a symphonic requiem, more a quiet and restrained twelve-bar blues: her life and her music showed us that a chill of deep awareness overtakes us when we eavesdrop on the hearsay of the heart and we listen to the soul confess what it doesn't know but feels. That's what funk music is and does. It is essentially about reconciliation of all opposites.

That basic notion of reconciliation, is, I believe, a valuable vehicle for fully appreciating the historical and contemporary parallels between even such seemingly disparate figures as Sister Rosetta Tharpe (who was essentially rapping for God), James Brown (who was grooving for his entire race), and Sharon Jones (who was the soulful inheritor of all three tongues and managed to speak them all with equal fluency).

When Sharon Jones is shown in the documentary on her life at a concert in Augusta, Georgia, late in her career, dressed in blazing red and erupting at the end of one of her signature songs into a breath-taking spirit trance that weirdly evokes a wild spontaneous rap of her own invention, it suddenly makes glaringly plain the overlaps between African juju, gospel testimony, soulful funk, and a drastically elevated hipping and hopping. She is almost speaking in tongues, so overcome is she by the energy of her faith-engine revving up beyond her control. No one is driving the soul train anymore; the train has left the tracks entirely, and she has given up control to some invisible conductor. This trajectory in the pursuit of evolutionary soul music has clearly taken us way outside the arbitrary borders between sacred and profane. It may even erase those divisions altogether. How else could we possibly come to understand the eerie spiritual bond between diverse African American poets such as Langston Hughes and Tupac Shakur, or between the seemingly divergent paths of Mahalia Jackson and Sharon Jones?

Perhaps the true secret to the Jonesian soul sound is encapsulated by her two biggest fans, Gabe Roth and Neal Sugarman, in their charmingly effusive liner notes for *Naturally*, her second album:

> What is it about a Sharon Jones show that leaves audiences mesmerized across the country? Is it the showmanship, the rhythm, the excitement? Of course it's all these things but more than anything else it's something deeper. Something so natural and beautiful it can barely be spoken of out loud. . . . Real SOUL is, was and always will be everywhere around us. . . . Sharon Jones has given us this rare gift of soul. Above all, open your mind, your body and your soul to Sharon Jones in the same way that she has opened her own to us: lovingly, passionately and naturally.

Amen again.

• • •

Toward the end of her life, Sharon Jones finally decided to acquiesce to the longtime request of her management (their plea, more like it) that she discuss her personal story and professional career in an autobiography. It was to be called *Got to Be the Way It Is: The Sharon Jones Story*, and it would surely have been a scintillating read, one that pulled at the heartstrings and left us admiring her combination of early struggles, her midlife triumph, and her late struggles. Alas, time was not on her side, and she was prevented from sharing the details with an author who could have helped shape her narrative. I'm pretty sure that the time required to reflect, remember, and recollect was instead spent trying to survive, to stay among us, and, of course, to continue performing live soul music for as long as she could do so.

If Aretha was the Queen of Soul, and Carla Thomas was the Queen of Memphis Soul, then given the hard work that Sharon Jones put in over the years, she must be the Lady in Waiting of Soul. The title of "Got to Be the Way It Is" once again contains something strongly akin to revivalist religious testifying in public, its boldly declaimed lyrics reminding us of the fates we must face and that the best way to deal with adversity is to transcend it by dancing your blues away. Any which way you choose it, you have to work it out—you have to face the way it is. That was definitely her credo.

New York–based DJ Jonathan Toubin, who did a high-profile dance show called *Soul Clap* and saw ever-larger crowds bouncing around his dance floors during Jones's roughly twenty-year-long recording career as evidence of a new soul music wave, also believes that Sharon Jones basically brought a whole new generation into soul music as a style through her persistent and passionate commitment to historically authentic funk. He expressed this rather poignantly to *Pitchfork*: "Sharon Jones knew her time might be short, she traveled with the specter of death by her side for almost four years. She had time to get to know it, maybe even to accept the idea of it, even though it had turned up way ahead of a reasonable schedule. And in her way, by continuing to take to the stage and give it her all, she was telling it [death] to sit down for a minute so she could ask us all to dance, just one more time."

Luckily for all of us, the deep connection Jones forged with her audience is also a phenomenon that may be perpetuated for some time to come. If Daptone has its way—and why shouldn't it?—the cult of Dap-Dippin' with Sharon Jones will continue to grow. As Gabe Roth told the *Los Angeles Times*, he wants the world to know that they're not done with her yet—not by a long shot. He insisted then that Jones would still be putting out records even after she's no longer around, "which is a good thing . . . I think it's important to get all the stuff out there."

Daptone's deep commitment to making a certain kind of music with a certain level of quality and sonic virtuosity tends to guarantee, it seems to me, that the posthumous Jones and the Dap-Kings body of work will be of a recognizably high standard. Roth and co. felt they owed it to her after she devoted so much of herself to making other people happy, and that she was so devoted to the wonderment of being alive that she left behind a huge chunk of her soul, and they want to treat that legacy with the proper respect it deserves.

This of course is welcome news to the growing cult of Dap, and they have been true to their word in honoring Jones's memory appropriately. Sure enough, on November 17, 2017, one day before the first anniversary of her passing, Daptone released *Soul of a Woman*, a final studio album collecting songs she and the band had been working on right up until the end. As I remarked in the earlier chapter on the band's albums with Jones, this final testament strikes a fine balance between the hunger for more material from a beloved artist and the responsibility to maintain the high technical and creative standards of a great label. This was a win-win situation, and even better, unlike the posthumous Amy Winehouse album, this one is *all* good. It also reaffirms the central mission of both the musicians and the company behind them.

Michael Barclay of the *Globe and Mail* offered a fine, elegiac profile of this ultimate late-bloomer while assessing the posthumous record that provided all the fire and energy that her adoring audience had come to expect over the years. In many ways, *Soul of a Woman* is a late-arriving spiritual telegram for listeners who so obviously miss her, but also one best summed up by her longtime producer, bass player, and friend, Daptone head honcho Gabe Roth. "It wasn't like we were trying to construct a goodbye letter. It wasn't a swansong, or a final opus. It felt the way all our records felt: it's about being alive, about that moment. And cancer was part of that moment."

In the absence of Sharon Jones, the Dap-Kings are trying to assess their next career moves. They have since backed up Smokey Robinson on a new album of his, and have other planned ventures, but unlike some bands who lost their singers to one fate or another, they have no plan to hit the road on their own. For Roth, "It's not even a question of taste or the optics of it. I don't care about that really." The more important aspect of the dilemma seems to be the long time—over twenty years—that they have spent building up a distinctive sound together as musicians who love being in the same spirit-space with each other.

In terms of carrying on the legacy of Daptone Records and its absent stellar stars, including Charles Bradley as well as Sharon Jones, and despite the fact that Daptone has begun branching outside soul into rock vibes on its subsidiary Wick Records, the label's core content will always have an authenticity that simply can't be faked. Sugarman expressed this as the fact that "Sharon had this way of making everyone who had seen the band feel connected to her. For those fans, I think the first listen (to the last record) is going to be incredibly difficult. But then you just get past that, and it's just great music."

It might be true that without those two anchors of Charles and Sharon, as Roth put it, "It might be a lot harder—but it's as important as ever—to keep making good music. We're still doing records we want to do, that sound the way we want them to sound, and we're not answering to the demands or the expectations of anyone in the music industry higher than the second floor of our own Daptone Studio."

Many of their planned projects together must remain forever hypothetical what-ifs, practically mythical now in tone (such as the full gospel album they had intended to create, inspired by Aretha Franklin's 1972 live gospel record, *Amazing Grace*). "It's been really hard for me that we weren't able to get that gospel record done because it was something really important to her," Roth lamented. "That record was huge for Sharon and she always wanted to do one like it. She had been singing gospel her whole life."

They've also been given some freedom to strike out in new and different directions as well, while having some mourning time to ponder the future of both band and label. A raft of releases, including new albums by Staten Island funk group the Budos Band and British R&B singer James Hunter, were let loose in 2018, while the Dap-Kings continued to undertake high-profile guest collaborations, most famously with Sam Smith on his recent album *The Thrill of It All*.

Sugarman admitted to constantly being asked the question, by the folks at *Billboard*, for example, about what the Dap-Kings are going to do now? To which he responded, "Nothing quite feels like the right direction to take. Everyone has a good suggestion, it seems, but there will never be another Sharon Jones. That's what this band was built for." Asked whether there were ever any thoughts of ending the band altogether, Sugarman wryly responded that they have had "all kinds of conversations." We'll all have to wait and see what those conversations may yield for the rest of us, hungry for more.

Gabe Roth also explained to *Billboard* that even though that intimacy is not an easy thing to say goodbye to, the flip side of the performing and recording puzzle is the special connection and exhilarating emotional boost they had with Sharon Jones herself as a person. "We know there's no sense in chasing that high. We were never higher than when we were behind Sharon on stage." I don't know, but that sounds like a swan song to me.

Returning briefly to the origins of the *Dap*-tone moniker and its heartwarming reference to a shared gesture of solidarity, there's a commonly understood explanation for the meaning of the actual word. It could be an urban legend, but even if it is, it's just so pertinent and perfect in the context of Sharon Jones that it's worth touching upon tenderly, in passing. The giving and getting of "d-a-p" in mutual recognition of a community of belonging and support is thought to convey three key words: "Dignity and Pride." If there's been one consistent link that binds together anyone who ever met her, performed with her, or even just enjoyed listening to her music and watching Jones taking care of business, it would be those three words. That's how she lived her life, and that's how she departed this world: with dignity and pride.

There's a piece by Diane Ackerman in her book *Going on Faith* that strikes me as eminently applicable to the life and work of Sharon Jones in terms of both her personal and professional legacy. Ackerman references a mystic who has implied that he didn't pray for faith, he prayed for wonder. "That is also my prayer," Ackerman observes. "Wonder is the heaviest element on the periodic table; a tiny fleck of it stops time. My periodic table of the heart also has many other elements, still unidentified by science. One of them is *unattainium*. That's the one that drives us forward whether or not we expect to succeed."

This sentiment seems not only very deep but also very, very wide.

Jones had that element of *unattainium* in abundance. It's what helped her succeed against all odds, even in her unexpected end itself, since she celebrated wonderment and used her music to stop time, again and again. When I remember her, I'm reminded of something the American poet Theodore Roethke said so well during the great soul year of 1965, in his essay *On Poetry and Craft*: "What we need are more people who specialize in the impossible." It often strikes me that this was her true specialty, and the lesson of her history: that the years know much more than the days could ever have imagined. It's also how Jones left us all with such a huge amount of her shared soul to experience: she left us the funky gospel according to Sharon.

Sharon Jones may indeed have been a long slow train, but when she finally pulled into the station, most people would agree on two things: that it was well worth the wait, and that she will be a long time missed.

AFTERWORD
An Appreciation by Barbara Kopple

I had the great good fortune and rare opportunity to make a film about Sharon and the Dap-Kings: it was called *Miss Sharon Jones!* Over the course of three years I filmed with Sharon, toured with the band, and sat with her in both studio green rooms and in hospital recovery rooms. I also saw firsthand the incredible family of musicians that Sharon had built up around her.

Sharon Jones turned my life around as a human being. As a documentary filmmaker I have the honor of meeting many extraordinary people from all walks of life. All of them made an impact on me. But no one has touched me as deeply as Sharon Jones did. She taught me what it truly means to have positive thinking and to use it daily. I used to think I was fearless, then I met Sharon, and she showed me what it really means: she was all about courage and love.

It was a trip to Sharon's hometown of Augusta, Georgia, that was among the most memorable experiences. To be at her childhood home, to drive through the streets where she grew up and first fell in love with music, to meet her family—this was seeing the real Sharon Jones. Away from the stages, recording studios and bright lights we got to see Sharon as she saw herself, as her mother's child. She loved her mother so deeply, and missed her so much. Sharon's mother didn't get to see her reach the heights of her career, but she saw the talent and passion in her daughter and nourished it. In the years since her mother's death, Sharon had taken on a kind of caretaker role for a large family of brothers, sisters, nieces, and nephews. She wasn't always there, but she was there when she was needed the most.

Sharon carried that love of family into her career. The amazing Dap-Kings and her manager, Alex Kadvan, were like brothers to her. Saundra Williams and Starr Duncan Lowe, her Dapette backup singers, were like sisters, always having each other's back and really loving one another deeply. Being with them all felt like being part of a real family. They spent twenty years playing together, sharing buses together, and recording those amazing albums. And what a huge blow losing her has been.

When she got sick, it was hard for Sharon to learn to be taken care of. It wasn't really her style. Megan Mast Holken was the angel who loved and took care of Sharon in her own home. They were best friends and they were seldom apart. Sharon was sunshine in any room, even when getting chemotherapy, and everyone who ever met her loved her. Sometimes I sat with her after long days in the hospital, when she was too exhausted to talk anymore. Even then, she would quietly hum old gospel songs she knew from her childhood. That music was inside her, through and through.

At the Toronto Film Festival, where our film had its world premiere, it was an absolute joy to be there with Sharon as she saw the film for the very first time. To see her laugh and cry and go through it all with the Dap-Kings and Dapettes: I spent almost as much time at that first screening watching them watch it as I did watching the film itself.

Sharon Jones was both beautiful and profound, especially while battling her way back to the stage after her first cancer diagnosis. She fought on and was fearless to the end. And that end came far too quickly for any of us who knew her to bear. Knowing Sharon and getting to tell her story was the greatest reminder of the honor of meeting someone unique who changed my life so much it's a challenge to describe. Someone like her is always with you and enriches your life in so many ways. Saundra Williams used to say that Sharon's voice was like a freight train coming onto the stage. She truly was a force of nature who inspired us all, brightened all our lives, and taught me personally what it means to embrace life to the fullest. It's a lesson I shall never forget.

SOURCES

AUTHOR'S INTERVIEWS
Alex Kadvan, Brilliant Corners Management
    (manager, Sharon Jones and the Dap-Kings)
Pastor Margo Fields
Willa Jones-Stringer
Saundra Williams
Starr Duncan Lowe
Barbara Kopple

BOOKS
Bayles, Martha. *Hole in Our Soul: The Loss of Beauty and Meaning in American Popular Music*. University of Chicago Press, 1994.
Bowman, Rob. *Soulsville USA: The Story of Stax Records*. Schirmer Books, 1997.
Cohn, Lawrence. Nothing But the Blues. Abbeville Press, 1993.
Cosgrove, Stuart. *Detroit '67: The Year That Changed Soul*. Polygon, 2016.
Darden, Robert. *People Get Ready: A New History of Black Gospel Music*. Continuum, 2004.
Guralnick, Peter. *Sweet Soul Music: Rhythm and Blues and the Southern Dream of Freedom*. Back Bay Books, 1986.

Haralambos, Michael. *Soul Music: The Birth of a Sound in Black America*. Da Capo Press, 1974.

Hirshey, Gerri. *Nowhere to Run: The Story of Soul Music*. Da Capo Press, 1994.

McDonough, Jimmy. *Soul Survivor*. Da Capo Press, 2017.

Nava, Alejandro. *In Search of Soul: Hip Hop, Literature, and Religion*. University of California, 2017.

Oliver, Paul. *Songsters and Saints: Vocal Traditions on Race Records*. Cambridge University Press, 1984.

Reed, Teresa. *The Holy Profane: Religion in Black Popular Music*. University of Kentucky Press, 2003.

Rudinow, Joel. *Tracking the Spiritual Roots of Pop, From Plato to Motown*. University of Michigan Press, 2010.

Sacré, Robert. *Religion, Blues, and (D)evil in African American Music*. Société liégeoise de musicologie, 1996.

Scaruffi, Piero. *History of Popular Music*. Perfect Press, 2003.

Seay, Davin, and Neely, Mary. *Stairway to Heaven: The Spiritual Roots of Rock n' Roll*. Ballantine, 1986.

Southern, Eileen. *The Music of Black Americans, A History*. W.W. Norton, 1997.

Sullivan, James. *The Hardest Working Man: How James Brown Saved the Soul of America*. Gotham Books, 2008.

Tennille, Andy, and George, Nelson (ed.). "The Return of Real Funk and Soul Music." *Best Music Writing 2008*. Da Capo Press, 2008.

Vincent, Rickey. *Funk: The Music, the People, and the Rhythm of the One*. St Martin's Press, 1996.

ARTICLES

Ayers, Michael. "Sharon Jones' Family Affair." *Village Voice*, April 6, 2010.

Barclay, Michael. "The Life and Death Behind Jones' New Album." *Globe and Mail*, November 11, 2017.

Blau, Max. "Sharon Jones on Beating Cancer, Going Onstage Bald, and Fighting for Soul." *Spin*, January 10, 2014.

Blickenstaf, Jacob. "Miss Sharon Jones: A Queen Among Kings." *New York Times*, November 23, 2016.

Blistein, Joel. "The Dap-Kings Remember." *Rolling Stone*, December 20, 2017.

Blyth, Antonia. "Singing Go Tell It on the Mountain, at the End." *Deadline Hollywood*, December 13, 2016.

Breihan, Tom. "Even in Death." Stereogum.com, November 21, 2016.

Browne, David. "Schooled in Hard Times." *Under the Radar*, November 19, 2016.

Chinen, Nate. "Master Linguists." *New York Times*, December 18, 2016.

Corcoran, Nina. "Sharon Jones' Five Most Legendary Performances." *Nerdist*, November 21, 2016.

Daley, Dan. "Gabe Roth, Recording for Daptone." *Sound on Sound*, June 2008.

Derrough, Leslie. "Fields Keeps It Strong." *Glide*, November 28, 2016.

Farberman, Brad. "Behind the Scene." Waxpoetics.com, April 6, 2010.

Fensterstock, Alison. "Sharon Jones Led the Soul Revival to the Dancefloor." *Pitchfork*, November 21, 2016.

Ferguson, Neil. "Diva Double Header." *The Horn*, 2013.

Fink, Matt. "Soul Survivor." *Under the Radar*, March 2014.

Fusilli, Jim. "Analog Soul." *Wall Street Journal*, April 1, 2010.

Gale, Ezra. "A Beginner's Guide to the Daktaris." *Village Voice*, March 4, 2009.

Gross, Terry. "Remembering Sharon." *Fresh Air*, NPR, November 23, 2016.

Hann, Michael. "Soul Star Sharon Jones." *Guardian*, November 19, 2016.

Himes, Geoffrey. "Remembering Sharon Jones." *Paste*, November 22, 2016.

Iannacci, Elio. "Remembering Sharon Jones." *Fashion*. November 22, 2016.

Kelly, Cathal. "The New Age of Nostalgia." *Globe and Mail*, December 24, 2016.

King, Bill. "Fond Memories." *FYI Music News*, November 21, 2016.

Kreps, Daniel. "Call On God." *Rolling Stone*, December 4, 2017.

Kreps, Daniel. "Sail On." *Rolling Stone*, December 4, 2017.

Lee, Adrian. "From the Archives." *Maclean's*, January 22, 2014.

Levenson, Max. "Soul of a Woman." *Bandcamp Daily*, November, 14, 2017.

Ma, David. "Sharon Jones." *Guardian*, November 20, 2016.

Mao, Jeff. " Gabe Roth Interview." Red Bull Academy, London, 2010.

Moore, Sarah. "Goldmining with Daptone." *PopMatters*, January 17, 2010.

Mugan, Chris. "Daptone Records Spreads Its Wings." *Independent*, August 18, 2016.

Nestruck, J. Kelly. "The Year of Staged Exits." *Globe and Mail*, December 24, 2016.

Newman, Jason. "Sharon Jones Fights On." *Rolling Stone*, July 29, 2016.

O'Falt, Chris. "Fuck Cancer!" *IndieWire*, December 21, 2016.

Pareles, Jon. "Sharon Jones, Powerhouse." *New York Times*, November 19, 2016.

Pareles, Jon. "Sharon Jones Says Farewell." *New York Times*, November 5, 2017.

Pelly, Liz. "New Imprint Brings Daptone Soul to Analog Rock 'n' Roll." *Guardian*, July 6, 2016.

Perry, Sarah. "Smokin Soul." *Atlas Society*, March 7, 2012.

Petrusich, Amanda. "Postscript: Sharon Jones." *New Yorker*, November 19, 2016.

Roberts, Randall. "She Didn't Want to Stop Singing." *Los Angeles Times*, November 20, 2016.

Ruffini, Nick. *Drummer's Resource*, July 17, 2017.

Schaller, Jeff. "Indispensable Funk." *Modern Drummer Magazine*, 2007.

Schneider, Jason. "Soul Survivors." Eclaim.ca, September 24, 2007.

Schwartzberg, Lauren. "Sharon Jones on Beating Cancer." *New York Magazine*, February 10, 2014.

Sexton, Paul. "The Sound That Gave Amy Soul." *Independent*, October 16, 2015.

Vozick-Levinson, Simon. "Solace Arrives." *New York Times*, November 12, 2017.

Wang, Oliver. "A Queen Among Kings." NPR Music, November 21, 2016.

Willman, Chris. "Sharon Jones, Remembered by Barbara Kopple." *Billboard*, November 19, 2016.

Wilstein, Matt. "When Prince Surprised Sharon." *Daily Beast*, November 18, 2016.

—"Is Gabriel Roth the Most Important Person in Modern Soul Music?" Craftpresents.com, July 15, 2015.

—Obituary Register. *Sunday Times* (London), November 21, 2016.

—"To Find Success." *PRI World*, November 23, 2016.

INDEX